Anglo-Saxonism and the
Construction of Social Identity

Anglo-Saxonism

University Press of Florida

Gainesville Tallahassee Tampa Boca Raton Pensacola Orlando Miami Jacksonville

and the Construction
of Social Identity

Edited by Allen J. Frantzen and John D. Niles

Frontispiece: "Tableau: Alfred the Great and His Subjects." One of a series of tableaux illustrating episodes and legends in the life of King Alfred acted out at the Guildhall, Winchester, September 19, 1901, to commemorate the thousandth anniversary of Alfred's death. "King Alfred" strikes the same pose as the statue of Alfred that was unveiled the next day as part of the same celebrations. Photograph by H. W. Salmon. From Alfred Bowker, *The King Alfred Millenary: A Record of the Proceedings of the National Commemoration* (London: Macmillan, 1902), facing p. 120.

Copyright 1997 by the Board of Regents of the State of Florida
Printed in the United States of America on acid-free paper
All rights reserved

02 01 00 99 98 97   6 5 4 3 2 1

Library of Congress Cataloging-in-Publication Data
Anglo-Saxonism, and the construction of social identity / edited by Allen J. Frantzen and John D. Niles.
p. cm.
Includes bibliographical references and index.
ISBN 0-8130-1532-4 (cloth: alk. paper)
1. Great Britain—History—Anglo-Saxon period, 449–1066—Historiography. 2. English literature—Old English, ca. 450–1100—History and criticism—Theory, etc. 3. National characteristics, English—Historiography. 4. Civilization, Anglo-Saxon—Historiography. 5. Civilization, Medieval—Historiography. 6. Anglo-Saxons—Historiography. 7. Middle Ages—Historiography. 8. Medievalism—History. I. Frantzen, Allen J., 1947–. II. Niles, John D.
DA152.A728 1997 97-270
941.01'072—dc21

The University Press of Florida is the scholarly publishing agency for the State University System of Florida, comprised of Florida A&M University, Florida Atlantic University, Florida International University, Florida State University, University of Central Florida, University of Florida, University of North Florida, University of South Florida, and University of West Florida.

University Press of Florida
15 Northwest 15th Street
Gainesville, FL 32611

Contents

Introduction

Anglo-Saxonism and Medievalism

Allen J. Frantzen and John D. Niles

I N THIS BOOK we bring together a series of essays that explore Anglo-Saxonism in a variety of forms and in a number of periods of history.

The term *Anglo-Saxonism* is used here to denote the process through which a self-conscious national and racial identity first came into being among the early peoples of the region that we now call England and how, over time, through both scholarly and popular promptings, that identity was transformed into an originary myth available to a wide variety of political and social interests.

The nine contributors examine how constructions of Anglo-Saxon history, language, and literature have evolved over time in response to a variety of political, religious, and social concerns, finding expression in texts that range from law codes and chronicles to scholarly books and children's literature. Authors in Part One address the origins of Anglo-Saxonism among the Anglo-Saxons themselves and analyze multiple political affiliations of early Anglo-Saxon texts, including Bede's *Ecclesiastical History of the English People* (finished in 731), the poetic entries that were incorporated into the *Anglo-Saxon Chronicle* under the years 942–75, law codes that were recorded in English before the Norman Conquest, and the Old English translation of St. Gregory the Great's *Pastoral Care*. The political dimension of several of these works extends to the period of the Renaissance, when manuscript texts written in Old English were published for the first time and drawn into service in

religious polemics. Contributors in Part Two call attention to nineteenth-
and early twentieth-century constructions of the Anglo-Saxon past while
tracing the relations between Anglo-Saxon studies and such other phenomena as nationalism, pedagogy, regional rivalries, and popular fiction.
These essays situate Anglo-Saxonism in larger geographical and cultural
contexts and point the way toward a more sharply historicized understanding of Anglo-Saxon scholarship as it exists today. The last essay, an
afterword, plays over some of the major and minor themes of the volume
and integrates Anglo-Saxonism into a more general theory of culture.

Anglo-Saxonism is a term of unclear origin.[1] In use only since the mid-
nineteenth century, it often refers to "the sentiment of being 'Anglo-
Saxon' or English ethnologically." The word generally implies a belief in
the superiority of "the Anglo-Saxon race," often (though not always)
with the understanding that "race" in such a formulation denotes not so
much a biological state as a social identity that is compounded of
ethnicity, culture, tradition, and language.

The adjective Anglo-Saxon is one of those terms with vigorous emo-
tive power that derives from its rather vague substantive content. In brief,
it is a word to conjure with. It parts company from such adjectives as
medieval and feudal in its relative freedom from sinister overtones. We
may speak of "medieval" punishments in the sense of cruel and barbaric
torments, for instance, or of "feudal" rule in the sense of the arbitrary
and tyrannical exercise of power, but "Anglo-Saxon" bears no such
negative weight. On the contrary, a person who speaks of Anglo-Saxon
political institutions is likely to think of them as enlightened and democratic. At worst, as in the acronym WASP (for "white Anglo-Saxon
Protestant"), the adjective Anglo-Saxon can carry a negative aura that
derives from its association with speakers who are irritatingly smug
about their own racial superiority. This acronym, which has not been
traced before the year 1962, has become almost a racial slur in itself as
well as a way of deflating the pretentions of the upper crust.[2] The term
WASP connotes inherited wealth, an Ivy League college, a career in
business, and connections to political leadership. A WASP wears Brooks
Brothers clothing (for the WASP is generally male), and he may even
speak with the trace of an English accent. The term is derogatory but
generally in a good-humored way.

Whatever its exact origins may be, the noun Anglo-Saxonism can
safely be said to have entered modern scholarly discourse in the title of
Reginald Horsman's study Race and Manifest Destiny: The Origins of

American Racial Anglo-Saxonism (1981) and in Hugh A. MacDougall's *Racial Myth in English History,* published the following year.[3]

Horsman treats Anglo-Saxonism as a particularly American form of another -ism, racialism. After tracing the emergence of scholarly and political interest in the Anglo-Saxon period during the English Reformation and the development of Anglo-Saxon political history in the context of disputes between the Crown and Parliament in the seventeenth century, Horsman focuses on mid-nineteenth-century debates that asserted the place of Americans of British descent as "a separate, innately superior people who were destined to bring good government, commercial prosperity, and Christianity to the American continents and to the world" (2). Even as Anglo-Saxon racialism emerged, Horsman observes, its claims were challenged by those who noted that England, the home of the Anglo-Saxons, had contained a mixture of races from its beginnings. But logical and historical inconsistencies were swept aside by the power of new "scientifically verified" arguments about the superiority and inferiority of races. In the political climate of the United States in the first half of the nineteenth century, Horsman shows, it was easy to insist that Americans were a new chosen people descended from the Anglo-Saxons, themselves a chosen people whose Aryan or Teutonic roots, scholars had now proved, could be traced to the Bible.

MacDougall treats Anglo-Saxonism as one of two competing origin myths for the English people (the other one being the myth of their Trojan origins, as set forth by Geoffrey of Monmouth and other medieval historians). Both of these rival myths hinge upon an imperturbable conviction of racial and national superiority. MacDougall makes clear that the power of any myth of origins resides not in its objective truth but rather in its being perceived as true; and he documents the gradual increase in the surety with which the people of England propounded their Anglo-Saxon origins during the period from the Renaissance to the beginning of the twentieth century.

A number of other scholars have traced the search for power, both academic and institutional, carried out by those who sought to control the Anglo-Saxon past and who claimed originary status from it. Three other books published in the last fifteen years have prepared the way for *Anglo-Saxonism and the Construction of Social Identity* and offer readings of complementary interest.

Anglo-Saxon Scholarship: The First Three Centuries, edited by Carl T. Berkhout and Milton McC. Gatch,[4] analyzes the achievements of a set of pioneering scholars from the sixteenth to the early nineteenth centuries. By focusing on the period of beginnings, this essay collection sidesteps the topic of racialism while showing how deeply the growth of Anglo-Saxon scholarship was implicated in three movements: the efforts of religious reformers to establish the Church of England on a secure foundation; the labors of academics to ascertain the early stages of the English language; and the politically motivated attempt to identify that language and the people who spoke it as branches of a larger Germanic tree.

In *Reversing the Conquest*, Clare A. Simmons explores the binary opposition of Saxons and Normans in British literature and historiography during the reign of Queen Victoria.[5] Simmons shows how the cult of King Alfred the Great as ideal monarch and the rise of professional Anglo-Saxon studies joined together in the service of a queen and royal consort who traced their lineage back to Germany. Such lineage was easily extended to ancient Germania, whence the Angles and Saxons had colonized Britain beginning in the mid-fifth century. The martial yet civilizing mission of the British Empire during the nineteenth century could thus be seen as replicating on a grand scale the beneficent influence of such a monarch as Alfred, who was venerated as both Germanic warlord and philosopher king.

In *Desire for Origins*, Allen J. Frantzen examines how ideological and political motives have shaped Anglo-Saxon studies from the first appearance of Anglo-Saxon texts in printed editions in the mid-sixteenth century to the late nineteenth century and the emergence of Old English as a university subject in Great Britain and North America.[6] Frantzen shows how Anglo-Saxonism developed hand in hand with what Edward Said has termed Orientalism.[7] Fascination with (and repulsion from) the exotic cultures and regions of the East has always tended to anchor itself on native ground peopled by loyal, four-square, fair-haired farmers and warriors. Frantzen combines deconstruction of the discipline of Anglo-Saxon studies with a call for the teaching of this subject with renewed vigor in the university curriculum, in part because "learning Anglo-Saxon is not only a good way to learn about language and history, but a good way to study the formation and conduct of scholarly disciplines themselves" (215).

Other scholars have exposed some of the investments and biases of Anglo-Saxon scholarship in a manner that contributes substantially to the understanding of Anglo-Saxonism. E. G. Stanley's *The Search for*

Anglo-Saxon Paganism, for example, lays bare the distortions and self-deceptions whereby nineteenth-and twentieth-century scholars systematically devalued the overt Christian content of numerous Old English texts while striving to reveal the hidden paganism that was thought to lie beneath them.[8] Stanley thus makes clear the part that the Romantic heritage has played in Anglo-Saxon scholarship of the recent past. Playing off Stanley's title in her own study "The Search for the Anglo-Saxon Oral Poet," Roberta Frank has exposed the wishful thinking involved in scholarly efforts to describe the Anglo-Saxon scop or bard.[9] As with the search for pagan belief and practice, the search for the oral poet has tended to tell more about the biases of scholars than about anything that can be objectively located in history.

Other studies have focused on specific aspects of the growth of a sense of the Anglo-Saxon past. After the Conquest, for example, even though the English language slipped from official use, some historical and ecclesiastical records written in Old English continued to be consulted and were either revised into contemporary English or translated into Latin. One of the earliest manifestations of Anglo-Saxonism after the Conquest can be traced in twelfth-century Middle English glosses on Old English texts, including those by the so-called "tremulous hand" of Worcester. Christine Franzen has argued that this glossator was seeking to update penitential texts, based on Anglo-Saxon models, so as to bring them into conformity with the reformed standards of Latin models. Among the texts glossed were a famous copy of Alfred's translation of the *Cura Pastoralis* in which there are fifty or more glosses per page, cribbed, Franzen finds, from a Latin source.[10] The tremulous hand also glossed the Old English translation of Bede and King Alfred's translation of Boethius, again evidently drawing on Latin versions.[11] We can see that writing on Old English in the Anglo-Norman period requires us to think in multilingual terms, more so even than in the period before the Conquest. Another manifestation of Anglo-Saxonism in this period is the translation of Alfred's English code of laws into Latin under the authority of Henry II (d. 1189). Through such acts of translation, key elements of the Anglo-Saxon past were made available to members of the francophone ruling class, who could then present themselves as custodians of a reputable English heritage. Much of this interest in Old English has been traced to St. Wulfstan (d. 1095, canonized in 1208). Bishop Wulfstan was so important to the emerging sense of an English national identity that King John asked to be buried next to him, and was.[12]

Studies such as those mentioned here have provided points of departure for the contributors to the present volume, each of whom pursues the argument about Anglo-Saxonism into new ground. At the same time as the authors address problems of interest to specialists, they also bring the subject of Anglo-Saxonism within the horizon of any readers interested in cultural history. The collection demonstrates how Anglo-Saxonism can be traced in a wide variety of texts and movements, both academic and popular, over a period of more than a thousand years. By linking current Anglo-Saxon studies to their early manifestations, we seek to contribute to the "new medievalisms" — that is, theoretically aware, institutionally focused, and interdisciplinary medieval studies — that are transforming the academy.

The volume begins by exploring how the Anglo-Saxons themselves thought about the origins of their national and racial identity. The textual records from the period before the Conquest show an emergent sense of Anglo-Saxon identity, of the English people as distinct from others, with a separate history and a distinct mission. Bede's *Ecclesiastical History,* examined in Allen J. Frantzen's essay, attempts to weld Anglo-Saxon kingdoms into a united Church if not a single nation. By employing "Angli" as a name for all the Christian peoples of the island, Bede succeeds in creating an English "nation" at least in name, if not in any genuine political sense. Bede proposes that such unity follows from Gregory the Great's mission to convert the English, a mission that Bede's own history consolidates and memorializes. Frantzen pairs Bede's work with a revision of this story by an important and little-known Renaissance scholar, John Bale, who drastically revises it — some might say "queers" it — by identifying its sexual subtext.

The essays by Janet Thormann and Mary P. Richards continue this effort to trace early manifestations of Anglo-Saxonism. Thormann analyzes the sequence of poems inserted into the tenth-century prose records of the *Anglo-Saxon Chronicle* for evidence of an early concept of national unity and mission. Much as historical writing in general "produces the idea of a nation," she argues, the vernacular poems of the *Chronicle* heightened the Anglo-Saxons' sense of nationhood by activating an ideological component derived from their heroic past. Richards locates an emergent sense of national identity in the vernacular law codes of Ine, Alfred, Athelstan, Edgar, and Æthelred. She thus calls attention to Anglo-Saxonism as a self-conscious process, both textual and political, through which the people of Britain simultaneously affirmed their Germanic heritage and their commitment to Christianity. These two essays reveal how the Anglo-Saxons established their identity as a people through vernacular textual traditions.

Suzanne C. Hagedorn focuses on the origins of modern Anglo-Saxon studies in partisan Renaissance scholarship. With the Reformation and the need for the Church of England to make a clean break from Rome, the search for native origins began in earnest. Homilies, penitentials, prayers, and other texts in Old English were published by Matthew Parker, chaplain to Queen Elizabeth I, in his attempt to document the origins of the Church of England in the Anglo-Saxon Church of half a millennium before. Hagedorn studies the reception history of a single canonical text, the famous preface to King Alfred's translation of the *Cura Pastoralis* of Gregory the Great, during the sixteenth century and in later times, up to the first complete edition of the *Pastoral Care* at the end of the nineteenth century. Her case history illustrates the changing faces of Anglo-Saxonism over a period of some time; in addition, it shows how the revival of interest in Anglo-Saxon manuscripts during the Renaissance led directly to modern Anglo-Saxon studies.

Prior to the Renaissance, the Anglo-Saxon period had rested in relative obscurity thanks in part to the influence of one historian with important Norman ties, Geoffrey of Monmouth. In his *Historia Regum Britanniae* Geoffrey systematically distorted and effaced Anglo-Saxon history, characterizing the English as little more than a band of cutthroats and intruders who had interrupted the providential flow of history from the ancient British past to a new glorious age that was soon to unfold.[13] Despite being little more than a tissue of colorful lies and fantasies, the Galfridian calumny dominated European historiography for four hundred years, as T. G. Kendrick has observed.[14] But by the time of the Renaissance, new versions of the past had begun to paint the Anglo-Saxons in a better light. This reconception of the early history of the English gained credibility once the political unity of the Anglo-Norman Empire had been succeeded by the Anglo-French rivalries of the Hundred Years' War (1337–1453). At this point an originary myth of "Saxon England" began to grow strong as a point of resistance to French political ambitions. This view constitutes a second strain of Anglo-Saxonism, a perspective in which the Anglo-Saxons are associated with a valorous and happy past and with religious and social traditions that need to be preserved.

The essays in Part Two explore different aspects of this new Anglo-

Saxon origin myth, one that has never ceased to inspire controversy and resistance, whether by those who look to classical Greece and Rome, to medieval France, or to Celtic or even pre-Celtic antiquity for important cultural precedents.

Robert E. Bjork shows that nineteenth-century Scandinavia offers clear lessons in the dangers of nationalistic bias. With the emergence of systematic language study and ethnography in the eighteenth century, the Anglo-Saxon past became involved in complex arguments, nearly every one of them spurious, either attempting to demonstrate a link between the Chosen People of biblical history and the languages and peoples of northern Europe or justifying one or another brand of nationalism. During this period, much as Swedish scholars were arguing that Sweden was the birthplace of civilization, Danish scholars were quick to proclaim their ancestors the progenitors of the English. Grímur Thorkelin's pioneering edition of *Beowulf* (1815) exemplifies the cultural appropriations that were then in vogue. For him, this Old English poem was no less than "a Danish poem in the Anglo-Saxon dialect" that had somehow to be loosened from the grasp of British scholars who were keeping Scandinavian treasures hostage. Competing nationalisms subjected Anglo-Saxon studies to enormous ideological strains in all parts of Europe and North America. In part because of the legacy of pseudoscholarship that derives from those movements, Anglo-Saxon studies are now in danger of being dismissed, on some sides, as being inherently ethnocentric and racialist— only one hundred years after they first generally gained a position of respect in the disciplines of the academy.

The next two essays explore the place of Anglo-Saxonism in nineteenth-century America. J. R. Hall discusses Charles Anderson and John Seely Hart as two key figures in the debate concerning the teaching of Old English in antebellum America, when few academies offered instruction in Old English despite Thomas Jefferson's belief that the success of the democratic experiment depended on citizens' knowledge of Anglo-Saxon language and culture. Hall reveals the contentiousness of language study in the early American educational curriculum. In particular, he shows how the issue of whether or not to teach Old English became swept up in the politics of a rapidly expanding nation and was thus dramatized in a public debate involving oratory.[15] In a complementary essay, Gregory A. VanHoosier-Carey turns his attention to Anglo-Saxonism in the postbellum South, when the myth of "Saxon England" provided inspiration for southerners resisting the consequences of the northerners' "conquest" of their beleaguered land. For a time, Anglo-Saxonism spoke with a southern accent. Just as previous to the war, southern slaveholders had looked to Anglo-Saxon England for justification of a slave economy that was viewed as the source of mutual benefit for both slaves and masters,[16] so during this later period, southern intellectuals made regional use of the idea of the Anglo-Saxons' resistance to the Normans and their eventual subversion of foreign authority through the triumph of their tongue.

In the last essay in Part Two, Velma Bourgeois Richmond directs attention to Great Britain at the beginning of the twentieth century and demonstrates how, again and again and with remarkable inventiveness, Anglo-Saxon themes were adopted into Edwardian juvenile fiction as part of an attempt to build "British character." This complex of virtues included manly comradeship in the public school spirit, the protection of women, and the defense of Christian values. Richmond relates this pedagogical aim to nationalist ambitions when the British Empire was at the apex of its power. Her essay builds on important studies of Victorian and Edwardian medievalism by such scholars as Alice Chandler, Mark Girouard, and Clare Simmons.[17]

To conclude the collection, John D. Niles offers an essay proposing a theory of culture that accommodates other essays in the volume. Niles approaches culture as a series of purposeful appropriations, a concept illustrated with examples that range from the site of Cardiff Castle to the competing uses made of the Celtic and Anglo-Saxon past in the contemporary tourist industry. According to the view presented here, the past is chiefly significant as something usable. People invoke it, reshape it, or discard it as they see fit according to prevailing ideologies and values, thereby continually shifting the ground on which they stand, often at the same time as they ignore that it has moved at all.

Because of constraints of length, we have been selective. Not every subject with important bearing on Anglo-Saxonism is addressed. For example, the collection offers only partial analysis of King Alfred the Great, who might well be considered the most successful—and certainly most discussed—promoter of Anglo-Saxonism before the Conquest. Readers with an interest in the historical King Alfred and the value of evidence thought to have bearing on his career are referred to a recent controversial book by Alfred P. Smyth.[18] Awaiting full treatment elsewhere is the story of the afterlife of Alfred since the Middle Ages, culminating in the late Victorian belief that "Alfred is, and will always remain, the typical man of our race, call him Anglo-Saxon, call him American, call him Englishman, call him Australian — the typical man of our race at his best and noblest."[19] In general, we have eschewed discussion of Anglo-Saxonism in the former British Empire, including Egypt, India, Canada, Australia, and New Zealand. Likewise, limitations of space preclude direct treatment of the Middle English period, of seventeenth- and eighteenth-century constitutional Anglo-Saxonism, and of important twentieth-century developments, including the Nazis' appropriation of Anglo-Saxon themes as part of their celebration of the Germanic past.[20] Our aim in this book is to stimulate thought in certain finite directions, not to address every relevant issue.

Neither do we strive for what could only be an artificial unity. In these diverse approaches to Anglo-Saxonism, the authors reinforce the contours of a field that has always resisted reduction to a single set of aims and methods. As editors we made no attempt to impose a single viewpoint on contributors. Several authors are more at home with antiquarian issues than with theoretical ones. Other contributors, fully at ease in the language of contemporary cultural criticism, would probably see antiquarianism itself as a potential vehicle for ideology in its tendency to promote particular political values (whether Whig or Tory, left-leaning or right-leaning) despite its apolitical facade.

While this book is directed to a primary audience of Anglo-Saxonists, it raises issues of importance to anyone engaged with intellectual history and the relations between scholarship, ideology, values, and national ambitions. In particular, it contributes to that heightened self-awareness concerning the uses of the past that is characteristic of medieval studies at the present time. This self-awareness has taken many different forms of late and can be summed up in the term *medievalism*, taken in a broad sense to refer to the uses to which the Middle Ages have been put during the postmedieval period. The current vogue of medievalism stems partly from the demise of positivist historicism, partly from the increasing willingness of scholars to see their own activities as part of a large and contentious social process rather than as situated in a timeless scholarly zone.[21]

The recent surge of interest in medievalism is evident in the eight volumes of *Studies in Medievalism*, edited by Leslie J. Workman, that have appeared since the inception of that series in 1979.[22] Two other recent essay collections focus on the reception history of the Middle Ages. One of these, edited by John Simons, includes chiefly British scholarship; the other, edited by R. Howard Bloch and Stephen G. Nichols, features work by Americans.[23] Although these books are noticeably lacking in attention to the Anglo-Saxon period, the many topics that they do encompass reflect the breadth of the contemporary cultural debate in which the theme of Anglo-Saxonism is embedded.[24] The virtual exclusion of Anglo-Saxon England from both these volumes and others deserves notice as evidence of one aspect of medievalism itself: namely, the struggle of scholars to allow competing voices from the past to be heard. The conception of the Middle Ages as something that begins in about the year 1200, like the conception of medieval English literature as, in essence, literature of the age of Chaucer, is something that Anglo-Saxonists have long had to contend with, seeing that the Anglo-Saxon period is clearly part of whatever we mean by medieval England. Inevitably, the struggle for a usable past is transnational. It crosses disciplinary boundaries and the limits that are set by historical periodization. It is multiethnic in character, in keeping with the increasing ethnic pluralism of North America and western Europe and the heat with which competing origin myths are being voiced.

By now it has become clear, in the words of medieval historian Norman Cantor, that the Middle Ages are the result of "an interactive cultural process" in which current scholarship is implicated at every turn. "In writing and reading history," Cantor writes, "we are visibly creating a psychoanalysis in which our own anxieties, hopes, fears, and disappointments become interactive" with the subjects of academic research. Absences, too, have a place in this process. Cantor himself has little to say about Anglo-Saxonism as one aspect of the modern invention of the Middle Ages. He devotes less than two pages of his history to "Anglo-Saxon lovers" who remain chiefly anonymous. Evidently, the marginalization of medieval studies within the academy is a phenomenon within which some medievalists' marginalization of Anglo-Saxon studies takes place.[25] Taking Cantor's argument one step farther, we might add that since the anxieties, hopes, fears, and disappointments that influence scholarly research are not the unique possession of solitary persons but are often common social property, the books and articles written by scholars about the Middle Ages contribute to a collective psychohistory of their own times.

As both part of this psychohistory and a commentary on it, we seek in the present volume to contribute to the more precise understanding of Anglo-Saxon England as a major historically contingent cultural construction. At every stage of its growth, this construction—which is only one aspect of the reception history of the past in general—has intersected with current controversies of a political, religious, racial, intellectual, pedagogical, or artistic nature. No historical period has stood apart from this contentious process, least of all our own. One of our chief purposes is to make visible the idea of Anglo-Saxon England *as an idea,* thereby displaying its influence in cultural history. Efforts of this kind are necessary if a high degree of scholarly self-awareness is to be maintained and if historically significant subjects are to be preserved from the oblivion into which they are always in danger of being thrust.

The origin of this collection was a conference on Anglo-Saxonism, held in Berkeley in March 1994, featuring Allen Frantzen as keynote speaker and organized by John Niles and the Old English Colloquium of the University of California, Berkeley. To supplement six papers drawn from that meeting and subsequently revised for publication, three additional papers were solicited to form a balanced collection that explores manifestations of Anglo-Saxonism from its beginnings to the twentieth century.

Notes

1. The following remarks rely on the entries on "Anglo-Saxon," "Anglo-Saxondom," "Anglo-Saxonism," and "WASP" in vols. 1 and 19, respectively, of the *Oxford English Dictionary,* 2d ed. For extended discussion of the first term, see Susan Reynolds, "What Do We Mean by 'Anglo-Saxon' and 'Anglo-Saxons'?" *Journal of British Studies* 24 (1985): 395–414.

2. The term seems to have entered mainstream use with E. Digby Baltzell, *The Protestant Establishment: Aristocracy and Caste in America* (New Haven: Yale University Press, 1964).

3. Reginald Horsman, *Race and Manifest Destiny: The Origins of American Racial Anglo-Saxonism* (Cambridge: Harvard University Press, 1981); Hugh A. MacDougall, *Racial Myth in English History: Trojans, Teutons, and Anglo-Saxons* (Montreal: Harvest House; Hanover, N.H.: University Press of New England, 1982).

4. Carl T. Berkhout and Milton McC. Gatch, eds., *Anglo-Saxon Scholarship: The First Three Centuries* (Boston: G. K. Hall, 1982). The collection includes a useful survey by Michael Murphy, "Antiquary to Academic: The Progress of Anglo-Saxon Scholarship" (pp. 1–17).

5. Clare A. Simmons, *Reversing the Conquest: History and Myth in Nineteenth-Century British Literature* (New Brunswick, N.J.: Rutgers University Press, 1990).

6. Allen J. Frantzen, *Desire for Origins: New Language, Old English, and Teaching the Tradition* (New Brunswick, N.J.: Rutgers University Press, 1990).

7. Edward Said, *Orientalism* (New York: Vintage, 1978).

8. E. G. Stanley, *The Search for Anglo-Saxon Paganism* (Cambridge, Eng.: D. S. Brewer, 1975).

9. Roberta Frank, "The Search for the Anglo-Saxon Oral Poet," *Bulletin of the John Rylands University Library of Manchester,* 75 (1993): 11–36. An entertaining companion piece for Frank's essay is Sam Smiles, *The Image of Antiquity: Ancient Britain and the Romantic Imagination* (New Haven: Yale University Press, 1994), chap. 4, "The Bards of England."

10. Christine Franzen, *The Tremulous Hand of Worcester: A Study of Old English in the Thirteenth Century* (Oxford: Clarendon, 1991), pp. 59–60.

11. Ibid., p. 78.

12. Ibid., p. 188.

13. See John D. Niles, "The Wasteland of Loegria: Geoffrey of Monmouth's Reinvention of the Anglo-Saxon Past," in *Reinventing the Middle Ages and Renaissance: Constructions of the Medieval and Early Modern Periods,* ed. William Gentrup (Turnhout, Belgium: Brepols, forthcoming).

14. T. D. Kendrick, *British Antiquity* (London: Methuen, 1950). See further Richard Waswo, "Our Ancestors, the Trojans: Inventing Cultural Identity in the Middle Ages," *Exemplaria* 7 (1995): 269–90.

15. On knowledge of the Old English language as one key element of Anglo-Saxonism, see also Clare A. Simmons, "'Iron-Worded Proof': Victorian Identity and the Old English Language," in *Medievalism in England,* ed. Leslie J. Workman (Cambridge, Eng.: D. S. Brewer, 1992 [= *Studies in Medievalism,* vol. 4]), pp. 202–14. Simmons documents the efforts of those Britons who "not only wished to establish the history of the English language, but also sought to use the evidence of language to determine the significance of being English" (p. 202).

16. See Eugene D. Genovese, "The Southern Slaveholders' View of the Middle Ages," in *Medievalism in American Culture,* ed. Bernard Rosenthal and Paul E. Szarmach (Binghamton, N.Y.: Center for Medieval and Early Renaissance Studies, 1989), pp. 31–52.

17. Alice Chandler, *A Dream of Order: The Medieval Ideal in Nineteenth-Century English Literature* (Lincoln: University of Nebraska Press, 1970); Mark Girouard, *The Return to Camelot: Chivalry and the English Gentleman* (New Haven: Yale University Press, 1981); and Simmons, *Reversing the Conquest.* For further discussion of some of the novels discussed by Richmond see also Billy Melman, "Claiming the Nation's Past: The Invention of an Anglo-Saxon Tradition," *Journal of Contemporary History* 26 (1991): 575–95.

18. Alfred P. Smyth, *King Alfred the Great* (Oxford: Oxford University Press, 1995), especially part two: "A Thousand Years of Deceit."

19. The words are those of Sir Walter Besant, Mayor of Winchhester, in an address delivered on November 9, 1897, quoted by Alfred Bowker, *The King*

Alfred Millenary: A Record of the Proceedings of the National Commemoration (London: Macmillan, 1902), p. 9.

20. One twentieth-century phenomenon, the afterlife of Anglo-Saxon themes and verse forms in the work of contemporary poets, is analyzed by Nicholas Howe, "Praise and Lament: The Afterlife of Old English Poetry in Auden, Hill, and Gunn," in *Words and Works: Essays in Medieval Language and Literature in Honour of Fred C. Robinson,* ed. Peter S. Baker and Nicholas Howe (Toronto, forthcoming). Howe builds on Robinson's own exemplary study "'The Might of the North': Pound's Anglo-Saxon Studies and *The Seafarer,*" *Yale Review* 71 (1982): 199–224.

21. Note in this connection Gerald Graff, *Professing Literature: An Institutional History* (Chicago: University of Chicago Press, 1987) and the collective volume *Redrawing the Boundaries: The Transformation of English and American Literary Study,* ed. Stephen Greenblatt and Giles Gunn (New York: Modern Language Association of America, 1992).

22. A ninth volume is due to appear in 1997 on the subject "Medievalism and the Academy."

23. John Simons, ed., *From Medieval to Medievalism* (New York: St. Martin's Press, 1992); Stephen G. Nichols and R. Howard Bloch, eds., *Medievalism and the Modern Temper* (Baltimore: Johns Hopkins University Press, 1996).

24. See the volumes cited in note 21.

25. Norman F. Cantor, *Inventing the Middle Ages* (New York: W. Morrow, 1991), pp. 38, 43.

Part One

Medieval and Renaissance Anglo-Saxonism

"Non Angli sed Angeli."
Illustration from *The Anglo-Saxon* 1:1 (London, 1849).
Reproduced with permission of the Newberry Library, Chicago.

1. Bede and Bawdy Bale

Gregory the Great, Angels, and the "Angli"

Allen J. Frantzen

W HAT DO WE mean by 'Anglo-Saxon' and 'Anglo-Saxons'?" asks Susan Reynolds in an important essay seeking to answer this question. To begin, she consults the *Oxford English Dictionary,* where *Anglo-Saxon* is a term used "rhetorically for *English* in its wider or ethnological sense" and also used to designate "all persons of Teutonic descent (or who reckon themselves as such) in Britain" and "all of this descent in the world, whether subjects of Great Britain or of the United States." With evident relief, Reynolds notes that these terms are now somewhat out of date, since "large parts of the world are subject formally neither to Great Britain nor to the United States." She continues: "Nonetheless, the passage [from the *OED*] exemplifies very well the link that was simply assumed to exist between language and biological descent all through history until it was made explicit in the eighteenth and nineteenth centuries as the fundamental premise of the philological nationalism that was then developing in Europe. The philologists themselves, of course, started from the universal assumption that language and descent went together, so that when they divided languages into Germanic, Latin, Celtic, and so forth, they thought that they were also dividing mankind into 'races' of common descent and common inherited characteristics."[1]

Language, common descent, and inherited characteristics are fundamental elements of Anglo-Saxonism in any period. I propose to examine their conjunction at an originary moment in the history of Anglo-Saxonism to which this volume contributes. That moment occurs in Bede's *Ecclesiastical History of the English People* when Gregory the Great encounters Anglian boys in a marketplace in Rome. I contrast Bede's account of this meeting with a version published by John Bale, a Reformation historian and anti-Catholic polemicist. Bale recasts the episode in a hostile light that exposes its sexual content and calls attention to the enduring power of Anglo-Saxonism to encode sexual norms in seemingly asexual narratives.

"Angli" and Angels

Bede's story of the Anglians in Rome, found at the start of book 2 of the *Ecclesiastical History,* is one of the most effective Anglo-Saxonizing gestures in the Old English period. Bede describes how Gregory, not yet pope, saw boys at a market and inquired about their race.

> It is said that one day, soon after some merchants had arrived in Rome, a quantity of merchandise was exposed for sale in the market place. Crowds came to buy and Gregory too amongst them. As well as other merchandise he saw some boys put up for sale, with fair complexions, handsome faces, and lovely hair. On seeing them he asked, so it is said, from what region or land they had been brought. He was told that they came from the island of Britain, whose inhabitants were like that in appearance. He asked again whether those islanders were Christians or still entangled in the errors of heathenism. He was told that they were heathen. Then with a deep-drawn sigh he said, "Alas that the author of darkness should have men so bright of face in his grip, and that minds devoid of inward grace should bear so graceful an outward form." Again he asked for the name of the race. He was told that they were called *Angli.* "Good," he said, "they have the face of angels, and such men should be follow-heirs of the angels in heaven." "What is the name," he asked, "of the kingdom from which they have been brought?" He was told that the men of the kingdom were called *Deiri.* "*Deiri,*" he replied, "*De ira!* good! snatched from the wrath of Christ and called to his mercy. And what is the name of the king of the land?" He was told that it was Ælle; and playing on the name, he said, "Alleluia! the praise of God the Creator must be sung in those parts."[2]

Gregory's puns were not original with Bede; a version of the story is found in the anonymous Whitby *Life* of Gregory the Great, probably written between 704 and 714 but unknown to Bede when he finished the *Ecclesiastical History* in 731.[3]

The Whitby *Life* recounts this episode with some important differences. One is the boys' age, which in the Whitby version is uncertain: "Now some say they were beautiful boys, while others say that they were curly-haired, handsome youths" ("Quos quidam pulchros fuisse pueros dicunt et quidam vero crispos iuvenes et decoros," 90–91). Bede says only that the Anglians were "boys put up for sale, with fair complexions, handsome faces, and lovely hair" ("pueros uenales positos candidi corporis ac uenusti uultus, capillorum quoque forma egregia," 132–33). Although Gregory calls the Angli "men" ("homines"), Bede raises the possibility that they were younger than seventeen or eighteen; he also elaborates the boys' physical beauty, which is described by the Whitby author more generally. Another point of difference concerns Gregory's motive. The Whitby author reports that the Angli were brought to Gregory at his own request because he was "prompted by a fortunate intuition, . . . puzzled by their new and unusual appearance, and . . . inspired by God" (91). This account portrays Gregory as a curious Roman who wants to see visitors of a different race and summons them; there is no accidental meeting and, more important, no marketplace. Gregory speaks directly to the boys (or youths) in the Whitby version, despite the language barrier between them; in Bede's account he relies on a translator. Finally, the Whitby version does not mention that the Angli were slaves.

Patrick Wormald notes that Bede seems to express some reservations about the truth of this anecdote, even though he included it.[4] The episode also impressed later Anglo-Saxon readers. Its general significance and much of its linguistic texture survive the translation of the *Ecclesiastical History* into Old English made at the end of the ninth century.[5] Ælfric's translation of the episode in his homily in St. Gregory likewise follows Bede's version.[6] Modern historians, literary and otherwise, perhaps like Bede, seem of two minds about the story. Although Sir Frank Stenton does not mention it, the episode is discussed by Peter Hunter Blair not once but twice.[7] In introductory grammars and readers, reliable measures of the cultural value attached to Old English narratives, references to this event are rare. Three standard grammars feature other episodes from Bede's *History* but not the story about the slave boys. Included instead are the conversion of Edwine, son of King Ælle (whose name so delighted

Gregory), which features the famous flight of the sparrow through the hall (2.9–11), and, inescapably, Cædmon's "hymn" (4.24). The story of Gregory and the boys can be found only in *Bright's Old English Grammar and Reader,* where it is excerpted briefly as part of a grammar lesson.[8] Yet this anecdote would seem worthy of more than routine attention, for it marks a symbolic point in the *History,* a transition from the pagan to the Christian phase of English history inaugurated by what Bede proudly calls Gregory's "earnest solicitude for the salvation of our race" (2.1, pp. 132–33).[9]

Following the example of Gildas, Bede adapts the story of the English to the motif of the Chosen People who violate their covenant with God and are destroyed as a result.[10] The British, Bede shows, drove out their Irish and Pictish assailants; their victory was followed by "an abundance of corn in the island as had never before been known. With this affluence came an increase of luxury, followed by every kind of foul crime. . . ." Both clergy and laity "cast off Christ's easy yoke and thrust their necks under the burden of drunkenness, hatred, quarrelling, strife, and envy and other similar crimes." Devastated by a plague, those who survived could not be awakened from "the spiritual death which their sins had brought upon them" (1.14, pp. 48–49). They called the Anglo-Saxons from across the sea, and soon "the fire kindled by the hands of the heathen executed the just vengeance of God on the nation for its crimes" (1.15, pp. 52–53).

Restored to peace for a time, the British kept alive the memory of this calamity; when that memory faded, however, they again lapsed into evil ways. "To other unspeakable crimes, which Gildas their own historian describes in doleful words, was added this crime, that they never preached the faith to the Saxons or Angles who inhabited Britain with them," Bede writes near the end of book 1. However, God did not abandon the sinners. Through Gregory, he appointed "much worthier heralds of the truth to bring this people to the faith" (1.22, pp. 68–69). Nicholas Howe suggests that Bede's positioning of the event "is a tribute to Gregory's achievement in making possible this shift in the destiny of the English."[11] Bede wishes to show a complete break between the lapsed early Christian communities and the heathen tribes Gregory's missionaries will convert. He stresses this hiatus in part because both his lineage, which he shared with the Anglian boys, and his *History,* which he dedicated to the Northumbrian king Ceolwulf, are implicated in it.

The boys were descendants of Anglo-Saxons who, 150 years after coming to Britain, were still pagan. What does it mean that they are called "Angli"? The glossary to the translation of the *Historia Ecclesiastica* by Bertram Colgrave and R. A. B. Mynors translates all occurrences of *Angli* and its derivatives as meaning "English." The *Dictionary of Old English* suggests that uses of the Old English equivalents to mean something other than "English" in such phrases as "kings of the English" or "nation of the English" are rare.[12] Colgrave notes that the boys Gregory saw were Northumbrian, although Gregory called them Angli.[13] Bede's understanding of Angli is clear in his description of the settlements of Germanic tribes. Bede locates the Jutes where the people of Kent live, and the Saxons where the West, East, and South Saxons live. He continues:

> Beside this, from the country of the Angles, that is, the land between the kingdoms of the Jutes and the Saxons, which is called *Angulus,* came the East Angles, the Middle Angles, the Mercians, and all the Northumbrian race (that is those people who dwell north of the river Humber) as well as the other Anglian tribes. *Angulus* is said to have remained deserted from that day to this. (1.15, p. 51).[14]

Therefore, unlike Boniface, who described himself as "of the race of the Angles,"[15] Bede can be understood to mean "Anglian" in the more specific sense of "Northumbrian." When he refers to himself as a boy who was born in the territory of Monkwearmouth-Jarrow (5.24, pp. 566–67), Bede tells us that he too is Northumbrian and Anglian as well as English.

The "Angli" are also, of course, "angels." Bede is careful not to overemphasize this meaning—it is enough, perhaps, for Gregory to establish this link—and little has been written about Bede's use of it. That the boys' beauty should make Gregory think of angels is significant, for there are many angels in Bede's *History,* but none of them merely symbolic. Rather, Bede's angels are busy escorting exemplary holy people to and from visions of the afterlife, or to their deaths.[16] Nowhere, apart from the story about Gregory, are humans described as "angelic." And nowhere else in Bede are angels used as they are so often in art, as androgynous measures of male (or, for that matter, female) physical beauty (although that sense perhaps emerges in reference to the vision of Cenred's thegn, in which the angels are described as "two most handsome youths" ("duo pulcherrimi iuuenes," pp. 500–501).

Bede suggests that Gregory's encounter with the boys motivated the mission to England, but in fact it would appear that the mission stemmed

from knowledge of conditions there that Gregory acquired after he had
become pope, and that the mission produced the anecdote, rather than
the other way around. Knowledge about the English might have reached
Gregory through Gaul, as Hunter Blair observes, since Bertha, the daughter of the Frankish king Chairbert, was married to the Kentish king
Æthelberht before Gregory became pope in 590.[17] In 596, "Gregory,
prompted by divine inspiration," according to Bede, sent Augustine and
several monks "to preach the word of God to the English race" (1.23, pp.
68–69). But because they were daunted by the prospect of preaching to
"a barbarous, fierce, and unbelieving nation whose language they did not
even understand," they turned back. Gregory sent one letter to encourage
the monks and another to Etherius, archbishop of Arles, to welcome
them. In this second letter Gregory also commended "the priest Candidus,"
who was sent "to take charge of a small patrimony of our church" (1.24,
pp. 72–73). Gregory had written to Candidus earlier (September 595),
asking him to buy "English boys who are seventeen or eighteen years old,
that they may be given to God and educated in the monasteries" ("pueros
Anglos qui sunt ab annis decem et septem vel decem et octo, ut in
Monasteriis dati Deo proficiant comparet").[18]

Hunter Blair suggests several possibilities for the presence of English
boys in Gaul—and therefore in Rome—at this time. "It is all too easy for
the reader to jump to the romantic conclusion that the boys whose
purchase was envisaged by Gregory were English slaves on sale in a
market-place," he warns. The boys might also have been held in service,
as four English boys were held in the service of Jews at Narbonne, or
prisoners of war, mercenaries, or "merely young men in some way bound
to the soil on Merovingian estates."[19] Among the "romantic" readers of
this episode Blair would have had to number Colgrave and Mynors and
David Pelteret, all of whom identify the boys as slaves.[20] Colgrave observes that the purchase of slaves by the Church was not an unusual
practice. "The custom of buying or ransoming slaves to turn them into
missionaries was known," he writes, and both Aidan and Willibrord
observed it.[21]

It is, one wants to reply to Hunter Blair, all too easy *not* to ask what
the boys were doing in the marketplace. There is no question that they
were on sale, and whether they were on sale as slaves, captives, or
"merely young men in some way bound to the soil" seems a small
difference. The boys about whom Gregory wrote were to be ordained
after they were freed. When Pope Leo I (d. 461) denounced the ordina-

tion of slaves as priests, it was because they had "not been able to obtain their freedom from their owners" and so were not worthy to be "raised to the dignity of the priesthood." He continued, "The sacred ministry is polluted by such vile company."[22] Positioned among "other merchandise," as Bede describes them, the boys in the marketplace are not so fortunate. They obviously are not going to be sold to someone like Gregory (he does not try to purchase them) who would arrange for their entry into a monastery.

Hunter Blair does not entertain the strong possibility that the Angli were slaves. Nor does he consider the significance of their age, even though the boys Gregory saw might well have been children, who were especially at risk in the slave trade. Parents could sell their children into slavery up to the age of six. The Penitential of Theodore of Canterbury explained the conditions under which this activity was permitted, and an Anglo-Saxon penitential of the late tenth century repeats them.[23] Referring to the laws of Wihtred of Kent (695), which permitted a freeman caught stealing to be sold "ofer sæ," Whitelock notes, "Except in Kent in very early days, it was strictly forbidden to sell people of English race across the sea, or into the control of foreigners, by which phrase the heathen Danes are primarily meant."[24] But in 1014 Wulfstan denounced those who sold their children into foreign servitude,[25] and foreign trade in slaves persisted until the Norman Conquest. Many sources testify to the importance of freeing slaves, or manumitting them, as a form of penance or an act of mercy.[26] In almost all cases the slaves in question are penal slaves, those forced into slavery because they could not pay debts or because they were being punished for some offense. The boys being sold in Rome were probably captives, perhaps too young to be penal slaves or to be sold as slave labor.

The boys are not the only slaves Bede tells us about. The most famous is Imma, the thegn who is bought by a Frisian trader and who is released from his chains of captivity through the prayers of his brother.[27] "Slave dealing seems to have been one of the earliest forms of continental trading in Anglo-Saxon times," Colgrave and Mynors observe in a note to the story of Imma, "and the slave boys seen by Gregory in Rome were probably taken there by Frisians."[28] This view is supported by Pelteret, who points to the existence of a Frisian colony in York in the mid-eighth century.[29]

The story of Imma shows that Bede approaches captivity figuratively as a representation of the bondage of sin from which true belief can release the captive. This sort of figurative release, not only for the boys but for the nation they represent, is evoked many times in Bede's narrative of the Chosen People, which seeks to valorize his own race and origins and to affirm their special place in the heart of the man who was to become, for Bede, the most important pontiff of the Church. In the service of Bede's Anglo-Saxonism, the boys represent a benign and neglected heathendom. The narrative exalts their innocence, youth, and beauty, but its real subject is their race, their nation, and their king, all three fortuitously predisposed to Gregory's apostolic design.

Neither corrupted nor fallen, "Angli" in three senses, the boys represent Bede's race in a pure state, which Gregory recognizes as that of a chosen people awaiting God's blessing. The boys aptly symbolize the absolute abjection of the Anglians—the English—that resulted from neglect of the faith by the British. They are, as Gregory says, enslaved by darkness. But that they might have been enslaved by more material forces does not seem an entirely "romantic" or incredible possibility. What was their value in the marketplace? Ruth Mazo Karras points out that sexual exploitation was among the many unfortunate facts of life for women slaves.[30] It is possible that boys were also sexually exploited and that their commercial value was directly related to their beauty and fairness.[31]

The sexual resonance of the anecdote, unremarked by Bede and by most of his readers, has, so far as I know, been discussed only by John Boswell. Boswell documents the Church's concern that abandoned children would be sold into slavery and used for sexual purposes. Some writers protested this practice but not for the reasons we might expect. Their concern was that fathers who abandoned their children might later accidentally buy them as slaves and commit incest by having intercourse with them! Boswell notes that the public sale of slaves continued in Rome long after the empire was Christianized and illustrates the practice with the episode as Bede recounted it.[32]

There is, it is true, little in Bede's *History,* in this anecdote or elsewhere, to draw attention to sexual behavior. Gildas is more forthcoming, but in his work too it is difficult to detect specific sexual practices. References to the archetypal disasters of Sodom and Gomorrah offer possible clues.[33] Shortly before the story about the boys, Bede, citing Gildas, deplores the "unspeakable crimes" of early British Christians (1.22, pp. 68–69). Earlier, he hints that sexual impropriety contributed to their downfall. With the affluence the Britons won, Bede writes, "came an increase of luxury, followed by every kind of foul crime . . . " (1.14, pp. 48–49). Sexual sins are included in the category of "luxury," which was often named as the chief sin of Sodom.[34] An admittedly tenuous connection to sodomy is possible, since a prohibition against mentioning this and certain other sexual sins seem to be observed when Bede called the crimes of the British "unspeakable."[35] We would not, for many reasons, expect Bede to comment on the sexual implications of Gregory's admiration of the beautiful boys in any negative way. Some seven hundred years after Bede's death, that task fell to John Bale.

Bale and Bede

In the 1540s, in the early phases of the English Reformation, Gregory's visit to the market attracted the attention of John Bale, a Carmelite priest who left the Church of Rome in the 1530s and became a prodigious instrument in the propaganda efforts of Thomas Cromwell.[36] Bale was the author of several large-scale surveys of English authors, the first biographer of Chaucer, and a collector of early manuscripts, including those in Anglo-Saxon, of which he owned a considerable number.[37] In his splendid study of *English Reformation Literature*, John N. King recognizes Bale as "the most influential English Protestant author of his time."[38]

Bale recounted the episode of Gregory and the slave boys in *The Actes of Englysh Votaryes*, a bold, even heroic revision of English history that describes the nation's struggles against the corrupt influences of the Church of Rome. The chief instrument of Roman domination, Bale argued, was clerical celibacy, which permitted the clergy to degrade marriage and to advocate virginity, all the while using its own religious houses for immoral purposes.[39] Bale vigorously defended the right of the clergy to wed and was convinced that Roman clergy who claimed to be celibate in fact indulged in every form of sexual corruption. His portrayal of the history of the Roman clergy in England, a steamy catalogue of the sexual excess of licentious men denied the right to marry, forms a prelude to his account of Gregory's visit to the marketplace:

> And as thys Gregorye behelde them fayre skynned and bewtyfullye faced, with heare upon their heades most comelye, anon he axed, of what regyon they were. Andswere was made hym, that they were of an yle called Englande. Wele maye they be called *Angli* (sayth he) for they have verye Angelych vysages. Se how curyose these fathers

were, in the wele eyenge of their wares. Here was no cyrcumstaunce unloked to, perteynynge to the sale. Yet have [has] thys Byshopp bene of all writers reckened the best sens hys tyme. (22a–b)

Bale mockingly reminds his readers to "[m]arke thys ghostlye mysterye, for the prelates had then no wyves." He does not directly accuse Gregory of "wele eyenge" the boys as sexual "wares," but he plainly implies that Gregory has sexual designs on them. Because priests were unmarried, Bale observes, with much sarcasm, "other spirytuall remedyes were sought out for them by their good prouvders and proctours, we maye (yf we wyll) call them apple squyres." "Apple-squires" here means pimp or panderer (OED). Stressing that this sale was not unique, Bale produces another witness, Machutus, who saw a similar event in Rome in 500 A.D. and bought the boys to protect them (22–22a). We are meant to conclude that Gregory, deprived of a wife by the Church's demand for clerical celibacy, sought out "other spirytuall remedyes" by purchasing boys for sex.

Bale's rewriting of the story of Gregory and the Anglian boys takes place in the context of an elaborate revision of England's Anglo-Saxon Christian history proposed in The Actes of Englysh Votaryes and The Image of Bothe Churches (two of ten books that he published in Antwerp in 1545 or 1546).[40] In The Image of Bothe Churches, Bale set forth a thesis about the Church in England that, as it was later developed by his better known contemporary, John Foxe, became a foundational strategy for Reformation anti-Roman polemic. This thesis is also at the heart of Bale's particular practice of Anglo-Saxonism. He argued that the Church had been divided during the reign of Constantine and that the See of Saint Peter stemmed from the corrupt division, while an isolated community of the faithful, who retained belief in the true Church, reestablished the true Church in England. Bale believed that the false Church of Rome had taken on the image of the true Church of antiquity. As Leslie P. Fairfield writes, Bale argued that "from the time of St. Augustine's mission in 597 to the repudiation of the papacy in 1533 the institutional English Church had been corrupt."[41] King shows that Bale's history of the early Church (wholly erroneous, needless to say) influenced the first book of Spenser's Faerie Queene, written in the 1590s, which stages this history of true and false images just as Bale imagined it: Red Cross Knight forsakes Una, the True Church, because Duessa, the false imitation that assumed the true Church's exact image, deceives him. Archimago is her partner, the "imago" here corresponding to the image-making power of Bale's title, *The Image of Bothe Churches.* The objective of his polemic was to unmask the false so that the true could be revealed.[42]

For Bede, the mission of Augustine marked the permanent conversion of Britain. Bale, as we have seen, reverses the significance of this event. The aim of *The Actes* is to teach its readers to judge false miracles used by "obstynate hypocrytes" still living under the pope's rules. Bale accuses Catholics of portraying "whoremongers, bawdes, brybers, idolaters, hypocrytes, traytors, and most fylthye Gomorreanes, as Godlye men and women" (2a). As he rails against them, Bale claims to want to teach Catholics the error of their ways. Still, he does not expect to reform what he calls servant slaves "to a most fylthye whore, and to her whoredome and whoremongers" (6b).

Like so many masters of diatribe, Bale was an idealist. His attack on the Roman clergy must be understood in the context of his idealization of marriage and his ardent defense of women's position. When he was a Carmelite priest, in the 1520s, Bale carried out extensive research into Carmelite archives and took special interest in the Church's view of women, in part at least because of his interest in Mary, the patron of the Carmelite order.[43] His recruitment to the Church of England came in the 1530s, when he lived in London and could see the drastic impact of Henry's marriage and decrees on all monastic orders, including his own. It was also at this time—in 1536—that Bale married, and undoubtedly this change in his life fueled his polemics about the Roman Church's demand for clerical celibacy.[44]

Marriage, Bale wrote in *The Actes,* was the "first order of religion," created in order to protect against "beastlye abusyons of the fleshe that shuld after happen" if men and women disobeyed God's command to increase and multiply (7b). The Church sought to dissuade holy men and women from marriage, broke up existing marriages, venerated only unmarried saints, and demonized women as "spretes" ("sprites," 3a-b); these were the acts of "the Sodomytycall swarme or brode of Antichrist" (4a). Bale fabricated a sweeping revision of the history of Anglo-Saxon saints, claiming that clergymen fornicated with cloistered nuns and pro-duced a race of bastards who were then venerated as saints, Cuthbert, Dunstan, Oswald, Anselm, and Becket among them (2b). Not all priests did so, of course. Those who refrained from women "spared not to worke execrable fylthyness among themselves, and one to pollute the other," an obvious reference to male homosexual acts (12b). Devout in his praise of Mary,[45] Bale was eager to insist that the mother of Jesus was not a professed nun, "as the dottynge papystes have dreamed, to couer their sodometrye with a most precyouse coloure, but an honest mannys wyfe" (13a). Bale attacked "spirituall Sodomytes and knaves" who wrote the lives of these sinful saints (18a): "Come out of Sodome ye whore-mongers and hypocrytes, popysh byshoppes and prestes" (18b). Bale used *sodometrie*—an obsolete word for sodomy, first used by Tyndall in 1530, according to the *Oxford English Dictionary*—to attack clergy who took the required vows of celibacy but who were unable to remain celibate: either men who had sex with each other because they could not have sex with women, or men who had sex with cloistered nuns who were virtually the male clergy's sexual slaves. Shortly before he recounts the story about Gregory, Bale tells of a large group of women who joined a pilgrimage, only to find that they had been taken from England to be forced into prostitution to the clergy on the Continent (21a).

Bale's definition of sodomy cannot be narrowed to male homosexual intercourse, but as he approaches the episode about the English boys (a center for my essay, not for his), Bale's denunciations of the "whorishness" of Rome focus more clearly on male homosexual acts. Echoing Gildas's treatment of the vice, Bale claims that sodomy was pervasive among the early Britons and that it was the reason for their overthrow by the Saxons (21a). Bale recognized the Saxons as the ancestors of the English (al-though his sense of ethnic identities is none too clear) and understood the boys as Saxons, who by implication were manly and virtuous, not sodomites like the early British against whom the Saxons fought. Bale repeats a tale (told by Gildas but gathered by Bale, along with others, from Geoffrey of Monmouth) concerning a monk named Maglocunus (Maglo), who became king and achieved great victories against the "Saxons, Normeies, and Danes." He was a "comelye" man who was also a sodomite, "which he had lerned in hys youthe of the consecrate chastyte of the holie clergye" (20b-21a).[46]

For Bale, as for Gildas, sodomy was a clerical vice as well as a vice of kings. The sin is not exclusively, or even primarily, a sexual offense, but rather broadly indicates impiety, injustice, and the improper use of God's gifts.[47] Bale's fullest exploration of sodomy is found in *A Comedy Concernynge thre lawes, of Nature, Moses, & Christ, corrupted by the sodomytes, Pharysees and Papystes,* published in 1538. According to Donald N. Mager, *A Comedy* is the only drama in sixteenth-century England in which Sodomy is a character.[48] The title juxtaposes sodomy with "nature" in a well-established paradigm that must be read against another opposition, that between Christ and "Papists." It is important to note that sodomy, which had long been the subject of extensive regulation in ecclesiastical courts, was criminalized for the first time in 1533, during the reign of Henry VIII.[49] Although Bale's account of Gregory and the slave boys does not mention sodomy, his sexual innuendo cannot be missed. For Bale, "sodomites" were not only the unjust and impious but also those who turned from the lawful union of marriage and had illicit intercourse either with the opposite sex or with their own. When he tells the story about Gregory's visit to the marketplace, Bale places Gregory in the long and infamous line of sodomitical Roman clergy who were denied lawful wives and who exploited boys instead to satisfy their lusts.

Bale's revision of this episode might profitably be considered an exercise in "queering," the critical (and political) act that seeks to uncover sexual tropes of which authors were not apparently aware, searching out same-sex relations in lives, institutions, and texts in which they have traditionally been overlooked. Bale, in the parlance of queer theory, can be said to "queer" Bede by calling attention to the possibility of homosexual relations in the culture Bede describes.[50] Jonathan Goldberg and other queer theorists are reluctant to characterize the work of queer theorists as "outing" because the general obscurity of all but a handful of Renaissance authors, and an even smaller group in the medieval period, precludes the political work that outing is intended to perform.[51] But outing in queer theory and queer politics is a self-conscious modern reflex of the narrower strategy—long despised and much indulged in—that Bale employs: the use of innuendo about sexual nonconformity to ridicule and destroy the opposition.[52] Such invective acquired measurable force in the Middle Ages, when (as James Brundage's survey of medieval canon law and handbooks of penance has demonstrated) deviant sexual acts, sodomy chief among them, came to indicate a lack of theological orthodoxy and were punished as heresy.[53] The term *sodomite* was used to describe those who held unorthodox theological beliefs as well as those who performed sex acts that were considered *contra naturam*, against nature, because they frustrated procreation. For Bale, the accusation of "sodomy" encompasses both theological and sexual sins and hence serves as a powerful weapon.

The conjunction of sodomy with sexual slavery drew Bale to the episode that was used by Bede to contrast the slavery of heathendom with the saving grace of Christianity. In Bale's view, the episode was not about redeeming heathens but about the enslavement of righteous Christians by the corrupt Church of Rome, and their subjection and sexual exploitation. For Bale, if not for us, the leering references to Gregory's "wele eyenge" of the boys in his search for "spirytuall remedyes" required no elaboration. Bale believed that he could document a long history of the Church's hostility to marriage—not just to the marriage of the clergy—and its contempt for women. Having repeatedly accused both earlier and contemporary figures of "sodometrye," Bale needed only to demonstrate Gregory's admiration for the boys' good looks; the implications were obvious.

Bale's accusations were sufficiently clear to his Catholic opponents, for whom Bede's text was seen as proof of a genuine and antique Christianity in England that needed no reform.[54] In 1565 Thomas Stapleton published the first translation of Bede's *History* in modern English, dedicated "To the Right excellent and most gratiouse princesse, Elizabeth by the grace of God Quene of England, Fraunce, and Ireland, Defendour of the Faith." Stapleton intended to juxtapose "a number of diuersities between the pretended religion of Protestants, and the primitive faith of the english Church," and contrasted the authority of Bede, who wrote without prejudice, with that of Bale, Foxe, and other "pretended doctors." Replying to Bale, Foxe, and others in the preface to his translation of the *History,* Stapleton protested that Bale deliberately misread this account in order to charge Gregory "with a most outrageous vice and not to be named." Stapleton obviously understood Bale to have accused Gregory of sodomy. Bede was a bee who made honey (beautiful meaning) out of this episode, said Stapleton. "Baudy Bale" was a "venimous spider being filthy and uncleane himself," an "olde ribauld," and "another Nero" who found "poisonned sence and meaning" in Bede's account.[55]

Is this indeed "poisonned sence and meaning," however? I will not attempt the impossible task of justifying Bale's attack on Gregory and the Church, but there is value in repositioning Bede between the artful simplicity of the Whitby account and Bale's extravagant reading. Bale suggests that the boys could well have been captives or victims of slave traders and that they are perhaps about to be sold into prostitution. He thereby forces us to consider what became of the boys after their beauty inspired Gregory's sending a mission to England and thus to reconsider Bede's treatment of the anecdote.

The most characteristic Anglo-Saxon aspect of Bede's *History* is its long-recognized aim of creating a unified English Church and people.[56]

Bede does this with a comprehensive concept of the "Angli" as a people elevated by their likeness, at least in Gregory's mind, to angels. Bale too makes use of the myth of a Chosen People who must be brought from captivity into freedom. For Bede these people are invaders who become Northumbrians, Anglians, and, finally, English. Bede's chosen people are brought to the promised land of Christianity; Bale's promised land is the Church of England, a new Christian church which, in *The Image of Bothe Churches*, he nonetheless claims to be the oldest church of all. In the context of Reformation theology, Bale's recasting of Anglo-Saxon history acquires a prominent sexual aspect if not a primary sexual character. The Anglo-Saxons are a people who naturally observe God's lawful commandment to be fruitful and multiply; their Roman oppressors, on the other hand, deny their clergy this right and, as a result, spread sexual corruption wherever they are to be found. Gregory's "wele eyenge" of the slave boys vividly emblematizes this exploitation in the heart of Rome itself.

"Those who find ugly meaning in beautiful things are corrupt without being charming," Oscar Wilde warned. "This is a fault."[57] This epigram prompts a reconsideration of both Bede and Bale. Bede asks us to see beautiful meanings in ugly things. The pathos that surrounds his account derives from this juxtaposition of their beauty and their abjection, and his addition of Gregory's "deep-drawn sigh" before he comments on the boys' beautiful faces is a sensitive touch. Yet Bede's interest is not in the boys. Given his own history, and his own identity as one of the "Angli," this lapse is curious. Young boys were sent to monasteries, as we know from Bede's own life: he came to the monastery of St. Peter and St. Paul at Monkwearmouth and Jarrow at age seven (5.24, p. 567). There the monks were involved in a discourse of sexualization, as the penitentials and monastic rules make clear. The Penitential of Cummean contains a long section on the "sinful playing of boys," and names there such sins as sodomy and mutual masturbation, specifying penances both for older boys and for the younger ones they corrupted.[58] Deriving this material from Theodore's Penitential, an Anglo-Saxon handbook repeats these prohibitions in chapters entitled "Concerning married men or boys, when they do wicked deeds in unnatural ways" and "Concerning young boys."[59] This discipline is in the spirit of the Benedictine Rule, which, like earlier monastic documents, specifies that older monks should sleep among the young ones (although one could not be sure that this practice guaranteed the boys' safety).[60] Bale's reading raises distasteful questions about the sexual corruption of youth by the clergy, a topic all too familiar today and, as we have seen, an issue not unknown in the Anglo-Saxon period.

Bale's Anglo-Saxonism differs from Bede's chiefly in one respect. For Bede, Anglo-Saxon origins supply a racial identity that permits harmonious relations with the Church in Rome and the lasting conversion of the English. For Bale, Anglo-Saxon identity emerges in a struggle against the enslaving bonds of Roman domination. Racial differences are observed, but vaguely (Maglo conquers "Saxons, Normeies, and Danes," for example), and matter less than the institution of marriage and the laws of sexual desire. I cannot say if Bale is the first writer to link Anglo-Saxonism to a sex-gender system that explicitly includes homosexual acts, but it seems undeniable that his Anglo-Saxonism values sex and gender above racial identity.

Bale has never been accused of being charming, although Stapleton certainly thought that he was corrupt. Wilde would agree, for Bale found ugly meanings in Bede's beautiful story about the slave boys. Keenly attuned to the alleged deceptions of the Church of Rome and skilled in deploying sexual innuendo against his opponents, he detected something in Gregory's visit closer to the truth than what Bede saw there. Bale points to the institution of slavery, which the Church accommodated comfortably, and to the sexual abuse of slaves—children, women, and men—that was an inevitable part of that system. He shows us the system flourishing under the smiling eyes of a man about to be pontiff, who rhapsodizes wittily about the boys' race, their ruler, and the name of their land, and seems genuinely sorry not that such beauty is wasted on the young but that it is wasted on pagans. It is as if Gregory could look through the boys to the English Church he hoped to establish. Gregory's gaze, so cruelly critiqued by Bale, had its counterpart, if not its origin, in Bede's own, which travels over the heads of these beautiful but miserable creatures back to the man in whose vision Bede saw both his history and his *History*.

Notes

1. Susan Reynolds, "What Do We Mean by 'Anglo-Saxon' and 'Anglo-Saxons'?" *Journal of British Studies* 24 (1985): 395–414; quotation from pp. 395–96.

2. Bertram Colgrave and R. A. B. Mynors, eds. and trans., *Bede's Ecclesiastical History of the English People* (Oxford: Clarendon Press, 1969; rpt. 1972),

book 2, chap. 1, pp. 132–35. Further references (to book and chapter number as well as page number) are given in the text.

3. Bertram Colgrave, ed. and trans., *The Earliest Life of Gregory the Great* (Cambridge: Cambridge University Press, 1985), p. 49. Further references are given by page number in the text.

4. Patrick Wormald, "Bede, the *Bretwaldas* and the Origins of the *Gens Anglorum*," in *Ideal and Reality in Frankish and Anglo-Saxon Society: Studies Presented to J. M. Wallace-Hadrill*, ed. Patrick Wormald, with Donald Bullough and Roger Collins (Oxford: Basil Blackwell, 1983), p. 124.

5. Thomas Miller, ed. and trans., *The Old English Version of Bede's Ecclesiastical History*, Early English Text Society vols. 95, 96, 110, 111 (London: Oxford University Press, 1890–98), 1: 96–99. What changes are made are not obviously significant: for example, Gregory is "warned to take such zealous care for the salvation of our people" ("he monad wære, þæt he swa geornfulle gymenne dyde ymb þa hælo ure þeode," p. 96, 3–4). The boys are less clearly young; they are called "cneohtas" and "men" in a sentence in which Bede calls them only "pueros." The puns in Old English are still effective, although the first is spoiled. The boys are said to be from "Ongli" and have "ænlice onsyne" (splendid countenances), their land is "Dere, *de ira eruti*," and their king is Ælle (p. 96, 21–32).

6. "Sancti Gregorii Pape. Urbis Romane Inclitus," *Ælfric's Catholic Homilies, The Second Series*, ed. Malcolm Godden, EETS SS no. 5 (Oxford: Oxford University Press, 1979), pp. 72–74. Ælfric, as we would expect, preserves the linguistic puns more effectively than the earlier translator. As I note in *Desire for Origins: New Language, Old English, and Teaching the Tradition* (New Brunswick, N.J.: Rutgers University Press, 1990), pp. 52–53, 60–61), Elizabeth Elstob, an important eighteenth-century Anglo-Saxonist, took the wordplay in this homily to extraordinary lengths, finding in the puns representations of her own name. See Elstob, *An English-Saxon Homily on the Birth-Day of St. Gregory: Anciently Used in the English-Saxon Church. Giving an Account of the Conversion of the English from Paganism to Christianity* (London, 1709), pp. 15–17. For a full discussion of Elstob's work, see Kathryn Sutherland, "Editing for a New Century: Elizabeth Elstob's Anglo-Saxon Manifesto and Ælfric's St. Gregory Homily," in *The Editing of Old English Texts*, ed. D. G. Scragg and Paul E. Szarmach (Woodbridge, Suffolk: D. S. Brewer, 1994), pp. 213–37.

7. Sir Frank Stenton, *Anglo-Saxon England*, 3d ed. (Oxford: Oxford University Press, 1971), pp. 103–4; Peter Hunter Blair, *An Introduction to Anglo-Saxon England* (Cambridge: Cambridge University Press, 1956), pp. 116–17, and *The World of Bede* (Cambridge: Cambridge University Press, 1970), pp. 41–48.

8. *Bright's Old English Grammar and Reader*, ed. Frederic G. Cassidy and Richard N. Ringler (New York: Holt, Rinehart and Winston, 1971), pp. 109–24 (Edwin), 125–34 (Cædmon); for the short excerpt about Gregory, see pp. 73, 76–77. See also Bruce Mitchell and Fred C. Robinson, *A Guide to Old English*, 5th

ed. (Oxford: Blackwell, 1992), pp. 216–19 (Edwin), 220–25 (Cædmon), and Bruce Mitchell, *An Invitation to Old English and Anglo-Saxon England* (Oxford: Blackwell, 1995), pp. 260–62 (Edwin), 263–64 (Cædmon). The story of Cædmon and Bede's description of the Angles, Saxons, and Jutes are included in *Sweet's Anglo-Saxon Reader in Prose and Verse,* rev. Dorothy Whitelock (Oxford: Clarendon Press, 1967), pp. 45–50 (the former), 42–44 (the latter). I have not made a thorough survey of earlier readers, but I note that Milton Haight Turk, *An Anglo-Saxon Reader* (New York: Scribner's, 1927), includes the story of Gregory and the boys, pp. 91–93, which Turk describes as a "charming and very famous tale" (p. 263, n.91).

9. After Gregory became pope (590), he sent preachers to the English with his encouragement and prayers. Their arrival and the early phases of the missionaries' work in England are described by Bede in earlier chapters (Bede, *Ecclesiastical History* 1.23–26, pp. 68–79). The success of the mission was so great that it was recorded on Gregory's tombstone (2.1, pp. 132–33).

10. Gildas, *The Ruin of Britain and Other Documents,* ed. and trans. Michael Winterbottom (London: Phillimore, 1978). See Nicholas Howe, *Migration and Mythmaking in Anglo-Saxon England* (New Haven: Yale University Press, 1989), pp. 33–49, for a discussion of Gildas and the pattern of prophetic history.

11. Howe, *Migration and Mythmaking,* p. 122.

12. The word means "the Angles" in many texts cited in Antonette di Paolo Healey and Richard L. Venezky, eds., *Microfiche Concordance to the Dictionary of Old English* (Toronto: Pontifical Institute of Mediaeval Studies, 1980; reprint, 1985). For example, "Angelþeod" refers to "the northern English, the Angles" in the preface to the Old English Bede. In Miller's edition, see chapter 2.2 and Bede 1.14.56.25 (cf. Latin 1.25, 72). "Angel" refers to the Anglian invaders from the Continent to Britain three times in this text: the heading to 1.8.9, Bede 1.12.50.20, and the heading to 1.8.13.

13. Colgrave, *The Earliest Life,* pp. 144–45, n.42. Recent studies of the meaning of "English" *Angli* as Bede uses the term do not discuss Gregory's role in choosing the name, presumably because it is seen as merely symbolic; see D. P. Kirby, *The Earliest English Kings* (London: Unwin Hyman, 1991), pp. 13–15, and H. E. J. Cowdrey, "Bede and the 'English People,'" *Journal of Religious History* 11 (1981): 501–23. See also Wormald, "Bede, the *Bretwaldas* and the Origins," pp. 121–24.

14. For an analysis of the ethnography operating in Bede's analysis, see John Hines, "The Becoming of the English: Identity, Material Culture and Language in Early Anglo-Saxon England," *Anglo-Saxon Studies in Archaeology and History* 7 (1994): 49–59.

15. Wilhelm Levison, *England and the Continent in the Eighth Century* (Oxford: Clarendon Press, 1946), p. 92.

16. Angels appear in Ercengota's death (3.8, pp. 236–37), in Fursey's vision (3.19, pp. 270–74), and in Begu's vision of Hild's death (4.23, pp. 412–13).

Angelic spirits accompany Herbert and Cuthbert at their deaths (4.29, pp. 440–41) and are mentioned in Theodore's epitaph (5.8, pp. 474–75). Chad's soul seeks the joys of heaven in the company of angels (4.3, pp. 340–43). Angels guide a wealthy man who comes back from the dead on a journey to heaven, purgatory, and hell (5.12, pp. 489–99). Angels bring the books of good and evil deeds to Cenred's thegn in a vision (5.13, pp. 499–503), and they attend Bede's own death (pp. 584–85). The reference to purgatory in the death of a wealthy man is significant. The man visits three realms, one of which holds those who confessed on their deathbeds; they now "have to be tried and chastened" in "flaming fire and awful cold" but will be released from this place by the prayers and alms of friends and the celebration of masses (5.12, pp. 494–95).

17. Hunter Blair, *World of Bede*, p. 47.

18. Colgrave and Mynors, *Bede's Ecclesiastical History*, p. 72n.1; the letter is found in A. W. Haddan and W. Stubbs, *Councils and Ecclesiastical Documents Relating to Great Britain and Ireland*, 3 vols. (Oxford: Clarendon Press, 1871), 3:5 (quoted here), and is translated in Dorothy Whitelock, ed., *English Historical Documents I, c. 500–1042* (London: Eyre Methuen, 1979), p. 790 (no. 161). Elstob comments on this letter and Gregory's "zeal" in freeing slaves and enlisting them in God's service and regards it as a practice that modern slave traders should emulate; see Elstob, *An English-Saxon Homily*, pp. xi–xii.

19. Hunter Blair, *World of Bede*, p. 45.

20. David Pelteret, "Slave Raiding and Slave Trading in Early England," *Anglo-Saxon England* 9 (1981): 99–114; see p. 104. See also Pelteret, *Slavery in Early Mediaeval England: From the Reign of Alfred until the Twelfth Century* (Woodbridge, Suffolk: Boydell Press, 1995).

21. Colgrave, *The Earliest Life*, p. 145n.43.

22. Quoted by Ross Samson, "The End of Early Medieval Slavery," in *The Work of Work*, ed. Allen J. Frantzen and Douglas Moffat (Glasgow: Cruithne Press, 1994), p. 105; see p. 112n.42.

23. "A father, if he is compelled by necessity, may sell his son into slavery up to the age of six years; after that age he cannot sell him (the son) without the son's consent." Translated from *Das altenglische Bussbuch (sog. Confessionale pseudo-Egberti)*, ed. Robert Spindler (Leipzig: Bernhard Tauchnitz, 1934), chap. 15, canon 18c (p. 183), taken from the Penitential of Theodore: "Pater filium suum necessitate coactus potestatem habet tradere in servitutem VII annorum, deinde sine voluntate filii licentiam tradendi non habet" (book 2, ch. 13.1); Theodore's Penitential is quoted from Haddan and Stubbs, *Councils and Ecclesiastical Documents*, 3:176–216.

24. Dorothy Whitelock, *The Beginnings of English Society* (Harmondsworth: Penguin, 1965), p. 112. See Pelteret, "Slave Raiding," p. 104, on the code of Whitred and a law of King Ine of Wessex prohibiting the sale of freemen into servitude abroad.

25. Whitelock, *Beginnings*, p. 111.

26. On manumission as an exercise of mercy and penitence, see Samson, "End of Slavery," pp. 108–10, 117–19.

27. For commentary on this episode, see Seth Lerer, *Literacy and Power in Anglo-Saxon Literature* (Lincoln: University of Nebraska Press, 1991), pp. 30–42, 48–52.

28. Colgrave and Mynors, *Bede's Ecclesiastical History,* p. 404, n.2.

29. Pelteret, "Slave Raiding," p. 105.

30. Ruth Mazo Karras comments on prostitution and female slaves in "Desire, Descendants, and Dominance: Slavery, the Exchange of Women, and Masculine Power," in *The Work of Work,* ed. Frantzen and Moffat, pp. 16–29. See also Elizabeth Stevens Girsch, "Metaphorical Usage, Sexual Exploitation, and Divergence in the Old English Terminology for Male and Female Slaves," in *The Work of Work,* pp. 30–54.

31. I raise the possibility that the Anglian boys were intended for sexual purposes in *Desire for Origins,* p. 47.

32. John Boswell, *Christianity, Social Tolerance, and Homosexuality: Gay People in Western Europe from the Beginning of the Christian Era to the Fourteenth Century* (Chicago: University of Chicago Press, 1980), pp. 143–44 and 144, n.35.

33. For a complete list of Gildas's references to Sodom, see N. J. Higham, *The English Conquest: Gildas and Britain in the Fifth Century* (Manchester: Manchester University Press, 1994), p. 61, n.48.

34. Many scholars have recognized that the sins of Sodom included sloth, luxurious living, and inhospitality to strangers. Boswell is unusual in claiming that, as early as the fifth century, many "Christian authors completely ignored *any* sexual implications of Sodom's fate" (p. 98, emphasis added), and that, as late as the fourteenth century, the sin of Sodom was represented as luxury rather than homosexuality. On the category of "luxury," see Mark D. Jordan, *The Invention of Sodomy in Christian Theology* (Chicago: University of Chicago Press, 1997), pp. 37–41.

35. In the *Ecclesiastical History,* Bede's "unspeakable crimes" are "inenarrabilium scelerum" ("Qui inter alia inenarrabilium scelerum facta," 1:22, pp. 68–69). In his Commentary on the Book of Genesis, Bede says that Ezekiel names all the sins of the Sodomites except the "unspeakable" or "unutterable" one of Genesis 19 ("excepto illo infando quod in sequentibus scriptura commemorat"). This passage from the commentary on Genesis is quoted by Richard Kay, *Dante's Swift and Strong: Essays on* Inferno *Canto XV* (Lawrence, Kan.: Regents Press, 1978), p. 384, n.49, translated pp. 229–30.

36. There is an informative survey of Bale's achievement in Leslie P. Fairfield, *John Bale: Mythmaker for the English Reformation* (West Lafayette, Ind.: Purdue University Press, 1976). See pp. 55–57, 121.

37. On Bale's Anglo-Saxon manuscripts, see David Dumville, "John Bale, Owner of St. Dunstan's Benedictional," *Notes and Queries* 41 (1994): 291–95.

38. John N. King, *English Reformation Literature: The Tudor Origins of the Protestant Tradition* (Princeton: Princeton University Press, 1982), pp. 56–62.

39. John Bale, *The Actes of Englysh Votaryes* (London, 1548), p. 2a.

40. Fairfield, *John Bale: Mythmaker*, p. 89.

41. Ibid., p. 121.

42. See King, *English Reformation Literature*, p. 62.

43. Fairfield, *John Bale: Mythmaker*, pp. 17–18.

44. This summary is based on Fairfield's analysis, pp. 31–49.

45. See Fairfield on Bale's devotion to Mary in his Carmelite years (pp. 17–18) and later years (pp. 42–43).

46. Geoffrey of Monmouth, *History of the Kings of Britain,* trans. Sebastian Evans, rev. Charles W. Dunn (New York: Dutton, 1958), book 11, chap. 7, pp. 238–39. Bale's probable source is the *Nova Legenda Angliae* of John Capgrave, whose narratives of saints' lives he grossly distorted. See Fairfield, *John Bale: Mythmaker,* p. 114, 121–22.

47. See Kay, *Dante's Swift and Strong;* Derrick Sherwin Bailey, *Homosexuality and the Western Christian Tradition* (London: Longmans, Green, 1955; Hamden, Conn.: Archon, 1975); and, on Renaissance understandings of sodomy, Alan Bray, *Homosexuality in Renaissance England* (London: Gay Men's Press, 1982), pp. 33–57.

48. Donald N. Mager, "John Bale and Early Tudor Sodomy Discourse," in *Queering the Renaissance,* ed. Jonathan Goldberg (Durham, N.C.: Duke University Press, 1994), pp. 141–61. Bale's other works underscore his charges of sodomy among Catholic clergy in *The Image of Both Churches.* See, for example, Bale, *The Pageant of Popes* (London, 1574), p. 36, an account of visitations to monasteries ordered by Henry VIII which found numerous "Ganimedes" there "giltye of sinne against nature" (36). This work, I note, both accuses Gregory of corrupting Christianity in England and praises him as "the best man of all these Romaine Patriarkes, for learning and good life" (34, 32). See also Bale, *Apology against a Rank Papist* (London, 1550), which charges that the Catholic clergy set aside marriage and virginity for "two unhappy gestes, called whoredom and buggery" (xii).

49. See James Brundage, *Law, Sex, and Christian Society in Medieval Europe* (Chicago: University of Chicago Press, 1987); Michael Goodich, *The Unmentionable Vice: Homosexuality in the Later Medieval Period* (Santa Barbara, Calif.: ABC-Clio, 1979); David M. Halperin, *One Hundred Years of Homosexuality and Other Essays on Greek Love* (New York: Routledge, 1990); Jonathan Goldberg, *Sodometries: Renaissance Texts, Modern Sexualities* (Stanford: Stanford University Press, 1992); Goldberg, ed., *Reclaiming Sodom* (New York: Routledge, 1994); and Goldberg, ed., *Queering the Renaissance.* Arguments about the tolerance of sodomy and other homosexual acts suggested in Boswell's work are

difficult to support, as I argue in "The Disclosure of Sodomy in the Middle English *Cleanness*," *PMLA* 111 (1996): 451–64.

The Tudor statutes had lasting consequences; the Supreme Court's 1986 *Bowers v. Hardwick* decision quotes them with approval. See Janet E. Halley, "*Bowers v. Hardwick* in the Renaissance," in *Queering the Renaissance*, ed. Goldberg, pp. 15–39.

50. "Queer theory" is understood here as a development of gay and lesbian studies with particular focus on redefining subjectivity within sexuality, emphasizing local and historicized conditions. Important formulations stressing that "queer" means an identity that does not have an essence and that shifts with its context are Michael Warner, ed., *Fear of a Queer Planet* (Minneapolis: University of Minnesota Press, 1994), pp. vii–xxxi; Judith Butler, *Gender Trouble* (New York: Routledge, 1991), pp. 223–42; Eve Kosofsky Sedgwick, *Epistemology of the Closet* (Berkeley and Los Angeles: University of California Press, 1990), pp. 1–61; and Sedgwick, *Tendencies* (Durham, N.C.: Duke University Press, 1993), pp. 1–20. It is worth noting that scholars of Renaissance and medieval cultures pioneered research in this area, beginning with Alan Bray in 1982, and medievalists had been working on homosexuality even before John Boswell's important study of 1980 (see note 32). See Bray, *Homosexuality in Renaissance England*, and "Homosexuality and Signs of Male Friendship in Elizabethan England," in *Queering the Renaissance*, ed. Goldberg, pp. 40–61. See also Brundage, *Law, Sex, and Christian Society*, and Goodich, *The Unmentionable Vice* (n. 49).

51. Jeff Masten, "My Two Dads: Collaboration and the Reproduction of Beaumont and Fletcher," in *Queering the Renaissance*, ed. Goldberg, pp. 280–309; see 302–3. I comment on queer theory and medieval studies in "Between the Lines: Queer Theory, the History of Homosexuality, and the Anglo-Saxon Penitentials," *Journal of Medieval and Early Renaissance Studies* 26 (1996): 245–96.

52. I say "narrower" here because activists do not out public figures in order to destroy them, as Bale sought to do when he accused his opponents of homosexual acts, but in order to force them to assume a public identity as a homosexual.

53. Brundage, *Law, Sex, and Christian Society*, pp. 313, 398–99.

54. Bede's text was being read by continental scholars—for example, by John de Grave, who edited the *History* in Antwerp in 1550. John Herwagen's 1563 edition took up this cause. I discuss this development in *Desire for Origins*, pp. 152–53.

55. Thomas Stapleton, *The History of the Church of England Compiled by Venerable Bede, Englishman* (Antwerp, 1565; rpt. Menston, England: Scolar Press, 1973), p. 3b. Stapleton's translation is used in the Loeb Classical Library, *Baedae Opera historica*, ed. J. E. King (London and New York, 1930).

56. See Colgrave and Mynors, *Bede's Ecclesiastical History*, p. xxx, for example, and Cowdrey, "Bede and the 'English People.'"

57. Oscar Wilde, "Preface," *The Picture of Dorian Gray* (New York: Random House, 1954), p. vii.

58. The Penitential of Cummean is possibly a seventh-century text. See Ludwig Bieler, ed., *The Irish Penitentials,* Scriptores Latini Hiberniae 5 (Dublin: Institute for Advanced Studies, 1963). The chapter concerning "the playing of boys" describes sodomy as anal intercourse, fornication "in terga" (in the rear or backside), and assigns penances of two years for boys, four years for men, and seven years for habitual sodomites (canon X.15; p. 128). I discuss this evidence in detail in "Between the Lines" (see note 51) and, from a different perspective, in "Where the Boys Are: Children and Sex in the Anglo-Saxon Penitentials," in *Becoming Male,* ed. Jeffrey Cohen and Bonnie Wheeler (New York: Garland, 1997), pp. 1–20.

59. Spindler, *Das altenglische Bussbuch,* pp. 177–79 (chap. 6, "De iuvenis"; chap. 8, "De maritis vel pueris, cum impie agant in pecora").

60. According to the Rule of St. Benedict, "The younger brethren shall not have beds next to one another, but among those of the older ones" (chap. 22, "How the monks are to sleep"). See *St. Benedict's Rule for Monasteries,* trans. Leonard J. Doyle (Collegeville, Minn.: Liturgical Press, 1948), p. 42. St. Basil's fourth-century warning against contact between young men is quoted by David F. Greenberg, *The Construction of Homosexuality* (Chicago: University of Chicago Press, 1988), p. 284; see also Greenberg's reference here to the *Rule,* n. 228. Goodich cites other examples of rules prohibiting same-sex contact in monasteries (*The Unmentionable Vice,* p. 18).

2. Anglo-Saxonism in the Old English Laws

Mary P. Richards

W HEN BEDE NOTED of the Kentish king Æthelberht that "among other benefits which he conferred upon the race under his care, he established with the advice of his counsellors a code of laws after the Roman manner," he called attention to features of the laws that made them distinctively Anglo-Saxon: "These are written in English and still kept and observed by the people. Among these [Æthelberht] set down first of all what restitution must be made by anyone who steals anything belonging to the church or the bishop or any other clergy; these laws were designed to give protection to those whose coming and whose teaching he had welcomed."[1] From the seventh century on, the laws of England were closely tied to Christianity through the rulers of its various kingdoms.[2] The choice of English as the language of the law, however, enabled the preservation of Germanic legal traditions that preceded the conversion. These traditions, together with the new commitment to Christianity, formed the basis of Anglo-Saxonism as expressed in the laws.

Although they have been cited in wide-ranging studies of the meaning of *Engla lond* and *Anglo-Saxon* by scholars such as Susan Reynolds and Patrick Wormald, the Old English royal codes have yet to be addressed as a body of material fundamental to the understanding of Anglo-Saxonism.[3] I hope to remedy this oversight by demonstrating how the laws capture and then expand the elements of Anglo-Saxon culture as expressed through two primary features: Christianity and the English language.

The several kingdoms of Anglo-Saxon England developed from the tribal origins of Germanic settlers, but geographical proximity and consequent opportunities for alliances, conquest, and overlordship inhibited the establishment of strong barriers among these groups. To the contrary, bonds created by mutually intelligible language and by conversion to Christianity fostered within diversity a unity that gave rise to the self-conscious national and racial identity we call Anglo-Saxonism. This progression manifests itself in the Old English royal codes, where the rulers of individual kingdoms legislated according to common assumptions of one language, a Christian constituency, an operative social and ecclesiastical hierarchy, and a definition of outsiders. Thus Anglo-Saxon culture—its development, definition, and preservation—constitutes a major theme in the laws that expands over time even as do the legal statements themselves. Whereas the earlier codes focus upon specific crimes and punishments, later codes deal with broader issues of national importance, such as protection of property and keeping the peace. Similarly, statements regarding ecclesiastical matters begin with a single reference in a lengthy code but later become a major preoccupation balancing secular issues in the laws.

Although he interprets the earliest appearance of a royal code for his own purposes, Bede makes the sole direct reference to an extant law code by a nonlegal source from the entire Anglo-Saxon period.[4] When coupled with the fact that all of the surviving compilations of the Old English laws are associated with ecclesiastical centers, and that Archbishop Wulfstan composed codes on behalf of King Cnut, the close connection between Christianity and the issuance of legal codes becomes clear. We cannot assume necessarily that written laws played a direct role in the consciousness of the Anglo-Saxon people. Administration of justice and general knowledge of the law were oral.[5] But when examined as materials preserving fundamental aspects of Anglo-Saxon culture and addressing common themes over time, the laws offer a unique view of Anglo-Saxonism.

Together with the *Anglo-Saxon Chronicle* and other official records such as charters, writs, and wills, the laws contribute to the body of vernacular prose documents characterizing the values, social structure, political aspirations, Christian foundation, and ideas of kingship that comprise Anglo-Saxonism. In so doing, the laws emphasize the protection of property, the importance of oaths, and the right of sanctuary. They assign penalties based upon the social status of criminal and victim. They offer special protection to the Church and its officials, and to the king and his household. They stress obedience to one's lord. The royal codes are especially important because they give voice to both the kings' aspirations and their frustrations as they look for ways to keep the peace, regulate interactions among their subjects and with peoples from neighboring kingdoms, and see that justice is administered, all the while drawing on the legislation of other kings and kingdoms and acknowledging that their authority is conferred by God. The standards thus developed and articulated by royal authority aim at defining behavior in support of a social hierarchy and political identity. Even as the royal codes express a clear awareness of the boundaries between kingdoms, they also convey an understanding of a shared heritage including religion, language, social structure, Germanic values such as the concept of *wergeld* (the monetary worth of a person), and royal authority.

Whereas there remains uncertainty as to the exact models for the earliest Anglo-Saxon legislation—Roman law, Frankish codes (especially the *Lex Salica*), or the redaction of Frankish materials by an intermediary such as the abbot Ansegisus[6]—there is no question that the Old English legal codes transcend those influences and forge their own tradition from the outset. Royal codes issued from various kingdoms over a period spanning the seventh through the early eleventh centuries provide rich evidence of this tradition. In fact, there seems to have been an expectation that Anglo-Saxon royal authority would assert itself periodically through legal decrees, even if those decrees had little new legislation to offer.[7] What they do show is a development away from particular crimes and punishments to larger issues of widespread concern, and an ever more active royal role in determining social policy and collecting the proceeds from violations thereof. The focus this essay takes is the emerging self-consciousness, portrayed mainly in the royal codes, of what it meant to be Anglo-Saxon—that is, to have a national identity in an island comprising rival kingdoms and ruled by the descendants of invaders, recent and not so recent. As an examination of the materials shows, contemporaries and successors, both royal and ecclesiastical, of the kings who issued laws regarded these as statements asserting the common culture of Anglo-Saxon England.

The choice of English as the language of the earliest laws was noted by Bede partly because it set the Anglo-Saxon codes apart from their continental predecessors. Frankish codes based on Roman models were always written in Latin and usually consisted of lists of offenses and punishments. Whereas the earliest Kentish codes, especially that of

Æthelberht, contain similar lists, they are written in English and reflect insular customs and terminology.[8] One important example is the concept of *mundbyrd,* or protection, as applied to people and places that were not to be violated. Wormald has speculated that the native oral tradition did not lend itself to transmission in Latin.[9] Although valid, this observation needs development.

As I have shown in a previous essay, the formal structure of the royal law codes resembles that of certain continental Germanic codes.[10] The main elements include a preface providing a context for the legal statements to follow and then the statements themselves, often in stylistically parallel constructions. The legal statements employ a body of Old English formulas and legal terms, some without Latin equivalents. Whereas the language of the codes evolved over time, it continued to preserve this special vocabulary, giving evidence not only of oral influences on the laws but also of a conscious effort to preserve these materials in traditional form. For example, an archaic, probably pagan, word such as *weofod* persists as the standard term for "altar" in the laws. Elsewhere, the phrases *we beodaþ, we læraþ,* and the ubiquitous *we cwædon* appear as formulas conveying the authority of oral pronouncements within the formal written codes. By contrast, the continental codes in Latin, while retrospective, lack a personal voice even in their prologues. The choice of Old English as the written medium thus sustained the connection to oral law, while at the same time providing means for continuous renewal in response to contemporary demands. Moreover, the language of the laws itself, being consistent from kingdom to kingdom and age to age, conveyed a bond of Anglo-Saxonism that was acknowledged every time a new code was promulgated.

In short, composition in English allowed for the laws to reflect a growing national identity. Just as the *Chronicle* was recorded in Old English year by year, so legal codes were issued by successive kings who built upon, rather than superseded, earlier legislation. Respect for legal tradition seems to have transcended historical rivalries and even linguistic variation among kingdoms. The West-Saxon King Alfred illustrates this point when he extols the laws of Kentish and Mercian kings in the preface to his code and appends the laws of his predecessor Ine to his own compendium.

Equally significant for the emergence of Anglo-Saxonism is the link between the written laws and the advent of Christianity in England. Soon after Æthelberht was converted by St. Augustine and his mission to

Canterbury, the first royal codes emerged as the earliest documents written in English. Given that literacy was the province of the Church, one might have expected Latin to be used as the language of record, especially since many of the laws addressed ecclesiastical matters. But preserving oral tradition in the language of the Anglo-Saxons was consistent with other phases of the conversion in England. There is some archeological evidence to support Bede's assertion that pagan temples were fitted out with Christian altars and put to new purposes, though rebuilding on Roman sites was more frequent.[11] The merger of pagan and Christian influences was fundamental to Anglo-Saxon culture, and its complexities are as evident in the laws as in Old English poetry.

I

The rubric to Æthelberht's law code (which may be a later scribal addition) links its origin to St. Augustine:

> Þis syndon þa domas, þe Æðelbirht cyning asette on Augustinus dæge.

> These are the decrees which King Æthelberht established in the lifetime of Augustine. (pp. 4–5)

As Bede notes, the first law in Æthelberht's collection sets compensation for thefts of God's property from the Church and from the bishop, priest, deacon, and clerk. It also compensates doubly breaches of the peace affecting a church. However, this is the only ecclesiastical law among the ninety items in Æthelberht's code. Thereafter many of the individual laws relate to statements in the Frankish codes, particularly the *Lex Salica*.[12] In this earliest Kentish code, traditional materials, both Frankish and pagan Germanic, are thus reworked, expanded, and given an ecclesiastical overlay.

Subsequent laws issued by kings of Kent underline the importance of Christianity to the developing self-consciousness of nationhood. The code of Wihtred is noteworthy because the prologue relates its genesis: a great council, convened in August of 695 at a place called Berghamstyde, brought the king together with Berhtwald, bishop over all Britain, the bishop of Rochester, and representatives of the Church and laity throughout the region to confer about a new set of decrees (p. 24). Although

Wihtred is called king of Kent (*Cantwara cyning*) and his decrees apply to the Kentish people, the reference to the *Bretone heahbiscop* expresses consciousness of a larger community to which Kent belonged. The church thus offered another cultural link among the various Anglo-Saxon kingdoms that was elaborated through the law codes.

Aside from its prologue, Wihtred's code gives ample evidence of the progress of Christianization, for fully twenty-four of its twenty-eight statements relate to the Church. The code states that people from outside the kingdom must abide by Christian practices or leave:

> Æltheodige mæn, gif hio hiora hæmed rihtan nyllað, of lande mid hiora æhtum 7 mid synnum gewiten.

> Foreigners, if they will not regularise their unions, [should] depart from the land with their possessions and with their sins. (4, pp. 24–25)

But the emergence of the kingdom of Wessex, as reflected in the legal codes of Ine and Alfred, coincides with a more strongly defined sense of Anglo-Saxonism than that found in the earlier Kentish codes. Not only do they embody nearly three centuries of Anglo-Saxon law, but they also serve as a reference point for future lawgivers. In particular these law codes reinforce the social structure, values, and sense of nationhood that appear as elements in the earlier royal codes.

Composed in the late seventh century, roughly contemporaneous with Wihtred's codes, Ine's laws always travel in manuscripts as an appendix to those of Alfred.[13] Since Alfred's prefatory remarks receive full treatment below, suffice it to say here that the physical wedding of the two royal codes in itself conveys a unity spanning nearly a century, the more so because as presented in manuscript collections, they are complementary in coverage. The individual legal statements are numbered consecutively in the table of contents and in the text. Together, Alfred's and Ine's laws address a wide variety of issues affecting the individual, the church, and the social structure of the kingdom.

The most striking feature of Ine's code is its relationship to Wihtred's. Whereas the earliest Kentish laws of Æthelberht comprise lists of compensations for crimes of various sorts, and the succeeding laws of Hlothhere and Eadric deal with more complicated situations including regulations within the arbitration process, Wihtred's laws address the various classes, both clerical and secular, with regard to offenses and accusations. Although it contains nearly three times the number of statements found in Wihtred's code, Ine's is equally concerned with ecclesiastical issues, crime and punishment segmented by class of the accused and victim, and the definition of outsiders. Even the genesis of the code described in the preface is similar, for it relates that Ine *Wesseaxna kyning* consulted broadly with his father, two bishops, his ealdormen, and many servants of God in the effort to establish just laws.

The theme of Ine's collection is announced in the first statement, which admonishes the clergy to observe their proper rule (*ryhtregol*) and commands the nation to obey *ealles folces æw 7 domas* (the law and decrees affecting the whole people; 1.1, pp. 36–37). The laws themselves offer a strong statement about the social hierarchy they impose. To a greater extent than Wihtred's code, Ine's addresses day-to-day living as well as the types of arbitration appropriate for the various classes. For example, fines are specified for fighting in several locations, the greatest punishment being reserved for fighting in the king's house: forfeiture of all property and possible execution (6, p. 38). A number of laws are devoted to keeping domestic animals, including a statement regarding the appropriate time to shear sheep (69, p. 58). Conditions leading to slavery, including a law forbidding the sale of slaves overseas, are covered in detail. Care is taken to define groups of marauders by the number of participants (13.1, p. 40). Whereas Wihtred's code deals with actions of the clergy—for example, how they should clear themselves of accusations—Ine's code covers other ecclesiastical matters such as baptism, payment of dues and tithes, and sanctuary, all of which impinge to some degree on the lives of the laity.

As mentioned, Ine's preface specifies that he as *Wesseaxna kyning* anointed by God has, together with his many counselors, considered means to ensure the salvation of all their souls and the security of "our kingdom" (*ures rices*) through the issuance of just laws (*Ine* prologue, p. 36). The reference to *ures*, "our," includes the king and his body of assembled advisors, all of whom seem to be West-Saxon since Ine refers to them as "my" people. But his *ryht æw 7 ryhte cynedomas* (just law and just decrees) have much in common with the contemporary Kentish code of Wihtred. As has been shown, the two royal codes share the inclusion of the Church in the development and administration of the law. They also have a common perspective on the organization of society and congruent attitudes toward outsiders. Both codes include an identical statement allowing individuals from afar to be taken as thieves if they do not identify themselves properly (*Wihtred* 28, p. 30; *Ine* 20, p. 42). Thus, although Ine's code does not acknowledge influences external to his kingdom, his laws clearly draw upon a common fund of legal tradition and address issues related to those considered by his neighboring ruler.

Ine's code is noteworthy because it goes on to address the subject of outsiders in detail. Within a set of statements dealing with the *wergeld* for foreigners, exact sums are specified for Welshmen (23.3, p. 42; 24.2, p. 43). Further on, an *Engliscmon* is distinguished from a *Wealh* primarily in the value of their respective wergelds and surety for their oaths, the Welshman always at considerably lower price. This distinction is made four times within Ine's code, always with reference to an *Englisc* rather than a West-Saxon man, a practice that continues through later royal codes. With its addition of laws dealing with outsiders, Ine's code expands the theme of Anglo-Saxonism in the common legal tradition and defines which peoples are not *Englisc,* that is, not the descendants of Germanic invaders.

The code of Alfred the Great also betrays a considerable debt to its Kentish predecessors, especially to Æthelberht's list of compensations. At the conclusion of his lengthy prologue, in which he traces his lawgiving to the law of the Old Testament balanced by the new law of Christ, Alfred calls himself king of the West-Saxons but indicates that he has borrowed statements from earlier lawgivers (his kinsman Ine, Offa of Mercia, and Æthelberht):

> Ic ða Ælfred cyning þas togædere gegaderode, 7 awritan het monege þara þe ure foregengan heoldon, ða ðe me licodon; 7 manege þara þe me ne licodon ic awearp mid minra witena geðeahte, 7 on oðre wisan bebead to healdanne. Forðam, ic ne dorste geðristlæcan þara minra awuht fela on gewrit settan, forðam me was uncuð, hwæt þæs ðam lician wolde, ðe æfter us wæren. Ac ða ðe ic gemette awðer oððe on Ines dæge, mines mæges, oððe on Offan Mercna cyninges oððe on Æþelbryhtes, þe ærest fulluhte onfeng on Angelcynne, þa ðe me ryhtoste ðuhton, ic þa heron gegaderode, 7 þa oðre forlet.
>
> Ic ða Ælfred Westseaxna cyning eallum minum witum þas geeowde, 7 hie ða cwædon, þæt him þæt licode eallum to healdanne.

Now I, King Alfred, have collected these [writings] and have
given orders for copies to be made of many of those which our
predecessors observed and which I myself approved of. But many of
those I did not approve of I have annulled, by the advice of my
councillors, while [in other cases] I have ordered changes to be
introduced. For I have not dared to presume to set down in writing
many of my own, for I cannot tell what [innovations of mine] will
meet with the approval of our successors. But those which were the
most just of the laws I found—whether they dated from the time of
Ine my kinsman, or of Offa, king of the Mercians, or of Æthelberht,
who was the first [king] to be baptised in England—these I have
collected while [leaving aside] the others.

I, then, Alfred, King of the West Saxons, have shewn these to all
my councillors, and they have declared that it met with the approval of all, that they should be observed. (*Alfred* preface, pp.
62–63)

Alfred regards these codes as part of a common heritage from which he is
free to draw those laws he considers the most just.[14] In so doing he makes
explicit the practice already visible in the laws of earlier kings. Although
he is aware of boundaries between kingdoms, those seem to carry more
dynastic than political implications for him. Noteworthy is his statement
about Æthelberht being the first king to be baptized in *Angelcynne,* a
term meaning "of English race" which Wormald has shown was applied
to the Germanic inhabitants of Britain from the time of Gregory the
Great.[15] Although *Anglo-Saxon* was not the preferred term among the
peoples themselves, it was synonymous with *English* in its various forms
and thus referred to the underlying heritage that the laws illustrate.[16]

By stating that his laws have been selected from codes that have stood
the test of time, Alfred enunciates the principle that acceptance implied
by longevity, rather than kingdom of origin, validates a given law. Keeping that perspective in mind, it is useful to review the major topics he
thinks worthy of inclusion. Not surprisingly, they are heavily ecclesiastical. The first is sanctuary in a monastery or church, a privilege granted to
fugitives under certain conditions for limited duration. A second is crimes
against women, including nuns. A third is fighting in the presence or on
the premises of a wide variety of individuals from king to commoner,
including the archbishop, bishops, and priests. A fourth is the obligation

to be loyal to one's lord and to defend him as necessary. Fines for offenses are doubled during Lent.

In a law decreeing the holidays to be observed by all free men, Alfred specifies days that would have been celebrated beyond his kingdom (43, p. 84). In addition to periods at Christmas and Easter, he includes the feast of St. Gregory the Great, who sent St. Augustine and his companions to Christianize England; the festival of Saints Peter and Paul, who were honored at Christ Church, Canterbury; and the four Ember fasts as designated by Gregory the Great for the English people. Surviving calendars from Anglo-Saxon England confirm that these religious days were celebrated widely in Alfred's time, hence they are part of a shared Anglo-Saxon culture reflected in his laws.[17] Furthermore, Alfred's is the first code to mention *halig ryht* (the laws of the Church) as an entity separate from the royal laws (40.2, p. 82). This fact furthers the impression that in compiling his collection he was thinking beyond the boundaries of his kingdom, possibly to canon law as understood in England.

There is no question that Alfred's royal successors perceived his laws as definitive for England: they referred to them as *seo domboc* (the book of laws), to which later decrees would be added. The so-called treaty between Alfred and the Danish king Guthrum, preserved in a manuscript containing *Alfred-Ine* among other Old English codes, provides yet an additional perspective on Anglo-Saxonism in Alfred's time with its purported description of the peace settlement between the English and the Danes (pp. 98–100). King Alfred, King Guthrum, *ealles angelcynnes witan,* and all the peoples of East Anglia agree upon the boundaries of the Danelaw and the means by which disputes will be settled. Defining the Danes as outsiders in the treaty reflects a characterization of non-English peoples noted in earlier royal codes, though it is doubtful that there were firm divisions in practice.[18] The point is that there was a strong sense of English law, as opposed to the practices of outsiders, that prevailed no matter what the kingdom or who the king.

The self-conscious Anglo-Saxonism embodied in Alfred's selection of laws, the celebration of his predecessors, and the relation of lawgiving to its religious context are confirmed in the earliest surviving copy of *Alfred-Ine* found in the Parker manuscript (Cambridge, Corpus Christi College, MS 173). Added about 950 to a genealogy of the West-Saxon royal line and a version of the *Anglo-Saxon Chronicle* (through 925), the law codes form part of a collection of historical and legal materials reflecting the achievements of the West-Saxon dynasty.[19]

As the *Chronicle* makes clear, the English people shared a common past dating from the time of their conversion to Roman Christianity, coincidental of course with the issuance of the first law code. By the ninth century, the kingdom of Wessex had taken the lead.[20] Moreover, Viking invasions had overthrown East Anglia, Northumbria, and Mercia, leaving the West-Saxon King Alfred to defend his own territory, devise a peace settlement, and contain the Vikings in a specified area, the Danelaw.[21] The *Chronicle* portrays forces from these various kingdoms uniting as Christians under Alfred's leadership (Annals 893 and 896) to engage a pagan enemy.[22] Indeed, peace negotiations required that the Danes embrace Christianity.[23] Within this historical context, the compilation of the Parker manuscript both celebrates the West-Saxon achievement and demonstrates its significance for Anglo-Saxon England. The laws themselves, through Alfred's prologue in particular, help to cast him as king of the Anglo-Saxons.

II

Given Alfred's accomplishments and reputation, it is not surprising that his successors (until the Scandinavian King Cnut) accepted his code as *seo domboc* and confined their own lawgiving to supplementary topics. The fact that six copies of *Alfred-Ine* survive to the present day is an indication of how widely it must have been disseminated in the Anglo-Saxon period.[24] The prologue to Edward the Elder's first code provides one example of Alfred's influence: the king commands his reeves to make legal decisions in accordance with the *domboc* and *folcriht* (customary law) on a fixed schedule (p. 114). His own ordinances then address buying and selling, topics not covered in *Alfred-Ine*. Anglo-Saxonism in the legal codes from the tenth and eleventh centuries is not restricted, however, to the recognition of *Alfred-Ine* as authority. *I Edward,* for instance, takes up the thorny issue of rights in *bocland* versus *folcland,* a matter of concern throughout Anglo-Saxon England from the eighth century onward.[25] Moreover, the aforementioned reference to *folcriht* is the first citation of English customary law within the royal codes. After *Alfred-Ine,* the Old English laws provide for the further development of a governance system uniquely Anglo-Saxon.

Laws associated with the next recorded lawgiver, King Athelstan, survive in various forms in Old English and Latin translation.[26] The body of this material extends the nationalistic perspective in Anglo-Saxon legislation in a number of ways. While strict on the issue of rendering tithes to crown and Church (*I Athelstan*), the king's legal statements also show compassion for the unfortunate that transcends political boundaries. For example, he orders his reeves to feed a destitute *Engliscmon* wherever they find one with revenues from royal rents, for the love of God (p. 126). The bulk of Athelstan's laws, however, result from national assemblies held at such locations as Grately, Faversham, Thundersfield, and Exeter.[27] Whereas these laws continue Edward's practice of referring to the *domboc* and *folcriht* as authorities, they naturally address matters of broad concern to Anglo-Saxon England.

In *II Athelstan,* thievery is an issue of central importance, especially as it implies the setting of *wergeld,* the surety of kinsmen, the definition of an outlaw, and procedures for the ordeal to determine the guilt or innocence of alleged criminals. Thus many of the themes traced through earlier royal codes emerge here to address a national problem. *II Athelstan* further sets jurisdictions for moneyers and for commerce generally and mandates attendance at national assemblies. As prefaces to his subsequent codes indicate, the king announced similar decrees at his various councils, modifying or expanding them as necessary along the way. The introduction to *V Athelstan* illustrates both his method and his frustration:

Æðelstan cyng cyþ, þæt ic hæbbe geahsod, þæt ure frið is wyrs gehealden ðonne me lyste, oþþe hit æt Greatanlea gecweden wære; 7 mina witan secgað, þæt ic hit to lange forboren hæbbe.

I, King Æthelstan, declare that I have learned that the public peace has not been kept to the extent, either of my wishes, or of the provisions laid down at Grately. And my councillors say that I have suffered this too long. (*V Athelstan,* pp. 152–53)

And again,

Ðis is seo gerædnes þe þa biscopas 7 þa gerefan þe to Lundenbyrig hyrað gecweden habbað, 7 mid weddum gefæstnod on urum friðgegyldum, ægðer ge eorlisce ge ceorlisce, to ecan þam domum þe æt Greatanlea 7 æt Exanceastre gesette wæron, 7 æt Þunresfelda.

These are the ordinances which have been agreed upon and confirmed with solemn declarations in our association, by the bishops and reeves who belong to London—by both nobles and

commoners—as a supplement to the decrees which were promulgated at Grately, at Exeter, and at Thundersfield. (*VI Athelstan*, pp.
156–57)

From his codes emerges a picture of Athelstan's energetic attempts to
bring order to a far-flung nation and to see that justice is enacted
efficiently. At the same time, his laws depend upon earlier legislation,
which was assumed to represent the underpinnings of the nation. Through
their bonds with Christianity and the language and the customs of the
people, the royal codes persist as a major vehicle for national unity and
the embodiment of the core values of the culture.

By contrast with the panegyric of poems in the *Anglo-Saxon Chronicle,*
the royal law codes do not assert the superiority of a particular king or
kingdom. Hence Athelstan thanks his councilors in Kent (*III Athelstan,*
Latin trans., p. 142) for their advice concerning peace in the land. What
the laws stress is a common tradition of governance and the necessity for
citizens from all areas to fulfill their social and religious obligations.
Athelstan's codes, then, command a degree of national consciousness
beyond that of *Alfred-Ine.* His successors King Edmund and King Edgar
build upon that foundation by calling together synods and councils to
strengthen both the religious and political fabric of the country.

Just as Athelstan promulgated a special code (*VI Athelstan*) for the
citizens of London to address issues of thievery, slavery, justice, and the
operation of the hundred (a geographical district defined by a hundred
hides of land), Edmund convoked a synod there in 942 to address
ecclesiastical matters, including tithing and proper conduct of those in
religious orders (*I Edmund*). Promoting Christian behavior is the stated
goal of his second code, devoted especially to the crimes of home-
breaking (*hamsocn*) and vendettas (*fæhðe*). In these instances, ancient
Germanic customs are directly contradicted by Christian prohibitions,
with the irony that one who commits these crimes can seek sanctuary in
the church.

Edmund's successor King Edgar covers many of the same issues as do
Athelstan and Edmund but in more detail. The first code attributed to
Edgar's reign concerns the administration of the hundred. The second is
devoted to church tithes and the third to the operation of the courts.
Although the hundred has earlier roots, *I Edgar* is the first royal code to
address its operations in Anglo-Saxon governance.[28] Edgar's fourth code
addresses the laity throughout the island:

Sy þeahhwæðere þes ræd gemæne eallum leodscype, ægðer ge Englum
ge Denum ge Bryttum, on ælcum ende mines anwealdes . . . .

The following measure, however, shall apply generally to the whole
nation—to the English, Danes and Britons in every part of my
dominion. . . . (IV Edgar 2a.2, pp. 32–33)

The law in question deals with the investigation of thieves. Edgar asserts
the Danes' rights to their own laws but states that in this instance his law
"shall apply generally to all of us who dwell in these islands" because it
promotes the security of the nation (14.2, p. 39). Frank Stenton observes
that with IV Edgar, the Danes are officially recognized as part of the
nation.[29]

It is interesting that the need to protect property drives the sense of
nationhood so strongly after the time of Alfred. In I Edgar, the first duty
of the hundred is to pursue thieves. III Edgar treats the issue of surety,
especially for those accused of thievery. In short, Edgar's codes give voice
to elements of Anglo-Saxonism that had not been treated directly in
earlier royal legislation. Because Edgar had the fortunate task of maintaining the peace and national unity established by his forebears, he was
able to build upon that foundation in his legislation, where he conveys
the social and ecclesiastical values of Anglo-Saxonism.

Æthelred II issued a number of legal codes, though among Anglo-
Saxonists he is known equally well for his attempts to appease Viking
invaders. His legislation survives in various stages of completion, but the
relative formality and chronology of the materials does not affect the
points made here. I Æthelred, "for the promotion of security wherever
English law prevails" (p. 53), sets forth the options of accused persons
and the types of punishment awaiting those found guilty. II Æthelred
outlines the conditions of a truce with the Vikings for which the king paid
22,000 pounds of gold and silver (7.2, p. 60). Among his statements, the
king characterizes his country as Anglalande and as subject to harrying
by enemy fleets. Despite his lack of resolve to fight the Vikings, Æthelred
conveys the sense that he represents a unified Christian country.

In the legislation just described, Æthelred continues the earlier practice of issuing legislation at national meetings of the royal councilors (I
Æthelred at Woodstock, III Æthelred at Wantage). These codes are
relatively unexciting except for their depiction of the king's humiliation
at the hands of the Vikings. His later legislation, by contrast, is written by

Archbishop Wulfstan, whose colorful style and concern with religious and social order adds a new flavor to the laws:

> Þis þonne ærest, þæt we ealle ænne God lufian 7 wurðian 7 ænne Cristendom georne healdan 7 ælcne hæðendom mid ealle awurpan; 7 þæt we habbað ealle ægðer ge mid worde ge mid wedde gefæstnod, þæt we under anum cynedome ænne Cristendom healdan willað.

> The first provision is: that we all love and honour one God, and zealously observe one Christian faith, and wholly renounce all heathen practices. We have confirmed, both by word and by pledge, our firm intention of observing one Christian faith under the authority of one king. (V Æthelred 1.1, pp. 78–79)

Specifically, Wulfstan employs homiletic rhetoric enriched by alliterating and rhyming word pairs to give urgency to the crimes he condemns. In so doing, he dramatizes the extent to which ecclesiastical influence has grown in the royal codes since the enactments of Æthelberht of Kent.

In V Æthelred the king is called "king of England," while his councilors affirm their intention to observe "one Christian faith under the authority of one king" (1, p. 79). Whereas V and VI Æthelred are general exhortations to ecclesiastical rectitude, VIIa Æthelred conveys a special urgency as it tells citizens to pray for God's help against the Vikings. VIII Æthelred revisits the topics of breaking the peace in various locations, of tithes, and of the comportment of ecclesiastical figures. With the addition of Wulfstan's concern for Christian order, these codes cover much the same issues as other royal legislation since Alfred's reign, again conveying the sense that certain issues of governance mattered most to Anglo-Saxons. Their desire to protect property, to keep the peace, and with God's help to determine the guilt or innocence of criminals drives the bulk of lawgiving from the period and, when couched in traditional legal language used even by Wulfstan, provides a sense of continuity with the Anglo-Saxon cultural context defined in the earliest codes.

Because Archbishop Wulfstan drafted legislation for both Æthelred and the last great royal lawgiver, King Cnut, there is substantial overlap between the codes attributed to those kings, most notably in issues related to the Church. In fact, I Cnut is little more than a recasting of Æthelred's ecclesiastical codes.[30] As an outsider, however, Cnut was

concerned to be accepted as king of England, hence he issued proclama-
tions declaring all he had done for the English people and used legislation
as a means to establish his authority over all England.[31] In *II Cnut*, which
is directed toward the laity, statements specify differences in custom
among Wessex, Mercia, East Anglia, and Kent, though elsewhere within
the same code the English are distinguished collectively from the Danes
(71a.2, p. 210; 83, p. 216). *II Cnut* further touches on themes central to
Anglo-Saxon culture as it emerges through the laws: the security of
home, the role of character witnesses for the accused, conditions of the
ordeal, breaking the peace, and Christian observances. Certain laws are
mentioned uniquely here—such as the dues and fines owed to the king of
England in Mercia and in the Danelaw (14, 15, p. 180)—but in general *II
Cnut* fits into the mainstream of royal legislation in Old English as it
developed a significant ecclesiastical component to balance secular matters. Cnut's laws are worthy of special attention because they are inclu-
sive and address those issues of greatest concern to all England:

> Se ðe ðas lage wyrde ðe se kyningc hæfð nu ða eallum mannum
> forgyfen, seo he Denisc sy he Englisc, beo he his weres scyldig wið
> ðone kyningc.

> He who violates the law which the king has now granted to all men,
> whether he be a Dane or an Englishman, shall forfeit his wergeld to
> the king. (*II Cnut* 84, pp. 216–17)

In his ability to issue laws for the whole of England rather than to make
selections from individual kingdoms, Cnut realizes the potential in Alfred's
sense of a common Anglo-Saxonism in the laws.

III

As is obvious from this survey of the royal codes, they have substantially
more in common than their language, format, and origin. Key themes
occupy the kings who issue legislation. Perhaps most striking is their view
that, in proclaiming laws, they are dealing with the heritage of the several
kingdoms and only augmenting the work of their predecessors. From the
beginning they convey the consultation and wisdom behind their codes
and stress their ties through Christianity to other kings and their peoples.

There is a strong sense that the various kingdoms have shared values in the laws and that these differ in relatively unimportant ways, such as the level of fines for offenses.

Remarkably, as they began to govern the conquered island, Norman rulers and ecclesiastics recognized the force of the Old English laws. William I's first ordinances were issued in English and offered the alternatives of trial by ordeal, the traditional English practice, or trial by combat, as was customary in France (Robertson, p. 232). Latin translations and compilations of the Old English codes were made and then used in Norman legislation.[32] Although French legal terms and processes eventually won out, English legislation was recognized by the Normans as a repository of cultural information useful for governance in the post-Conquest era.[33]

In subsequent centuries, the laws retained their fascination as objects of study. During the sixteenth century Laurence Nowell and others in his circle worked with collections of laws in Sir Robert Cotton's library and fortunately copied from manuscripts that later were damaged or destroyed. Eighteenth-century antiquarians such as Elizabeth Elstob made copies of the *Textus Roffensis,* the most complete surviving collection of the Old English laws. Among the earliest printed texts of Old English were royal law codes, and their language was studied in early grammars and vocabulary lists. Though interesting in themselves, the laws were appreciated especially as providing a window on the origins of Anglo-Saxon culture that gave rise to a distinct nation.[34] Their ability to reconcile the pagan Germanic heritage of Anglo-Saxon England with its strong commitment to Christianity, then to transcend the borders of rival kingdoms, and ultimately to help forge a self-conscious nationalism is little short of marvelous.

Notes

1. Bertram Colgrave and R. A. B. Mynors, eds. and trans., *Bede's Ecclesiastical History of the English People* (Oxford: Clarendon Press, 1969; rpt. 1972), book 2, chap. 5, pp. 150–51. Bede's views and their importance for understanding Anglo-Saxonism are analyzed by Patrick Wormald in "Bede, the *Bretwaldas* and the Origins of the *Gens Anglorum*," in *Ideal and Reality in Frankish and Anglo-Saxon Society: Studies Presented to J. M. Wallace-Hadrill,* ed. Patrick Wormald with Donald Bullough and Roger Collins (Oxford: Basil Blackwell, 1983), pp. 120–23, and "*Engla Lond:* The Making of an Allegiance," *Journal of Historical Sociology* 7 (1994): 1–24. The standard edition of the laws is by Felix Liebermann, *Die Gesetze der Angelsachsen,* 3 vols. (Halle: Niemeyer, 1903–16;

rpt. 1960). For ease of reference, quotations in this essay are drawn from F. L. Attenborough, *The Laws of the Earliest English Kings* (Cambridge: Cambridge University Press, 1922; rpt. 1974), and A. J. Robertson, *The Laws of the Kings of England from Edmund to Henry I* (Cambridge: Cambridge University Press, 1925; rpt. 1974). Citations consist of the numbered legal statement followed by the page reference. Henceforth "Liebermann," "Attenborough," and "Robertson" refer to these three editions. Attenborough is cited for the codes of Æthelberht, Wihtred, Ine, Alfred, and Athelstan, and Robertson for the codes of Edmund, Edgar, Æthelred, Cnut, and William I.

2. Patrick Wormald, "*Lex Scripta* and *Verbum Regis*: Legislation and Germanic Kingship from Euric to Cnut," in *Early Medieval Kingship,* ed. P. H. Sawyer and I. N. Wood (Leeds: University of Leeds, 1977; rpt. 1979), pp. 130–31.

3. Susan Reynolds, "What Do We Mean by 'Anglo-Saxon' and 'Anglo-Saxons'?" *Journal of British Studies* 24 (1985): 395–414, and Wormald, "Making of an Allegiance." The role of a common language in assertions of identity is explored by John Hines in "The Becoming of the English: Identity, Material Culture, and Language," *Anglo-Saxon Studies in Archaeology and History* 7 (1994):49–59.

4. Patrick Wormald, draft entry for *Sources of Anglo-Saxon Literary Culture,* s.v. *Laws of Æthelberht.*

5. See Patrick Wormald, "The Uses of Literacy in Anglo-Saxon England and its Neighbours," *Transactions of the Royal Historical Society,* 5th series, 27 (1977): 111–13, and Simon Keynes, "Royal Government and the Written Word in Late Anglo-Saxon England," in *The Uses of Literacy in Early Mediaeval Europe,* ed. Rosamond McKitterick (Cambridge: Cambridge University Press, 1990), pp. 228–29, 243–44.

6. Wormald, "*Lex Scripta* and *Verbum Regis,*" pp. 110, 130–34.

7. Ibid., p. 118. The evolution of the royal codes from Roman form to Roman purpose, whereby Ine and his successors used legal decrees as a means of social control, is analyzed by Wormald in "Inter-Cetera Bona . . . Genti Suae: Law-Making and Peace Keeping in the Earliest English Kingdoms," *La Giustizia Nell'Alto Medioeva,* Settimane di Studio del Centro Italiano de studi sull'alto medioevo 42 (Spoleto: La Sede del Centro, 1995), pp. 963–93.

8. *Lex Salica,* entry by Mary P. Richards in *Sources of Anglo-Saxon Literary Culture: A Trial Version,* ed. Frederick M. Biggs, Thomas D. Hill, and Paul E. Szarmach, Medieval and Renaissance Studies 74 (Binghamton, N.Y.: SUNY Press, 1990), pp. 134–35.

9. Wormald, "*Lex Scripta* and *Verbum Regis,*" p. 115.

10. Mary P. Richards, "Elements of a Written Standard in the Old English Laws," in *Standardizing English: Essays in the History of Language Change,* ed. Joseph B. Trahern Jr., Tennessee Studies in Literature 31 (Knoxville: University of Tennessee Press, 1989), pp. 1–22.

11. Colgrave and Mynors, *Bede's Ecclesiastical History,* book 1, chap. 30, pp. 106–8. See Barbara Yorke, *Kings and Kingdoms of Early Anglo-Saxon England* (London: Seaby, 1990), pp. 38–39, and Bridget Cherry, "Ecclesiastical Architecture," chap. 4 of *The Archaeology of Anglo-Saxon England,* ed. David M. Wilson (Cambridge: Cambridge University Press, 1976), esp. pp. 156–58.

12. Richards, *Lex Salica,* p. 134.

13. Mary P. Richards, "The Manuscript Contexts of the Old English Laws: Tradition and Innovation," *Studies in Earlier Old English Prose,* ed. Paul E. Szarmach (Albany, N.Y.: SUNY Press, 1986), pp. 173–74.

14. Allen J. Frantzen, *King Alfred* (Boston: Twayne, 1986), pp. 13–16, presents a concise analysis of Alfred's preface.

15. Wormald, "Making of an Allegiance," pp. 12–13.

16. Reynolds, "What Do We Mean," pp. 402–5.

17. The most recent analysis of pre-and post-Conquest calendars is found in chap. 2, "The Calendar," by Richard W. Pfaff, in *The Eadwine Psalter: Text, Image, and Monastic Culture in Twelfth-Century Canterbury,* ed. Margaret Gibson, T. A. Heslop, and Richard W. Pfaff (London and University Park, Pa.: Pennsylvania State University Press, 1992), pp. 62–87; on this point, see pp. 67–69. Texts are presented in Francis Wormald, ed., *English Kalendars before* A.D. *1100,* Henry Bradshaw Society 72 (London, 1954).

18. Reynolds, "What Do We Mean," pp. 408–9.

19. Malcolm B. Parkes, "The Palaeography of the Parker Manuscript of the Chronicle, Laws and Sedulius, and Historiography at Winchester in the Late Ninth and Tenth Centuries," *Anglo-Saxon England* 5 (1976): 166.

20. H. R. Loyn, *The Governance of Anglo-Saxon England 500–1087* (London: Edward Arnold, 1984), p. 60. Chap. 3 on the reign of Alfred, pp. 61–78, focuses on the king's role as lawgiver and the interconnection between royal and ecclesiastical governance.

21. Simon Keynes and Michael Lapidge, *Alfred the Great* (Middlesex: Penguin, 1983), p. 23.

22. Ibid., p. 41.

23. Wulfstan's version of the treaty entitled *Edward and Guthrum* provides later testimony to this condition. See Attenborough, p. 102.

24. Keynes and Lapidge, *Alfred the Great,* pp. 303–4; Keynes, "Royal Government," p. 232.

25. Frank M. Stenton, *Anglo-Saxon England,* 3d ed. (Oxford: Oxford University Press, 1971), pp. 309–12. *Bocland* is usually understood as land held under royal charter, whereas *folcland* refers to land held under *folcriht,* or common law.

26. Wormald, "The Uses of Literacy," p. 112; Keynes, "Royal Government," pp. 235–41.

27. Stenton, *Anglo-Saxon England,* pp. 349–52.

28. Robertson, p. 300.

29. Stenton, *Anglo-Saxon England,* p. 371.

30. The text as presented in Liebermann, vol. 1, pp.278–307, shows the extent of indebtedness to the later codes of Æthelred in the marginal notations. Both are the work of Archbishop Wulfstan.

31. Stenton, *Anglo-Saxon England,* pp. 409–11.

32. For a discussion of these Norman redactions of the Old English laws into Latin, see Mary P. Richards, *Texts and Their Traditions in the Medieval Library of Rochester Cathedral Priory,* Transactions of the American Philosophical Society (Philadelphia: APS, 1988), pp. 46–52.

33. M. T. Clanchy, *England and Its Rulers 1066–1272: Foreign Lordship and National Identity* (Glasgow: Fontana, 1983), pp. 58–60.

34. Allen J. Frantzen, *Desire for Origins: New Language, Old English, and Teaching the Tradition* (New Brunswick, N.J.: Rutgers University Press, 1990), pp. 42–43, 47–55.

3. The *Anglo-Saxon Chronicle* Poems and the Making of the English Nation

Janet Thormann

HE *Anglo-Saxon Chronicle* makes history as it records events. Through the effort of arranging lists of events in a chronology, maintaining those records over a period of time in various manuscripts, and combining and rewriting those manuscripts in various compilations,[1] the writing of the *Chronicle* produces the idea of a nation, an Anglo-Saxon England that may legitimately lay claim to power. The textual records produced in this manner constitute a national past; they support the conviction of the nation's persistence in time. The nation, that is, is a symbolic product. In this essay, I discuss the role of three of the four poems that appear as tenth-century *Chronicle* entries in order to demonstrate how each performs significant ideological work in producing a nation and a history.[2]

The keeping of a chronicle does not in itself constitute the writing of a history. Chronicle lists are like genealogies, in that they are ruled by chronology; their syntax is a parataxis governed by succession in time.[3] In such a chronology, no discursive relation other than sequence links the separate years or the events entered for each year of the chronicle record: the grammar of chronicle writing is juxtaposition. Any chronology assumes a point of origin, an arbitrary foundation, as a means of ordering the counting of years. For the dating system of the *Anglo-Saxon Chronicle,* that foundation is the birth of Christ. The *Chronicle* entry for the year 1 A.D. notes that *Crist wæs acenned,* "Christ was born,"[4] and that beginning orients all previous and subsequent dating in relation to *Cristes geflæscnesse,* "the incarnation of Christ." Counting, the marking of years in a list, does not, of course, constitute a discourse but only a system of symbolic articulation, a rule for noting difference.

The principle of chronicle listing is the principle of the calendar, and, in fact, the writing of the *Anglo-Saxon Chronicle* may have originated in the context of the Easter table, with prose entries added as notes to chronological tables used to find the date for Easter.[5] The notation of dates in a chronicle, as in a calendar, allows time to be ordered and mastered as a system of differences. Such a basic indication of differentiated time, the marking of difference as such, is the precondition for the recording of events in writing. Hayden White's description of the records of events in early continental annals and chronicles may apply also to the *Anglo-Saxon Chronicle:* according to White, the listing of dates in an annal or a chronicle "confers coherence and fullness on the events by registering them under the years in which they occurred. To put it another way, the list of dates can be seen as the signifieds of which the events . . . are the signifiers. The 'meaning' of the events is their registration in this kind of list."[6]

The symbolic articulation of time in a notation of difference may in fact be a primary function of chronicle writing. Charles Plummer explains that the *Chronicle* was intended "to *characterize* the receding series of years, each by a mark and sign of its own, so that the years might not be confused in the retrospect of those who had lived and acted in them."[7] In fact, many *Chronicle* entries, throughout the years of the record's maintenance, simply register the number of the year, suggesting that the written notation of the date is significant in itself. As Peter Clemoes argues, one of the functions of chronicle records is to provide a continuous list of dates: "The series of year numbers starting from Christ's birth must have been significant in its own right and its significance must have lain in its very continuity. . . . By following one another the numbers represented the line of events leading to the happenings of the present from an illustrious origin, just as a 'so-and-so was the son of so-and-so' series authenticated a person's descent from a distinguished ancestor."[8] The articulation of a symbolic system composed of a series of dates that establishes continuity is in itself meaningful for chronicle writing. In a historical discourse, however, in contrast to a chronicle, a regulating meaning directs the paratactic structure of sequence and chronology in order to motivate narrative.

History takes form as a discursive production when chronological

succession is motivated and directed by law, by the imposition of an
arbitrary rule governing human relations, a rule which, in turn, depends
on power. White suggests that a list of dates in a chronicle lacks "a notion
of a social center by which to locate [events] with respect to one another
and to charge them with ethical and moral significance."[9] Power and
superior force must enter into a particular relation to language in order
to become lawful authority, and lawful authority will then, reciprocally,
motivate and direct language. The conquest of territory and the coercion
of force are not sufficient to establish nationhood. It can only be when
power is reconfigured in discourse that language produces the idea of a
nation as legitimate rule.[10]

A common language undoubtedly provides a population speaking that
language with an idea of community. It may motivate an idea of common
nationality, as well. The history and continuity of the English language is
obviously crucial to an English national identity.[11] Nevertheless, a common language alone does not make a nation. The idea of an English
nation took form only during the tenth century, as Roberta Frank has
noted, when the concern "to establish in the present an ideological basis
for national unity" developed in Britain.[12] It was at this time that the
several competing local territories of lowland Britain were unified under
the hegemony of a single power. At this time, writing identified and
naturalized hegemonic power as a nation, as a social and political unity
authorized in tradition and law.

A body of traditional poetry, as well as the awareness of a common
spoken language, may work to define a sense of community, and Frank
shows how *Beowulf* may have served national ambitions. John D. Niles
also emphasizes the ideological purposes of that poem when he writes
that "*Beowulf* was a vehicle for political work in a time when the various
peoples south of Hadrian's Wall were being assimilated into an emergent
English nation." In his view, "the poem is a site where cultural issues of
great magnitude and complexity are contested."[13] Niles describes a "tenth-
century renaissance" in vernacular culture as a vehicle for a developing
nationalism, so that as early as "Athelstan's reign, for the first time, it is
possible to speak of an English nation."[14] According to this line of
reasoning, the text of *Beowulf* is a significant result of that national
consciousness and, at the same time, a significant contribution toward it.

It is in the writing of the *Chronicle,* however, that the English nation is
most clearly revealed to be an "imagined community"[15] and takes shape
as a textual production. The *Chronicle* was first compiled during Alfred's

reign, possibly under Alfred's direction, as part of the large cultural, educational, and political program that was directed at his court.[16] This common stock of early entries, ending in 891, collected and translated from various sources,[17] may be read to support a West-Saxon cultural and political program. While it is generally acknowledged that the accumulation and distribution of the common stock of manuscripts was motivated by political purposes, it is not until the tenth-century continuations of the *Chronicle*,[18] and most obviously in the tenth-century poems, that an English nation is identified, when reference to an Anglo-Saxon England comes to supersede references to territorial kingdoms and peoples. Whatever Alfred's part was in motivating, directing, or distributing the early common stock, the *Chronicle* refers to Alfred as a king of England only after his death, in the entry for 900:

> Se wæs cyning ofer eall Ongelcyn butan ðæm dæle þe under Dena onwalde wæs.

> He was king over all England except for that part that was under Danish domination.[19]

The idea of an England emerges when Alfred has secured the conditions for West-Saxon hegemony. Thereafter, the *Chronicle* poems celebrate West-Saxon rulers as kings of an English people, Edmund in 942 as *Engla þeoden* ("lord of the English," 1), Edgar in 973 as *Engla waldend* ("ruler of the English," 1) and in 975 as *Engla cyning* ("king of the English," 36).[20]

Antonia Gransden compares the early core of the *Chronicle* with a Russian doll: "it incorporates earlier annals which in their turn incorporated still earlier ones, and so on."[21] Such intertextuality is characteristic of the *Chronicle*'s writing, as Martin Irvine shows in a complex analysis.[22] According to Gransden, additions to the core were made after that core "was sent to monasteries throughout England for copying . . . [and was] continued by the addition of installments which the monasteries received from some sources now unknown. These covered the periods from 894 to 924, 925 to 975 and 983 to 1018."[23] Not all the copies dispersed through the country contain all the core material: some northern copies integrate other chronicles, notably the Mercian Register, and some use material from Bede; and after 1018 additional new material was entered in some manuscripts. It is obvious that the history of the compilation, of its extensions and processes of accumulation, testifies to a prolonged and widespread effort to give textual materiality to an "imagined community." At the same time, the texts would have provided support and encouragement for furthering the imaginative elaboration of a nation.

The tenth-century *Chronicle* poems imagine the nation through a developing ideology. That that ideology should first become apparent in poetry may be due to the change of register from prose to poetry.[24] No longer just a recording of dates and of notable events, the *Chronicle* becomes the site, in these poems, of a change in textual self-awareness. This textual reflexivity is at the same time a political reflexivity. Because the traditional language of oral, vernacular poetry was habitually used to invoke a common heroic past, this language could readily fulfill political demands for defining a common past and a shared political community, when it was deployed in the *Chronicle*'s poems.

Four poems listed for the years 937, 942, 973, and 975 are usually grouped together.[25] The four poems all appear in MSS A, B, and C, and all share common characteristics. All are occasional, responding to par-ticular events. According to Jeff Opland, the poems are "as far as we know without precedent in the written literature of the Anglo-Saxons" in that each "celebrates an event: they do not describe or tell the story of the event, but are produced on the occasion."[26] All are panegyrics, praising the person or the acts of West-Saxon kings. All elaborate the genealogy of the kings they celebrate, thereby asserting the natural continuity of legitimate rule. All identify the kings as rulers of an English nation.

Standing out in their prose contexts, and extending over a period of less than forty years, the poems work to naturalize West-Saxon hege-mony when they proclaim military conquest to be lawful right. They assert the existence of an English nation even as they take part in the process of constructing that nation as legitimate power. The ideological effect of the poems is to produce West-Saxon domination as synonymous with England and to confirm West-Saxon power as traditional authority.

The entry for 937, *The Battle of Brunanburh,* has received extensive critical attention and demands separate treatment as a significant work. The poem celebrates King Athelstan's military victory over an alliance of Vikings, Irish, and Scots to secure West-Saxon control of territory that could now be identified as England. Elsewhere I show that in *Brunanburh* the authority of poetic language represents the battle as the continuation of a tradition of heroic action.[27] The West-Saxon leaders, Athelstan and his brother Edmund, are cast as actors in a heroic role they inherit through their genealogy. Martin Irvine describes the effect of the poem's traditional language and genre as follows: "The traditional form was used to create an image of unbroken tradition of national and racial heroic glory extending from the earlier kings in the Anglo-Saxon royal genealogy to the house of Alfred: the poetic medium for representing the heroic past was appropriated for representing a new 'heroism' of the English kings in the creation of a national kingdom."[28] The language of poetic tradition in *Brunanburh* constructs the battle site as a memorial space commemorating military victory. Success in war is read as a confirmation of rightful, inherited power: violence and the triumph of superior force are the performance of natural right. In addition, when the poem reads the present as a repetition of the heroic past, it manipulates the "myth of migration" that has been the subject of recent discussion by Nicholas Howe.[29] The poem exalts victory in war as the playing out of a national destiny and marks the battle as the achievement of the unity and historical continuity of an English nation.

The three *Chronicle* poems to be discussed here are less distinguished than *Brunanburh*. Their language is generally viewed as bland and redundant; appositive phrases pile up and lists accumulate; plain facts are reported in tortuous periphrasis. John D. Niles refers to the manipulation of apposition in one of the poems as a "parade of synonymous expressions,"[30] and Joseph Harris cites "an almost painfully archaizing traditional style" of praise for royal deeds.[31] In contrast to the drive and enthusiasm of the patriotism in *Brunanburh,* their tone is flat. Whatever the limits of their style, however, the very presence of traditional poetic language in *Chronicle* entries is itself significant. The poems have symbolic force and authority as a consequence of their reenactment of conventional language; their deployment of poetic tradition accomplishes political and ideological work. The *Chronicle* poems stage and enact a claim to authority in their imitation of traditional alliterative verse and of traditional formulaic heroic style.[32]

The prestige and traditionality of the verse language sponsor West-Saxon power as a national identity. In this sense, the poems are performances: they reactivate poetic tradition in order to assert a new discourse of history. The following analysis of the poems shows that, first, they imitate the diction of heroic poetry; second, they draw upon the formulas and themes of Christian narrative and elegy, appropriating the conventions of religious poetry for secular purposes; and, finally, they offer a symbolic guarantee of providential design that gives meaning to human and natural events. In so doing, the poems produce the idea of a national history that legitimizes West-Saxon power as national authority.

The poem entered for 942, sometimes known as "The Conquest of the Five Boroughs," records Edmund's military conquest of Mercia, naming the Five Boroughs in particular as conquered territory, and praises Edmund for freeing the Anglo-Danish population from the control of Norsemen. The accumulation of the names of battle sites and conquered territories is a standard feature of *Chronicle* writing, but the celebration of the king as Christian warrior in this poem is exceptional. Appositive half-lines repeatedly cast Edmund as the hero of traditional poetry. Edmund is designated *Engla þeoden* ("lord of the English," 1) and *Eadmund cyning* ("King Edmund," 1 and 13). Repeated epithets enlist the habits of traditional diction to naturalize the West-Saxon ruler as king of an English people. As *afera Eadweardes* ("Edward's heir," 13) he assumes a natural succession to power through his genealogy. As *mæcgea mundbora* ("guardian of the kindred," 2), *wiggendra hleo* ("protector of warriors," 12), and *dyre dædfruma* ("fierce performer of deeds," 3), he reenacts the role of heroic warrior invoked in the conventional formulas.[33]

Like the other *Chronicle* poems, the entry for 942 imitates the traditional heroic style when it establishes Edmund, a warrior hero, as king of an English nation by virtue of both his inheritance of royal power and his inherent worth, as demonstrated by his military might. West-Saxon power is represented to be the natural continuation of the past and thereby as legitimate authority over a whole people. Power is inserted into history by being written as the continuation of poetic convention.

The list of Edmund's conquests leads to a celebration of the king's victory over the Norsemen:

> Dæne wæran æror
> under Norðmannum   nyde gebegde
> on hæþenra   hæfteclommum
> lange þrage,   oþ hie alysde eft
> for his weorþscipe. (8–12)

The Danes had been oppressed by force under the Norsemen, in heathens' chains for a long time, until he freed them again, to his honor.[34]

The military campaigns and the claims to territories involving competing Danish, Norse, and West-Saxon interests in the ninth and tenth centuries are a tangle of alliances and betrayals and of short-lived periods of stability.[35] If the Danish population of the Five Boroughs did not welcome the control of Norse invaders in 942, the ancestors of that same population had invaded the land in the ninth century and had terrorized the island's inhabitants; in the eleventh century, Danish armies would take control of the island. Now, in the poem, however, the Danes stand as representatives of the native inhabitants, settled down on the land as natural English subjects. Frank Stenton claims that the poem "brings out the highly significant fact that the Danes of eastern Mercia, after fifteen years of Athelstan's government, had come to regard themselves as the rightful subjects of the English king."[36] Whether or not this claim is justified, it does seem clear that West-Saxon power regards the population as rightful subjects: the poem describes the Danes as dependents, in need of West-Saxon rescue and redemption.

The poem's diction represents the military campaign of 942 to be a spiritual liberation. One of the commonplaces of Old English literary history is that religious poetic narrative adopted the language of heroic epic. Christ as warrior in "The Dream of the Rood," *Elene*'s narrative as sacred epic, and "The Seafarer" as heroic elegy teaching Christian wisdom are just a few examples of the appropriation of heroic conventions for religious purposes.[37] Now in this *Chronicle* poem, the language of religious poetry is appropriated for political ends. The territories were formerly held "in heathens' chains." Edmund's conquest by force is phrased as if it were a spiritual restoration: Edmund "freed (or redeemed) them again, to his honor" (11–12).[38] Edmund fights as a Christian warrior to deliver the spiritually oppressed; his war is a type of Christian redemption. If Christ is the archetypal redeemer, then Edmund as a Christian warrior engaged in an act of redemption imitates Christ. The poem of 942, then, adopts for political purposes vocabulary carrying strong religious connotations. Military hegemony over the Five Boroughs is written as spiritual liberation; West-Saxon conquest is made to impersonate Christian typology. Edmund as heroic warrior consequently becomes a figure of sacred kingship.

The poem entered for 973, celebrating the consecration of Edgar, further develops an ideology of sacerdotal rule. This poem, sometimes named "The Coronation of Edgar," reports that Edgar was consecrated

king in Bath, on Pentecost, in the company of a great number of priests
and monks, when he was thirty years old. Nearly one-third of the poem
(that is, six and a half lines) carefully and redundantly restates the year of
the event and gives written authority for that dating:

> And ða agangen wæs
> tyn hund wintra   geteled rimes
> fram gebyrdtide   bremes cyninges,
> leohta hyrdes,   buton ðær to lafe þa get
> wæs wintergeteles,   þæs ðe gewritu secgað,
> seofon and twentig;   swa neah wæs sigora frean
> ðusend aurnen,   ða þa   ðis gelamp. (10–16)

And then ten hundred years had passed from the birth of the
glorious king, the guardian of light, except there were remaining yet
seven and twenty of counted years, as books say; so nearly a
thousand years of the Lord of victories had passed when this
happened.

The wordy elaboration works to establish the significance of the occasion. At the same time, the poem's effort to secure the certainty of the
ritual's date may be a self-referential citation, since the *Chronicle* might
itself be one of those cited books whose chronology ensures the date of
this ritual and of dating generally. The elaboration would then work to
call attention to the prose context of the report, that is, to the *Chronicle,*
and to the poem itself as a representation of the historic moment. What
the quoted passage most obviously emphasizes, however, is the poem's
concern with the dating as such and its meticulous attention to establishing the accuracy of the year. A similar concern with dating is evident in
the report of Edgar's death in the poem for 975, where instead of the
number of the year, the number of the day of the month is foregrounded.
The attention to dating in both poems signifies that the notation of time
in a symbolic system, the marking of time itself, continues to be an
essential purpose of the *Chronicle.*

The poem for 973 presents the consecration ceremony as a grandiose
spectacle. Since Edgar had already assumed the office of kingship fifteen
years earlier, it would seem that he intended the rite as a political act.

According to Richard Humble, the ritual of consecration would have been a carefully planned performance, the result of an alliance between secular and ecclesiastic interests.[39] Perhaps in imitation of the ritual consecration of a priest, the ceremony was carried out when Edgar was thirty. The elaborate diction of the poem emphasizes his age:

> And him Eadmundes   eafora hæfde
> nigon and XX,   niðweorca heard,
> wintra on worulde,   ða þis geworden wæs
> and þa on ðam XXX wæs   ðeoden gehalgod. (17–20)

And Edmund's heir, strong in battle, had passed twenty-nine years in the world when this came about, and in the thirtieth he was consecrated king.

Thirty was the earliest age at which a man could be ordained, because thirty was the age of Christ when he began his ministry and at the same time the age at which entry into the priesthood was allowed in Old Testament practice.

The poem's diction emphasizes the theocratic implications of the spectacle. Signifiers with religious denotations fill out half-lines resonant of heroic praise poetry: *Þær wæs preosta heap, / micel muneca ðreat* ("there was a band of priests, a great crowd of monks," 8–9); *gleawra gegaderod* "([a throng] of wise men gathered," 10). This *heap*, the troop or armed band (in the language of heroic poetry), is a company of priests rather than warriors, and the *ðreat*, the crowd, is made up of monks and wise men in attendance. The representation of the scene draws on the traditional heroic figuration of the leader surrounded by his retainers. Monks take the place of thegns to compose a sort of ecclesiastical comitatus to function as witnesses for the spectacle.

In contrast to the report of the ceremony of 973, the *Chronicle* reports other consecrations in comparatively bare prose entries: Athelstan in 924 was simply "consecrated at Kingston" (*æt Cyngestune gehalgod*).[40] Æthelred in 979 was "consecrated on Sunday, fourteen days after Easter, at Kingston, and present at his consecration were two archbishops and ten bishops." Kingston, a royal manor close to the border of Wessex and Mercia, was the usual site for tenth-century consecrations. In contrast, the language of the poem for 973 emphasizes that Edgar is anointed in the ancient city of Acemannesceaster (*on ðære ealdran byrig, Acemmanesceastre,* 4), a Latinate name for Bath.[41] The place is given two names, and the importance of Bath as the location for the ceremony is thereby stressed: *eac hi igbuend oðre worde / beornas Baðan nemnað* ("men dwelling on the island name it Bath by another name," 4–5). The rite, then, is related to a historic past, because it is located at a place associated with a Roman presence. The rite is also located in sacred time, for it is held at Pentecost. Sacred and legendary time and space are thus both simultaneously invoked, and the poem constructs the occasion as a historic event by representing it as a continuation and reenactment of the past. Pentecost occurs again on an ancient site, and the political rite of coronation coincides with the recurring moments of the sacred calendar.

But a particular past seems to be deliberately invoked here in order to support political claims. The associations with Bath suggest that this coronation was constructed as a statement of imperial kingship. Because Bath was an important center of Roman military occupation, its connotations of Roman imperial history would impress Edgar's claim to extensive power: in Pauline Stafford's view, "Bath symbolized the Roman, imperial connotations of the occasion."[42] The contemporary claimant to the inheritance of that imperial rule, the German emperor Otto the Great, may have provided a model for Edgar's ceremony in his own coronation in 952. Otto was married to Athelstan's sister and would therefore have had a close connection to Edgar's family, so that his influence on the English consecration ritual is not unlikely. The christening of Edgar's son, Edmund, in 966 had already adopted the Ottonian ceremonial model in a rite that was, according to Stafford's description, "a great family gathering at Winchester [and] a demonstration of family unity [that] stressed the continuity of the dynasty, their claims to power as a family."[43] The imperial connotations of Edgar's coronation would have been apparent as well in the anointing of Edgar's queen, for as Cannon and Griffiths have pointed out, "so far as is known, this was the first time that a double coronation like this had taken place in England."[44]

Further evidence for the construction of Edgar's rule as an imperial kingship comes from other *Chronicle* entries that record the subordination of local rulers to his domination.[45] The same entry that gives notice of his consecration in the D and E *Chronicle* manuscripts implies that Edgar enlisted a ritual of subordination to extend his power:

> . . . Se cyng geleadde ealle his sciphere to Lægeceastre. 7 þær him
> comon ongean .vi. cyningas. and ealle wið trywsodon þæt hi woldon
> efen wy[r]hton beon on sæ 7 on lande.[46]

> . . . The king led all his fleet to Chester where six kings came to him
> and pledged that they would be his allies on sea and on land.

Frank Stenton relates this event to another report of homage: "on one
occasion all the kings in Britain, eight in number, Cumbrians and Scots,
came to him on a single day and acknowledged his supremacy."[47]

As well, two entries found in only some manuscripts of the *Chronicle*
confirm Edgar's national ambitions and his deliberate cultivation of
international interests.[48] Both praise Edgar for his command of subordi-
nate rulers, and both identify Edgar's person, the king as an individual
exerting his will, rather than his deeds or his military might, as the
ground of power and cause of celebration. The first of these is the entry
for 959 in the D, E, and F manuscripts of the *Chronicle,* which, immediately after notice of Edgar's accession, celebrates the king's supremacy
over submissive leaders. Edgar is represented to be a figure commanding
subordination and exerting control:[49]

> . . . Ciningas 7 eorlas
> georne him to bugon.
> 7 wurden underþeodde to þam þe he wolde.
> 7 butan gefeohte eal he gewilde,
> 7 þet he sylf wolde.

> . . . Kings and earls eagerly submitted to him and became subject to
> whatever he wanted. And without battle he ruled all that he wanted.

The diction that identifies Edgar's power with his will, *eal he gewilde,
/ þet he sylf wolde,* seems to be formulaic: the entry for 946 similarly
states that submissive peoples swore to king Eadred "that they would
agree to all that he wanted," *þæt hie wolden eal þæt he wolde.* The
repeated phrasing indicates that by the middle of the tenth century the
person of the king has come to stand for a political power sufficient to
replace the coercion of military force. The king's will directs the nation,
and the power of the king's person substitutes for the force of physical
violence.

Edgar's political domination may be associated with what the entry for 959 suggests to be his cultural ambitions, as it goes on to criticize the king's patronage of foreigners and of foreign and heathen manners.[50] The criticism in itself is evidence of the operation of imperial power by means of a cultural politics:

> . . . He ælþeodige unsida lufode.
> 7 hæðene þeawas, innan þysan lande,
> gebrohte to fæste.
> 7 utlændisce hider in tihte.
> 7 deoriende leoda bespeon to þysan earde.

> . . . He loved bad, foreign customs and brought heathen practices too firmly within this land. And he brought foreigners here and drew harmful people to this country.

The identification of foreign influences here suggests a strong sense of national identification, a political and cultural basis superseding a local or tribal basis for defining identity. At the same time, the entry implies that this sense of Englishness remains precarious, for it must be defended from contaminating contact with strangers.

The second entry recorded only in the D and E manuscripts of the *Chronicle* substitutes for the more common poem on Edgar's death a different poem for 975 that eulogizes the dead king.[51] This alternate entry for 975 underlines widespread subordination to Edgar's rule:

> Cuð wæs þet wide
> geond feola þeoda
> þæt aferan Eadmund[es]
> ofer ganetes bað
> cyningas hine wide
> wurðodon side
> bugon to cyninge
> swa wæs him gecynde.

> That was widely known among many nations that kings far and wide over the seas honored Edmund's son, paid homage to the king, as was his right by birth.

The language of this entry asserts Edgar's dynastic claim to power, inherited through his genealogy, and sponsors his right to homage. No longer a territorial ruler, Edgar as figure of national kingship gains international recognition and dominance. These two poems entered for 959 and 975 in some manuscripts of the *Chronicle,* then, amplify the suggestions in the *Chronicle* poem for 973 that Edgar's coronation was intended as a display of quasi-imperial power.

The *Chronicle* poem of 973 celebrating the coronation of Edgar takes up the voice of the oral poet in order to produce the rite as a historic event, an occasion to be commemorated and remembered. Writing now ensures the credibility and prestige that oral transmission provided in the past. The poem appropriates the memorial functions of oral poetry for the record it is engaged in producing when it merges references to oral and written transmission. So the traditional voice of the oral poet reports the coronation with the phrase *mine gefrege* ("as I have heard," 9), the traditional formulaic phrase for oral transmission, as if the *Chronicle* poem were perpetuating oral knowledge and information. Such an assumption of the oral poet's voice acts as a guarantee of information and a proof of the reliability of the poem's report. In addition, because the oral poet traditionally spoke for the community he represented, the poem's assumed oral voice authenticates the values and purposes of the coronation ritual when it purports to speak for the large national body that the ritual intends to address and to represent. But even as the poem calls on the voice of the oral poet, it also calls upon written evidence in order to date the rite in relation to Christ's birth: *þæs ðe gewritu secgað* ("as books say," 14). If writing maintains accurate records from the past to speak in the present, the implication of the assumed, oral voice of the poem is that the writing of the *Chronicle* poem confirms and preserves the truth of the present to be read in the future. Demonstrating an incipient self-consciousness of its historical status, the poem thereby reflexively establishes both itself and the *Chronicle* in which it is written to be reliable records to be transmitted to the future.

Edgar died only two years after the rite of sacred kingship was carried out. The poem for 975, customarily titled "The Death of Edgar," first reports the king's death in the month of July and his son Edward's succession. It then states that Cyneweard, bishop of Wells, departed the country. Then a series of disasters are listed: Christian worship is violated in Mercia; Osric, ealdorman of Northumbria, is exiled; a comet appears;

and famine is widespread. Finally, it asserts that God restored prosperity to all the English.

The report of the king's death is elaborated in traditional diction. Like the hero of poetic narrative who actively chooses death, Edgar *ceas him oðer leoht* ("chose the other light," 2).[52] Other variations reporting Edgar's death recall the lessons of elegy and didactic Christian wisdom literature in their insistence on the transitory brevity of earthly life: *þis wace forlet, / lif þis læne* ("he abandoned this fragile, transitory life," 3–4) and *geendode eorðan dreamas* ("he ended earthly joys," 1). As James Earl writes, the notion that "the things of this world and the world itself are given to us only for our temporary use," that our lives and pleasures are *læne* in the sense of "loaned," is "perhaps the most familiar formula and theme" in Old English poetry.[53] The accumulation of appositive phrases and traditional themes reporting Edgar's death composes an example of what T. D. Hill has studied as the "variegated obit." According to Hill, the practice of variation in obituaries developed among medieval Latin history writers, who were themselves adopting biblical phrasing in order to elaborate an expansive style.[54] The *Chronicle* poem, then, enlists a stylistic feature of Latin historical writing for the vernacular record, drawing upon established features of Christian scholarship and instruction, as well as on models of religious and secular heroism, for its synonymous expressions of death.

The start of the second half of the poem, following the reports of Edgar's death and Edward's succession, is marked by the formulaic phrase of oral transmission, *mine gefræge* ("as I have heard," 16). This second half breaks into three parts, each unit marked by the introductory conjunction Ða or the transitional phrase *þa wæs* or *þa wearð,* "then it happened," each phrase developing a single narrative moment. In this section of the 975 poem a fully realized discourse of history becomes explicit for the first time in the *Chronicle*. The list of events constituting the *Chronicle* record is no longer simply a metonymic sequence; instead, a relation of cause and effect links the particular events introduced by the transitional phrase. The consecutive elements are directed by an overriding design, that is, by a logic and narrative meaning. That logic and meaning is God's purpose and will, an intention and motivation manifested as what happens in time. The logic of providential design explains human events as the consequence of God's justice: divine will here becomes the origin and guarantee of meaning.

In the absence of such a guarantee, without any principle of interpretation to explain causation or to provide relation between discrete events, *Chronicle* listings can only be structured through juxtaposition and contiguity. Succession in a chronology provides a principle of order, but it does not assign significance. To return to White's analysis, because of the "lack of causal connections between the events recorded,"[55] the meaning of the entries in a chronicle remains unclear. Typically, semantic ambiguity results from the sequential order of the *Chronicle*'s listing of events, since contiguity may indicate only an accumulation of detail or it may imply a hidden relation. This is not to say that entries cannot constitute narratives, for clearly many *Chronicle* entries are quite extensive narrations. But the meaning of the individual notations, the relations between the notations, and even the reasons for their selection are not clear. It is this indeterminacy that gives the impression that the prose implies or suggests more than it states directly. Hence semantic ambiguity in the *Chronicle* takes the form of an indeterminacy concerning the presence as well as the content of meaning; in the absence of narrative continuity or of clear logical relation between elements in an entry or between entries, nothing indicates whether or not juxtaposition asserts a logical relationship between the units, and nothing suggests what such a relationship might be. Juxtaposition or parataxis may imply the existence of some sort of meaningful link between the listed events, or the events may only mark the chronological sequence and differentiate the years.

Suggestive ambiguity is especially obvious in early entries. For instance, the early ambiguity of the record is exemplified in the entry for 734:

Her wæs se mona swelce he wære mid blode begoten. 7 ferdan forþ Tatwine 7 Bieda.

In this year the moon seemed as if it were covered with blood. And Tatwine and Bede died.

Similar ambiguity marks the entry for 773:

Her oþiewde read Cristesmel on hefenum æfter sunnan setlgong. 7 þy geare gefuhtan Mierce 7 Cantware æt Ottanforda, 7 wunderleca nedran wæron gesewene on Suþseaxna londe.

In this year a red cross appeared in the sky after sunset. And this
year the Mercians and the people of Kent fought at Otford. And
marvelous snakes were seen in Sussex.

Is the bloodied moon a symptom of Tatwine's and Bede's deaths? What
bearing do marvelous snakes and a heavenly cross have on a battle? The
listing lacks an interpretative principle, a basis for explaining causation
and relation. Unexpected natural appearances and human misfortunes
are listed consecutively, as if they belonged to the same order. In such a
symbolic structure, occurrences in nature and in human culture are
analogies, sharing likenesses and resemblances to one another and par-
ticipating in a common, unified world. But the meaning of each event and
the relations among all events are not identified. What happens in culture
seems to participate in nature, and all events are equally important,
without subordination to a controlling logic.

Changes in the characteristics of the *Chronicle*'s prose begin to emerge
with additions to the common stock after 891. Cecily Clark notes that
the terse, laconic, semiformulaic style of the early entries give way to
greater subordination, to efforts at interpretation, and to some linkage
between entries. Nevertheless, during most of the tenth century "there is
little sense of any control of events as a whole, nor is the formal continuity controlled by any real plan of exposition; indeed, at times the mere
sequence of events is unclear."[56]

Gransden describes a similar general tendency toward greater detail in
chronicle writing as an effect of the advent of literacy and of political
purposes: "The early chronicles are often cryptic and their significance is
sometimes lost today because of the passage of time. . . . A chronicle
appealed to those who shared its author's folk memory. As the written
record gained in importance over oral traditions, chronicles became more
detailed and specific . . . partly because the authors intended to support
the established order by emphasizing its antiquity and continuous history
and the prowess and success of some rulers."[57] However, even in the
tenth century when the *Chronicle*'s writing begins to become more elaborate and full, parataxis continues to govern the grammar and to provide
the narrative principle.

A historical discourse develops out of the *Chronicle*'s listing when
discrete events and appearances become references to a spiritual meaning. The imposition of a transcendent meaning on the recorded events
maintains the paratactic grammar that has characterized the *Chronicle*'s

writing, but it links the separate, sequential elements in a logical relation. So in the 975 poem on Edgar's death, juxtaposition still orders the sequence of events: a wise man is exiled, a comet appears, a famine occurs. Sublating sequence now, however, is a system of signification under the direction of divine will. In this semiotic system, events and appearances—all of what happens in time—are signifiers. Natural occurrences, supernatural appearances, and human events no longer serve equally as marks differentiating the years in which they occur. Rather, events and appearances in nature and in culture are to be read as references to an intention and thereby take on meaning. All events convey meaning because they refer to God's will. Time now becomes history, and history now is the signification of a law.

The law of God's justice and purpose is the discursive principle that allows history to emerge as a meaningful narrative in the *Chronicle*. Hence the poem for 975—*hungor ofer hrusan* ("hunger throughout the earth," 35)—can read famine as punishment for breaking God's law, just as prosperity—*blisse gehwæm . . . þurh eorðan westm* ("favor to each person from the abundance of the earth," 36–37)—is God's reward. Sacrilege is the cause of calamity, calamity the effect of divine vengeance. The violation of law, *þa man his riht tobræc* ("then God's law was violated," 23), and the rejection of proper worship—*waldendes lof / afylled on foldan* ("worship of the Lord was destroyed on the earth," 17–18)—are responsible for causing hunger; misfortune is a just punishment. The exile of Oslac, "the valiant man," is another example of impious practice.

Providential design here provides a law that supersedes the *Chronicle*'s grammar of contiguity, connecting and relating individual events in a discursive logic. At the same time, providential design serves an ideology supporting West-Saxon ambitions. For if God's enemies, those who break the law, are the traditional foes of the West Saxons, West-Saxon power must be understood to be the vehicle for God's intentions. Accordingly, the 975 poem claims that it is in Mercia that right worship is rejected. In some *Chronicle* manuscripts (D and E), the name of the Mercian leader who instigates the lawlessness is given as Alfhere, and his particular crime is identified as destroying monasteries that King Edgar had established. What well might be a regional rebellion against West-Saxon domination—a rebellion likely to occur upon the death of a ruler and a consequent perceived weakness, just the kind of internecine warfare that fills the pages of the *Chronicle*—is constructed in the late tenth-century poem as the drama of a national theology. According to the logic of providential history, West-Saxon political purpose takes on a transcendent national significance. When West-Saxon territory becomes identified with an English nation, God, as *brego engla* ("leader of the English," 36), acts in historical time as ruler of an English people.

Even while this entry for 975 provides the first statement in the *Chronicle* of the discourse of a providential history, such a discourse would long have been available in Anglo-Saxon culture for a political ideology, particularly through Bede, as Patrick Wormald shows,[58] and through Orosius and ultimately, of course, the Old Testament.[59] The *Chronicle* here enlists the well-established theological discourse of history to enable a vernacular historical discourse that provides an ideology to buttress a particular regime of power. The formal, rhetorical development of the *Chronicle*'s writing then both results from and strengthens West-Saxon ambitions.

However strong and stable West-Saxon rule in the tenth century may have been, the *Chronicle* makes it clear that no West-Saxon leader was free of rebellion, invasion, treachery, and the pressures of separate interests pursuing opportunistic strategies. West-Saxon hegemony was from the start continuously challenged and reasserted in response to contingent events; it was tied to the death of rulers, to invasions, and to military loss and victory. West-Saxon power could become synonymous with England, with an Anglo-Saxon nation, only when that power was inscribed as a symbolic production. The *Chronicle* poems produce just such an inscription; they further a national ideology when they develop a discourse of history. The discourse naturalizes military conquest and the temporary consolidation of sovereignty; the ideology that determines that discourse supports power by reconfiguring it as inherited, lawful rule. Eventually, the authority deriving from a tradition of lawful rule comes to survive the disintegration of the power that that tradition was initially installed to validate. The production of a historical discourse in the *Chronicle* poems works to create the idea of an English nation when it identifies West-Saxon hegemony as the manifestation of divine will. In other words, the idea of a nation is a powerful fiction.

Notes

An early version of this paper was written at an NEH Summer Seminar at Harvard University in 1993. I want to thank Peter Richardson and Marion Aitches for conversations and suggestions on earlier drafts, and Joseph Harris and T. D. Hill for their generous, careful, and companionable teaching.

1. Descriptions of the manuscripts and histories of their compilation are given by Charles Plummer, *Two of the Saxon Chronicles Parallel* (Oxford: Clarendon Press, 1892–99), vol. 2, pp. xvii–cxxxvii; Dorothy Whitelock, *The Anglo-Saxon Chronicle* (New Brunswick, N.J.: Rutgers University Press, 1961); and J. M. Bately, *The Anglo-Saxon Chronicle: A Collaborative Edition*, gen. eds. David Dumville and Simon Keynes, vol. 3, *MS A* (Cambridge: D. S. Brewer, 1986), pp. xiii–clxxvii. See also Bately, "The Compilation of the Anglo-Saxon Chronicle, 60 BC to AD 890: Vocabulary as Evidence," in *British Academy Papers on Anglo-Saxon England,* ed. E. G. Stanley (Oxford, 1990), pp. 261–97; Bately, *The Anglo-Saxon Chronicle: Texts and Textual Relationships* (Reading: University of Reading, 1991); and Antonia Gransden, *Historical Writing in England c. 550 to c. 1307* (Ithaca: Cornell University Press, 1974), pp. 29–41. Audrey L. Meaney, "St. Neots, Æthelweard and the Compilation of the *Anglo-Saxon Chronicle:* A Survey," in *Studies in Earlier Old English Prose,* ed. Paul E. Szarmach (Albany, N.Y.: SUNY Press, 1986), pp. 193–243, provides a discussion of the scholarship on the manuscript relations. Given the complex history of the individual manuscripts, reference to a single *Anglo-Saxon Chronicle* may be artificial or even misleading, since the records do not constitute a single text; nevertheless, common editorial practice refers to the *Anglo-Saxon Chronicle* as a record composed of several versions.

2. Although all four poems are not found in all manuscripts of the *Chronicle,* they are all in the A, B, and C manuscripts, the first two recorded in manuscripts A, B, C, and D, the last two in manuscripts A, B, and C, with the 973 poem of A entered for 974 in B and C. See Katherine O'Brien O'Keeffe, *Visible Song* (Cambridge: Cambridge University Press, 1990), pp. 110–11, for a discussion of the use of the A manuscript for a standard version of the poems and pp. 113–16 for a critical treatment of their editing.

3. The West-Saxon genealogies are discussed in Kenneth Sisam, "Anglo-Saxon Royal Genealogies," *Proceedings of the British Academy* 39 (1953): 287–348; D. N. Dumville, "The Anglian Collection of Royal Genealogies and Regnal Lists," *Anglo-Saxon England* 5 (1976): 23–50; and Craig Davis, "Cultural Assimilation in the Anglo-Saxon Royal Genealogies," *Anglo-Saxon England* 21 (1992): 23–36.

4. Unless otherwise noted, all quotations from the *Chronicle* are from the A manuscript, also known as the Parker manuscript, ed. Bately. This is generally acknowledged to be the earliest surviving copy and the closest to an original. See M. B. Parkes, "The Palaeography of the Parker Manuscript of the *Chronicle,* Laws and Sedulius, and Historiography at Winchester in the Late Ninth and Tenth Centuries," *Anglo-Saxon England* 5 (1976): 149–71, for a description of the manuscript and a possible history of its compilation. Martin Irvine, in *The Making of Textual Culture* (Cambridge: Cambridge University Press, 1994), ascribes "a single-mindedness to the Parker compilation that opens a window onto the function and meaning of the Chronicle poems" (p. 456). For a summary of manuscript relationships see Bately, *The Anglo-Saxon Chronicle,* p. 62. All translations are my own.

5. See F. M. Stenton, *Anglo-Saxon England* (Oxford: Oxford University Press, 1962), p. 15, and Gransden, *Historical Writing in England,* p. 30. In "The Narrative Mode of *The Anglo-Saxon Chronicle* Before the Conquest," in *England Before the Conquest,* ed. Peter Clemoes and Kathleen Hughes (Cambridge: Cambridge University Press, 1971), Cecily Clark ascribes the terse, formulaic style of the writing of early entries in the *Chronicle* to that work's origin in marginal notes to Easter tables: "such notes, being adjuncts to the calendar . . . were also factual and objective. . . . The objective manner of the primitive annals abstracted from such tables (although not their extreme brevity) was imitated in annals independently composed" (p. 218). Parkes, "The Parker Manuscript of the *Chronicle,*" concurs that the "exemplar was based closely either on something resembling Easter tables or on a collection of material abstracted from notes to Easter tables" (p. 154) but argues for a continental influence motivating the early compilation. However, Whitelock, *The Anglo-Saxon Chronicle,* p. xxii, rejects the idea that the *Chronicle* originated in Easter tables.

6. Hayden White, "The Value of Narrativity in the Representation of Reality," in *On Narrative,* ed. W. J. T. Mitchell (Chicago: University of Chicago Press, 1980), p. 9.

7. Plummer, *Two of the Saxon Chronicles,* p. xix.

8. Peter Clemoes, "Language in Context: *Her* in the 890 *Anglo-Saxon Chronicle,*" *Leeds Studies in English* 16 (1985): 31.

9. White, "Value of Narrativity," p. 11.

10. For discussion of ideology as understood here, see Slavoj Žižek, *The Sublime Object of Ideology* (London, 1990), *For They Know Not What They Do* (London: Verso, 1991), and *The Metastasis of Enjoyment* (London: Verso, 1994), part 1, pp. 5–85. Karl Mannheim, *Ideology and Utopia* (New York: Harcourt Brace, 1936), is a classic treatment of ideology as an expression of class hegemony.

11. See Patrick Wormald, "Anglo-Saxon Society and Its Literature," in *The Cambridge Companion to Old English Literature,* ed. Malcolm Godden and Michael Lapidge (Cambridge: Cambridge University Press, 1991), pp. 17–19.

12. Roberta Frank, "The *Beowulf* Poet's Sense of History," in *The Wisdom of Poetry,* ed. Larry D. Benson and Siegfried Wenzel (Kalamazoo, Mich.: Medieval Institute Publications, 1983), p. 63.

13. John D. Niles, "Locating *Beowulf* in Literary History," *Exemplaria* 5 (1993): 107.

14. Ibid., p. 91.

15. I borrow this term from Benedict Anderson, *Imagined Communities* (London: Verso, 1983). In tracing the birth of nineteenth-century nationhood and nationalisms, Anderson foregrounds the role of print technologies and textual communities in creating the idea of a nation. See also Brian Stock, *The Implications of Literacy: Written Language and Models of Interpretation in the Eleventh and Twelfth Centuries* (Princeton: Princeton University Press, 1983), for the

formation of textual communities. My use of the term *imagined community* is intended to underline the constructed character of nationhood.

16. See Whitelock, *The Anglo-Saxon Chronicle,* p. xxiii, and Bately, "The Compilation of the Anglo-Saxon Chronicle."

17. See the introductions to the books by Plummer, Whitelock, and Bately cited in note 1.

18. Parkes, "The Parker Manuscript of the *Chronicle,*" argues that the history of the compilation of the A manuscript "suggests a conscious attempt on the part of [the] compiler, active some time during or after the reign of Athelstan, to preserve the tradition of the West Saxon royal house in its purest form. . . . The form of the compilation of the Parker manuscript in the mid-tenth century emphasizes the previous achievements of this dynasty" (p. 167).

19. According to Frank Stenton, even in his law code, Alfred "gives himself no higher title than King of the West Saxons," (*Anglo-Saxon England,* p. 273). In contrast, Patrick Wormald claims that Alfred "was the first king whose titles [*rex Angulsaxonum / Anglorum Saxonum*] claimed rule over all the English" ("Anglo-Saxon Society and Its Literature," p. 13). The meanings of the designations of rulership are complicated and not always clear, especially in the early years of the *Chronicle;* see Patrick Wormald, "Bede, the *Bretwaldas* and the Origins of the *Gens Anglorum,*" in *Ideal and Reality in Frankish and Anglo-Saxon Society,* ed. Patrick Wormald et al. (Oxford: Blackwell, 1983), pp. 96–129. While a discussion of Alfred's titles is beyond the scope of this essay, it nevertheless remains important to note when the *Chronicle* records begin to refer to rule over England, rather than to a West-Saxon or Anglo-Saxon kingship.

20. All quotations of the poems are from *The Anglo-Saxon Minor Poems,* ed. Elliott Van Kirk Dobbie, The Anglo-Saxon Poetic Records, vol. 6 (New York: Columbia University Press, 1968). Dobbie gives precedence to the version from the A manuscript for each. Unless otherwise indicated, reference to each *Chronicle* poem here will refer to the A manuscript version printed in Dobbie.

21. Gransden, *Historical Writing in England,* p. 38.

22. Martin Irvine, "Medieval Textuality and the Archaeology of Textual Culture," in *Speaking Two Languages,* ed. Allen J. Frantzen (New York: SUNY Press, 1991), pp. 181–210.

23. Gransden, *Historical Writing in England,* p. 38.

24. Little can be asserted confidently about the authorship of the poems and about the process of their inclusion in the *Chronicle* manuscripts. As Katherine O'Brien O'Keeffe writes, "These poems cannot be ascribed to identifiable authors, and they offer remarkably little information on the facts of their composition" (*Visible Song,* p. 108). Alistair Campbell, in the introduction to his edition of *The Battle of Brunanburh* (London: W. Heinemann, 1938), implies that the compiler was not the poet: whoever compiled the *Chronicle* manuscripts, writes Campbell, "he realised that he was providing poor fare for his monkish readers, so he added two poems. . . . His interest was, like the writers of these poems, in

the past and in the glory of his present rulers" in 937 and 942. The poem for 975 may be the product of two authors, since "it is possible that the original poem ended at line 12 . . . and that the chronicler is responsible only for the continuation from 13 to the end" (p. 36). In *Anglo-Saxon Oral Poetry: A Study of the Traditions* (New Haven: Yale University Press, 1980), pp. 172–77, Jeff Opland develops Campbell's suggestion of skaldic influence to posit a revival of eulogistic court poetry during the reign of Athelstan. In his view, "the appearance of poetry in the *Anglo-Saxon Chronicle* may well be a reflection of trends in the oral tradition" (p. 172). Although Opland does not explain the exact relation between the poets, "drawing on their living oral traditions," and the compilers of the *Chronicle,* he does indicate their influence on the texts: "A reanimated tradition of eulogistic poetry in praise of rulers might then have ensured the legitimacy of written poems such as those that were entered in the *Chronicle*" (p. 174). Opland's view that the poems were produced in the context of the court is consistent with Dobbie's description of the poet of the *Battle of Brunanburh:* whether the poet "was a cleric or a layman seems immaterial; he is perhaps best described, in Klaeber's words, as a 'gifted and well trained publicist' of the West Saxon court" (Dobbie, *The Anglo-Saxon Minor Poems,* p. xl). In contrast, Patrick W. Conner argues that the poems could have been composed at Abingdon, although probably not by the same person, "when Abingdon was developing its recension of the *Chronicle,*" that is, the C manuscript: Patrick W. Conner, *The Anglo-Saxon Chronicle: A Collaborative Edition,* vol. 10, *The Abingdon Chronicle* (Cambridge: D. S. Brewer, 1996), p. lxxxiii.

25. These are the accepted dates for the poems, as they are entered in the A manuscript and known in the literature. Inconsistencies in dating may result from scribal errors, from differences in collated sources, or from different methods of dating the start of the year. For the dating of the year see Plummer, "On the Commencement of the Year in the Saxon Chronicles," in his *Two of the Saxon Chronicles,* vol. 2, pp. cixl–cxli. See O'Keeffe, *Visible Song,* p. 109, for a record of the revisions of the datings.

26. Opland, *Anglo-Saxon Oral Poetry,* p. 173. Opland analyzes the poems as panegyrics in "Scop and Imbongi, IV: Reading Praise Poems," *Comparative Literature* 45 (1993): 97–120.

27. Janet Thormann, "*The Battle of Brunanburh* and the Matter of History," *Mediaevalia* 17 (1994, for 1991): 5–13.

28. Irvine, "Medieval Textuality," p. 202.

29. Nicholas Howe, *Migration and Mythmaking in Anglo-Saxon England* (New Haven: Yale University Press, 1989); see esp. pp. 28–32 for discussion of the *Chronicle* poems.

30. John D. Niles, *Beowulf: The Poem and Its Tradition* (Cambridge: Harvard University Press, 1983), p. 61.

31. Joseph Harris, "Old English Heroic Poetry: An Essay," unpublished manuscript, p. 52. Harris considers all the poems to be panegyrics, with "faint

traces of continued contact with oral [poetry]," p. 52. I am grateful to Professor Harris for allowing me to read this manuscript.

32. Martin Irvine, similarly, claims in *The Making of Textual Culture* that the "very form of the traditional diction, formulae, and meter [of these poems] was ideologically encoded to link the present to the heroic past" (p. 453). I do not agree that the poems reflect "a nostalgia for a lost, or at least historically prior, oral past," however, or that "the poetic form itself had become a vehicle for nostalgia" (p. 452). The poems produce an ideology by repeating and manipulating traditional language and thematic matter. Rather than expressing a nostalgia for a lost past, the language performs the present as an extension of the authority of the past. Such an "always present past authority" is, in part, what the nation is.

33. The formulaic character of these epithets is evident. With *maga mundbora* compare *meahtig mundbora* (*Resignation* 109) and *modig mundbora* (*Guthlac* 695); with *wiggendra hleo* compare *wigendra hleo* (*Beowulf* 899, 1972, 2337); with *dyre dædfruma* compare *dior dædfruma* (*Beowulf* 2090).

34. The reading of manuscript A, *Dæne wæran æror* (8), contrasts with the reading of manuscript B, *Denum wæron æror*. If *Denum* is the correct reading, the meaning of the lines would be that the territories "had been oppressed by force under the Danes, the Norsemen," with Danes and Norsemen in apposition. However, Dobbie comments that the "reading *Denum*, which makes the Danes (of the Danelaw) and the Norsemen (of Northumbria) the same people, is unsatisfactory" (*The Anglo-Saxon Minor Poems*, pp. xli–xlii).

35. For an outline of the complex and shifting political situation in England at this time, see for example Richard Humble, *The Fall of Saxon England* (London: A. Barker, 1975), pp. 89–137.

36. Stenton, *Anglo-Saxon England*, p. 354.

37. See for example Robert E. Diamond, "The Diction of the Signed Poems of Cynewulf," *Philological Quarterly* 38 (1959): 228–41; Donald K. Fry, "Themes and Type-Scenes in *Elene*," *Speculum* 44 (1969): 35–45; and especially Michael D. Cherniss, *Ingeld and Christ* (The Hague, 1972).

38. *Alysan* (11) means "to free, deliver, or liberate," and the word appears in Bosworth and Toller primarily in religious contexts with the meaning "redeem."

39. See Humble, *The Fall of Saxon England*, p. 116.

40. Plummer, *Two of the Saxon Chronicles*, MS D, vol. 1, p. 105.

41. See note in Plummer, vol. 2, p. 161, for Latinate forms of the place name. Plummer's note suggests that the foundation of the baths "was ascribed to Julius Caesar" and that it "is possible that the first part of the name contains the Latin 'aquae.'"

42. Pauline Stafford, *Unification and Conquest: A Political and Social History of England in the Tenth and Eleventh Centuries* (London: E. Arnold, 1989), p. 56.

43. Ibid., p. 53.

44. John Cannon and Ralph Griffiths, *The Oxford Illustrated History of the British Monarchy* (Oxford: Oxford University Press, 1988), p. 30.

45. Michael Wood, "The Making of King Æthelstan's Empire: An English Charlemagne?" in *Ideal and Reality in Frankish and Anglo-Saxon Society,* ed. Wormald et al., pp. 250–72, presents a convincing case for the imperial dimensions of Athelstan's rule. My focus here, however, is the evidence from the *Chronicle* poems, which suggests imperial associations and sacerdotal implications during the reign of Edgar.

46. Plummer, MS E under the date 972, in vol. 1, p. 119.

47. Stenton, *Anglo-Saxon England,* p. 364.

48. If the authorship and the context of the *Chronicle* poems generally cannot be resolved, treatment of the origin and even the character of these two entries can only be even more speculative. Plummer prints as poetry both the 959 entry in the D, E, and F manuscripts and the 975 entry in the D and E manuscripts that substitutes for the more familiar poem on Edgar's death. Whitelock, in contrast, states that the 959 entry "is written in alliterative prose, and is in the style of Archbishop Wulfstan of York" (*The Anglo-Saxon Chronicle,* p. 74), and that the beginning of the entry reporting Edgar's death in the D and E manuscripts is distinct from the prose that follows in that it "is strongly rhythmical with some assonance and rhyme" (p. 77). Campbell writes that the compiler "deemed the insertion of verse an admirable way of producing an impressive continuation of the *Chronicle,* but the scholarly and correct, if feeble, verse" of the earlier compilation "did not please him. He thought that his readers would prefer some specimens of a new sort of jingling verse, which had developed among the popular poets" (*The Battle of Brunanburh,* p. 37). Accordingly, Campbell understands these entries to echo a tradition of popular poetry in the *Chronicle.* In the absence of any consensus or of any certain means of evaluation, I am following Plummer in printing the entries as poems.

49. Quotations are from Plummer, MS E, in vol. 1, pp. 114–15.

50. Although Opland does not discuss the 959 entry, the criticism of the king here fits his conception that the function of the eulogistic court poet was to "apportion praise and sometimes blame" (*Anglo-Saxon Oral Poetry,* p. 173). Gransden, in contrast, cites this criticism as evidence that "a gradual alteration in the attitude to the ruling house can be detected. As the unification of England proceeded, the Chronicle began to reflect incipient national feeling. This could involve criticism of the king. . . . The Chronicle identifies itself with the English people rather than the king" (*Historical Writing in England,* p. 40). If such a separation between West-Saxon and English interests is at all possible at this early a date, it would represent the paradoxical success of West-Saxon ideological ambitions in supporting the idea of an England that could exist independently of West-Saxon rule.

51. Quotations are from Plummer, MS E, in vol. 1, p. 121.

52. Compare *godes leoht geceas* (*Beowulf* 2469).

53. James Earl, *Thinking About Beowulf* (Stanford: Stanford University Press, 1994), p. 62.

54. T. D. Hill, "The 'Variegated Obit' as an Histographic Motif in Old English Poetry and Anglo-Latin Historical Literature," *Traditio* 44 (1988), 101–24.

55. White, "Value of Narrativity," p. 9.

56. Clark, "The Narrative Mode," p. 224. Clark identifies a significant shift in the *Chronicle*'s narration to a greater subjectivity "from about 991" when the annalist "begins to offer explanations of the events he records, and also comments on them" (p. 225). In later, eleventh-century entries, Clark finds evidence of a sense of causation and a growing interest in participants' thoughts, motives, and feelings, along with growing partisanship. Clark does not discuss the tenth-century poems, since she is investigating changes in the prose. In contrast, my focus here has been on the way a historical discourse, supported by an ideology, emerges in the poetry.

57. Gransden, *Historical Writing in England*, p. 30.

58. Patrick Wormald, "The Venerable Bede and the 'Church of the English,'" in *The English Religious Tradition and the Genius of Anglicanism*, ed. Geoffrey Rowell (Oxford: IKON, 1992), pp. 13–32.

59. See Gransden, *Historical Writing in England*, especially pp. 29–41, to identify the larger context of historical discourses.

4. Received Wisdom

The Reception History of Alfred's Preface to the Pastoral Care

Suzanne C. Hagedorn

K ING ALFRED THE GREAT's letter exhorting his bishops to join him in promoting an ambitious program of vernacular education and translation is, as T. A. Shippey has remarked, "one of the most familiar of Anglo-Saxon texts, translated annually as an exercise by hundreds of undergraduates, and first conned by most scholars at an age when their critical faculties are hardly developed."[1] Many people who study Old English literature first encountered it as I did—in *Bright's Anglo-Saxon Reader* (or a similar introductory handbook) during the first term of an undergraduate Old English course. That a letter lamenting the sorry state of English learning and attempting to persuade Anglo-Saxon bishops of the need for bilingual education has itself become a frequently used pedagogical tool ought to occasion some reflection about how and why this text has been appropriated in the millennium or so since Alfred sent copies to Wulfsige, Wærferth, Plegmund, and Hehstan. That such reflections have only rarely intruded into critical studies of Alfred's letter may be regarded as a symptom of the degree to which scholars (usually unconsciously) collaborate in the fiction that their access to Alfred's text is unmediated by the accidental historical processes of its textual transmission.[2]

In speaking of the "reception" of Alfred's letter, a text usually known as his preface to the *Pastoral Care,* I employ the term in the sense of Hans Robert Jauss and his followers, who see reception as a process in which the audience participates. As Jauss writes, "In the triangle of author, work, and public the last is no passive part, no chain of mere reactions but rather itself an energy formative of history."[3] For Jauss, a literary work "is not a monument that monologically reveals its timeless essence. It is much more like an orchestration that strikes ever new resonances among its readers and that frees the text from the material of the words and brings it to a contemporary existence."[4] Moreover, like a musical score, a literary text is transmitted by recopying or reprinting, and is thus subject to the interventions of its scribes, editors, and critics. The residues of textual criticism—including emendations, interpolations, and punctuation—are signs of interpretive activities that inevitably become part of a subsequent reader's experience of the work whether that reader is conscious of them or not. In order to understand better the presuppositions on which current scholars build their interpretations, we need to investigate the process of textual transmission with an awareness of the cultural contexts that enable and govern particular moments in a work's reception. Thus, Jerome McGann argues for a "more comprehensive sociohistorical view of texts" as material objects, pointing out that "the language in which texts speak to us is not located merely in the verbal sign system. Texts comprise elaborate arrangements of different and interrelated sign systems. It makes a difference if the poem we read is printed in *The New Yorker, The New York Review of Books,* or *The New Republic.* Textual and bibliographical criticism generates, in relation to the works we read, a great deal more critical information than a calculus of variants or a record of emendations."[5]

In examining the reception of Alfred's preface, I will therefore be calling particular attention to issues that can be broadly called codicological. The typeface, the layout, and even the size of a book can give nonverbal clues to its cultural context and intended readership, just as the author's or editor's prefaces and dedicatory epistles help to situate it in a world of social and political relationships. By tracing the material forms and the circumstances in which this single text has been presented to various communities of readers over the centuries, we may be able to see in microcosm the larger cultural forces that have informed the discipline of Anglo-Saxon studies as a whole.

✠

The earliest reception history of Alfred's preface to the *Pastoral Care* can be at least partially reconstructed from a study of its manuscripts. Since this phase in the text's transmission is closest to the "originary moment" of Alfred's composition, Anglo-Saxonists have concentrated their energies on exploring it, studying the cultural context of Alfred's publication and distribution of his work and carefully describing the various manuscripts and their vicissitudes.[6] Likewise, the ways in which later Old English writers made use of Alfred's preface to the *Pastoral Care* have also attracted some scholarly attention: Bernard Huppé has argued that Alfred's preface served as a model for Ælfric's preface to Genesis, while N. R. Ker has identified some of the glosses to the preface in Bodleian MS Hatton 20 of the Old English *Pastoral Care* as those of the eleventh-century homilist Wulfstan or someone closely associated with him.[7]

The Old English manuscripts of the *Pastoral Care* also indicate that the text was studied during the Middle English period, as Henry Sweet was the first to observe in his 1871 edition of the Hatton manuscript. Describing the Latin glosses in the early part of the manuscript, Sweet concluded that "the work seems to have been used as a text-book for the study of Old English in the thirteenth and following centuries."[8] In more recent investigations, Christine Franzen and R. I. Page have argued that two of the Old English manuscripts of the *Pastoral Care* served precisely that purpose for an anonymous thirteenth-century scribe dubbed the "tremulous hand of Worcester" from his characteristically shaky annotations. Interlinear Latin glosses in this hand, evidently copied from Gregory's text, appear in both the Hatton 20 and the Corpus Christi College Cambridge 12 manuscripts of the Old English *Pastoral Care*.[9] In the case of Alfred's preface, of course, the scribe could not have worked with a Latin original and would have had to rely upon comparative studies of other Old English texts or his own knowledge, which might explain Franzen's observation that the Worcester scribe's glossing of the preface in Hatton 20 is much less frequent than the glossing of the main text and is in a more mature state of his hand. She also notes that the scribe chose to flag Alfred's famous comments on the decay of learning—a passage that may have seemed particularly meaningful to someone who was trying to master a language that had itself fallen into disuse.

Although the efforts of the Worcester scribe and other monastic glossators indicate that there was some isolated interest in Anglo-Saxon during the Middle English period, the language lay largely neglected until the sixteenth century, when the dissolution of English monasteries under Henry VIII provided an impetus to collect and preserve Anglo-Saxon manuscripts. In the latter half of the century, religious controversies pushed Matthew Parker, Queen Elizabeth's first Archbishop of Canterbury, to marshal historical evidence from the Anglo-Saxon period to support Anglican views on the Eucharist and on vernacular translations of the Bible.[10] From the 1560s until his death in 1575, Parker coordinated an ambitious program of collection, publication, and translation of early chronicles and documents relating to medieval English history—a program that resulted in the first editions of many Anglo-Saxon texts, among them Alfred's preface.

As R. I. Page has shown, Parker and his circle left numerous traces behind them as they read and translated the Anglo-Saxon manuscripts they later published; the manuscripts of Alfred's preface are no exception.[11] Parker's secretary John Joscelyn copied Latin glosses from CCCC 12 into Hatton 20, and may also have been responsible for an interlinear translation inserted into Cambridge University Library MS Ii.2.4., a text that is closely linked to the translation published by Parker in 1574.[12] Furthermore, two other sixteenth-century translations—one a transcription and translation of Hatton 20 by Joscelyn, the other an anonymous sixteenth-century translation with a heading in Parker's distinctive hand— indicate a high degree of interest in Alfred's preface at this period.[13] Why did Parker's circle find Alfred's preface so compelling? Perhaps, Page suggests, because Parker himself could identify both with Alfred's complaints about uneducated priests and with the king's wish to justify a translation program.[14]

In fact, Alfred's preface and his translation program were directly or indirectly invoked in Parkerian publications to provide a venerable precedent for the archbishop's own biblical translation project. In the 1568 "Bishop's Bible," a new translation made by a group of Anglican prelates at his request, Parker's preface echoes Alfred's preface to the *Pastoral Care,* as the archbishop rebukes those who forbid scriptural translation as being unwilling to follow in the track of their illustrious forebears:

> Yea, they be farre unlike their olde forefathers that have ruled in this realme, who in their times, and in divers ages did their diligence to translate the whole bookes of the scriptures to the erudition of the laytie, as yet at this day be to be seene divers bookes translated into the vulgar tongue, some by kynges of the realme, some by bishoppes, some by abbottes, some by other devout godly fathers.[15]

But Parker was not content merely to assert that the Anglo-Saxon scriptures existed; in 1571 he had them printed as a "testimonie," along with a preface by the martyrologist John Foxe. In his preface dedicating *The*

Gospels of the fower Euangelistes to Queen Elizabeth, Foxe points out the relevance of Anglo-Saxon studies for secular and legal history, but he is mainly interested in Old English texts as evidence to support contemporary Anglican church policy on biblical translation. In his defense of vernacular translations of scripture, Foxe cites Alfred's "learned preface before the Saxon Pastoralles,"

> in which he doth declare that the Hebrues had the law of God in their tounge, the Grecians had it turned into their tounge, and the Romanes by their skilfull interpreters had it in their tounge, and all other Christian people, as he sayth, have some part of those thinges in their owne proper language: And thereupon he thinketh it meete that all bookes that be nedefull for men to know, to have them turned into the tonge which all men do know.

Here, Foxe's close paraphrase of the text of Alfred's preface suggests that Parker and his circle had furnished him with their translation.

Parker and Foxe's introductions demonstrate the utility of Alfred's preface as an authoritative proof-text to sixteenth-century scholars engaged in ecclesiastical controversies. At the same time, Alfred's preface was also used as historical ammunition in a more down-to-earth controversy—the longstanding squabble over whether Oxford or Cambridge was the older university. Matthew Parker's friend and fellow Cambridge alumnus John Caius refers to Alfred's letter in a 1568 treatise aimed at refuting Oxford's claims to have been founded before Alfred's time. Citing the king's comments on the decay of learning to prove that no grammar school existed in the entire western part of England—and certainly not at Oxford—Caius describes the preface approvingly as "ipsam Aluredi epistolam (in qua sui temporis inscitiam dolet) sapientiæ eius verum testimonium" ("that letter of Alfred's in which he laments the ignorance of his age, a letter that is a true witness to his wisdom").[16] Here, Caius uses the preface as an emblem of the king's interest in learning, a role it also plays in Matthew Parker's 1574 edition of Asser's life of King Alfred, titled *Ælfredi Regis Res Gestæ*.[17] In his introduction to Asser's history, Parker refers to the preface to illustrate Alfred's commitment to the pursuit of knowledge. To reinforce his point, he published the Old English text of Alfred's preface with an interlinear gloss and a Latin translation as an appendix to Asser's history.

Besides providing a tangible example of Alfred's wisdom, Parker's *editio princeps* of Alfred's preface may also be an early attempt to convert the king's epistle into a language-learning tool. In his introduction to Asser, Parker argues that studying Anglo-Saxon is a rewarding pursuit, since one will have the pleasure of comparing the contemporary English language with the "Saxon" in order to see their similarities; he says that he has caused the Gospels to be published with a marginal gloss in English for this very reason. Placed in this context, Parker's decision to publish the text of the preface with an interlinear English gloss and Latin translation appears to be another manifestation of the archbishop's wish to encourage the study of Old English.

The form of Parker's edition may also help explain why Alfred's letter to his bishops has been canonized under the title "Alfred's Preface to the *Pastoral Care,*" an appellation which Francis P. Magoun, for one, has rejected as inaccurate.[18] Parker's edition begins with the following heading and interlinear gloss: "Ðis is seo forspræc hu S. Gregorius þas boc gedihte þe mon Pastoralem nemnað" ("This is the Preface how S. Gregorie this booke made, which men the Pastoral doe call"). Although this heading clearly applies to Gregory's introduction to the *Pastoral Care,* it is here attached to Alfred's words. Possibly as a result of this association, the term *preface* began to be applied to Alfred's letter—a practice which Parker himself adopts in his introduction to *Ælfredi Regis Res Gestæ,* and which has continued to the present day.[19]

Parker may or may not have intended his edition of Alfred's preface as an Anglo-Saxon primer, but that is precisely the aim of Bonaventura Vulcanius's reprinting of the king's letter in 1597. In *De Literis et Lingua Getarum Sive Gothorum,* a slim pamphlet in octavo, Vulcanius provided commentary on and specimens of the Gothic language, to which he appended fragments of Old German, Old English, Persian, Basque, Frisian, Welsh, Icelandic, and even Nubian.[20] Vulcanius, also known as Bonaventura De Smet, was a humanist scholar who edited many classical literary and historical texts. Around the time that *De Literis et Lingua Getarum* appeared, he was occupied with the publication of various Latin and Greek writers on the Goths—Jordanes, Isidore, and Procopius. His little pamphlet on the Gothic language thus forms a companion piece to the collection of chronicles he had published in the same format that year.[21] Vulcanius's work could be considered an early exercise in comparative philology, for Alfred's preface is of interest to him less as a historical or religious document than as a linguistic curiosity. His Latin introduction to this "Specimen of the Ancient Saxon Language" gives some historical background about Alfred's reign that largely recalls Parker's introduction. In the text that follows, Vulcanius follows Parker's edition of the preface almost exactly, preserving the typographical format of Old English text with interlinear English gloss, so that "the studious reader can compare the Old Saxon with English and our Teutonic language."[22]

During the seventeenth century, Anglo-Saxon scholars were apparently content with Parker's edition of Alfred's letter and saw no need to revisit the manuscripts themselves. The antiquarian William Camden, for instance, simply reprinted Parker's edition with a few typographical errors in his 1603 *Anglica, Normannica, Hibernica, Cambrica, a veteribus scripta,* a collection of medieval chronicles.[23] Toward the end of the century, Obadiah Walker did the same, reprinting Parker's Old English text of the preface and its Latin translation as an appendix to his 1678 Latin edition of Sir John Spelman's *Life of King Alfred the Great.*[24] The important exception to this general rule was the Dutch scholar Francis Junius, the greatest of seventeenth-century Anglo-Saxonists. Junius produced a transcript of MS Cotton Tiberius B.xi, which contained Alfred's translation of Gregory's *Pastoral Care* along with the prefatory materials composed by Alfred.[25] Twentieth-century Anglo-Saxonists consider this one of the earliest manuscripts of Alfred's work, if not the exemplar kept at the king's administrative headquarters.[26] With the exception of a single leaf that became detached and was then preserved in the binding of a manuscript at Kassel, the manuscript was reduced to a few charred fragments in the Cotton Library conflagration of 1731. As a result, scholars must largely rely upon Junius's transcription to reconstruct the text of this manuscript, although comparisons of the transcript with that portion of the text found on the Kassel leaf have cast doubt on his reliability as a transcriber.[27] Nevertheless, even if its value to modern scholars trying to reconstruct the lost Cotton manuscript is diminished by its inaccuracies, Junius's transcript remains an important document in its own right, since it manifests his interest in manuscript studies and provides information about the whereabouts of a manuscript that was apparently completely unknown to Parker and his circle during the previous century.

If Junius's work on Alfred's preface illustrates the philological vein of seventeenth-century Anglo-Saxon scholarship, Sir John Spelman's biography of King Alfred, which also makes use of the preface, shows how political agendas intersected with historical scholarship during this tumultuous period. An ardent royalist, Spelman wrote his *Life of King*

Alfred the Great from 1642 to 1643 while living in Oxford, where he had been summoned by Charles I after the king had made the city the headquarters for royalist forces. Spelman's portrayal of Alfred as an exemplary king beset by foreign invasions in the *Life* is clearly not only an expression of Spelman's antiquarian interests but also a veiled commentary on the contemporary political situation.[28]

Spelman died in 1643 before his biography could be printed. It remained in manuscript until after the Restoration, when Obadiah Walker, the master of University College, Oxford, had it translated into Latin and published with copious annotations. Walker was not only an ardent royalist but also was suspected by many to be a secret Roman Catholic.[29] His notes disputing Spelman's claim that King Alfred and the pope had clashed were therefore taken as evidence of his "popish" sympathies, and in 1679, the Oxford historian Anthony à Wood reported that Walker's edition of Spelman's *Life of Alfred* had been denounced in Parliament as being among the "popish books" printed by the university press at the Sheldonian Theatre.[30]

Spelman's work was eventually published in English and without Walker's controversial notes when the antiquary Thomas Hearne "sent it abroad in it's own Natural Dress" in 1709.[31] In his biography of Alfred, Spelman includes an English translation of the preface as evidence for Alfred's spirituality. As he writes, "The Preface containeth many very remarkable Things, in which, above all other, we may behold the King's Zealous Care to revive Religion, and to restore the true Knowledge and Service of God, and to increase the Prosperity of his People."[32] Spelman probably translates from Parker's edition, for he says that the preface is directed to Wulfsige, as it was in the manuscript Parker printed. Spelman's translation turns Parker's gloss into readable English, yet it sticks closely enough to Parker's wording throughout to show that he used the interlinear gloss of Parker's edition as his trot. Furthermore, Spelman repeats some of the translation errors made in Parker's gloss; for instance, within the first few lines of the preface, he translates "ge heora sybbe ge heora sydo" as "both in war and peace" instead of "both their peace and their customs" and "mid wige ge mid wisdome" as "in knowledge and in wisdom" instead of "in warfare and in wisdom." Since Anglo-Saxon lexicography was still in its infancy, such lapses are hardly surprising.

Although Spelman wrote that he would include Alfred's preface and a translation at the end of his book, Hearne's notes on this passage say that the projected appendix is not in Spelman's manuscript. In the 1678 Latin edition, however, Walker fulfilled Spelman's wish by reprinting Parker's edition of Alfred's preface. In this reprinting, the modern English interlinear gloss is eliminated and Parker's Old English and Latin texts are printed side by side, a layout that discourages the comparison of words that Parker's arrangement of text and gloss allowed. Unlike Parker, Walker and his collaborators were not interested in promoting Anglo-Saxon scholarship. Rather, their large and elegant Latin volume seems designed for a learned audience by those who wanted to show off their own erudition. And indeed, this was precisely their motive; Walker and various other members of University College undertook the publication of *Ælfredi Magni Anglorum Regis* after a successful fund-raising campaign to rebuild the large quadrangle of the college "that the world should know that their benefactions are not bestowed on mere drones."[33] One wonders whether major contributors received complimentary copies.

In terms of the transmission history of Alfred's preface, Spelman's work is mainly important for its improved English translation, which came to be used and reprinted by later scholars. Nevertheless, the patriotic context provided for the preface by Spelman's biography is as important as the translation itself. Although contemporary Anglo-Saxonists may regard Spelman's history as merely a quaint curiosity, for close to two centuries his work was considered the authoritative biography of the king, and as such it provided a historical basis for the glorification of Alfred and his reign in the popular imagination.[34]

The publication of the encyclopedic *Linguarum Veterum Septentrionalium Thesaurus* by George Hickes and various collaborators in the early eighteenth century ushered in a new era of Anglo-Saxon studies, but this landmark work apparently had little effect on the study of Alfred's preface.[35] Hickes's *Thesaurus* is most useful to modern scholars because of volume 3, the *Catalogus Historico-Criticus* of the great paleographer Humfrey Wanley, which lists and describes all the Anglo-Saxon manuscripts that Wanley could find. Wanley's descriptions are invaluable not only because of his expertise but because he was able to view manuscripts that have since been lost to the ravages of fire. Like Junius's transcript, Wanley's catalogue entries on the manuscripts of Alfred's preface provide important clues about the text's transmission history. Wanley noted that MS Cotton Tiberius B.xi once was prefaced by a note saying that "+ Plegmunde Arcebisc. is agifen his boc and Swiðulf Bisc. ⁊ Werferðe Bisc." and that the text of Alfred's preface preserved in it has a blank where the

addressee's name should be, facts which have led modern scholars to
believe it to have been very near to Alfred—possibly even the copy
belonging to the king's administrative headquarters.[36] One would think
that the wealth of information provided by Wanley's *Catalogus* would
have encouraged renewed interest in manuscript studies and might even
result in improved editions of Anglo-Saxon texts. This did not happen
with Alfred's preface, as Francis Wise's 1722 edition of the text demonstrates.

In Wise's *Annales Rerum Gestarum Ælfredi Magni,* Alfred's preface
again appears as an appendix to Asser's life of Alfred. Here, for the first
time, Alfred's preface is published using sources other than Parker's
edition, as its heading proclaims: "Ælfredi Regis Præfatio ad Pastorale
Sancti Gregorii è Cod. MS. Junius LIII" ("The Preface of King Alfred to
St. Gregory's Pastoral Care from MS. Junius 53").[37] Wise's notation of
the manuscript he works with in the heading at first sounds promising,
but his work can best be described as an *attempt* at a critical edition.
Though he consults the Hatton manuscript and sets up an *apparatus
criticus,* his choice of texts to include in it is not particularly useful.
Instead of working with MS Cotton Tiberius B.xi directly, Wise uses
Francis Junius's transcript, even though the manuscript was still extant.
Strangely enough, Wise makes this transcript the basis of his edition
instead of the Hatton manuscript, which he cites only in the apparatus of
variants. Finally, in the apparatus he cites variants from both Parker's
and Camden's printings of the preface—as if these two publications were
independent editions of different manuscripts rather than an edition of a
single manuscript and a faulty reprint thereof. Wise prints the Old
English text in special Anglo-Saxon type with the apparatus at the foot of
the page; he follows it with a Latin translation, which is simply a reprint
of Parker's translation with the name of Bishop Wulfsige left out of the
first line. He does not include any discussion of manuscripts or historical
commentary on the preface; the reader is left to divine its significance
without editorial aid.

After examining Wise's edition of Alfred's preface, one concurs with
W. H. Stevenson's judgment that Wise was not a discerning textual
critic.[38] It is clear that his editorial choices were dictated by the materials
easily accessible to him. His apparatus includes the printed editions of the
preface as well as the Hatton manuscript and Junius's transcript, which
were both in the Bodleian where Wise worked as a sublibrarian; the
Cambridge manuscripts and those in the Cotton library at Westminster

are omitted. After Wanley's *Catalogus,* there could be no excuse for not knowing about these other manuscripts of the preface. Wise could have used them but apparently did not. His edition of Alfred's preface, like his edition of Asser as a whole, must therefore be regarded as a missed opportunity.

At the close of the eighteenth century, Wise's edition of Alfred's preface was translated and put in the service of Alfredian hagiography in Sharon Turner's *History of the Anglo-Saxons.* Turner's patriotic appropriation of Alfred's preface in his history forecasts the role that Alfred's text would play in several other nineteenth-century publications.[39] Turner, a London attorney who spent his spare time in the British Museum exploring the Cotton collection and other Anglo-Saxon manuscripts, began publishing his four-volume history in 1799.[40] In the 1823 edition, Turner translates nearly all of Alfred's prose preface from Wise's edition in order to illustrate the king's "own mind giving voice to his patriotic and his intelligent feelings."[41] At various points he interrupts his translation with editorial comment. At the end of the preface, for example, Turner approvingly concludes, "What a sublime, yet unostentatious character appears to us in these artless effusions! A king, though in nation, age and education, almost a barbarian himself, yet not merely calmly planning to raise his people from their ignorance, but amid anxiety, business, and disease, sitting down himself to level the obstacles by his own personal labour, and to lead them, by his own practice, to the improvements he wished."[42] Here, Alfred is taken at his word (and Asser's) on the decay of learning in the kingdom; further, the king's carefully crafted piece of epistolary rhetoric is taken for "artless effusions," in accordance with the romantic medievalism of Turner's age. In this section of his work at least, Turner justifies Edward Irving Carlyle's estimate that "Turner's Anglo-Saxon work stands in something of the same relation to the revival of the study of history as Horace Walpole's 'castle' at Strawberry Hill to the later revival of Gothic architecture."[43]

In describing Alfred's achievements in his 1842 *Biographia Britannica Literaria,* the antiquarian Thomas Wright takes a more measured tone than Turner. Wright, a student of the renowned Anglo-Saxonist John Mitchell Kemble, made a career of publishing works of early English literature. Besides being elected a fellow of the Society of Antiquaries, he served as an officer of two newer literary and historical societies, the Camden Society and the Percy Society, for which he edited various poetic and historical texts.[44] The *Biographia,* undertaken for the Royal Society of Literature, was a "Biography of Literary Characters of Great Britain and Ireland, arranged in Chronological Order." Wright completed volumes on the Anglo-Saxon and Anglo-Norman periods. In the former volume, his entry on Alfred describes the extant manuscripts of the *Pastoral Care*. Although Wright's manuscript descriptions appear to come from his own observations, when he publishes Alfred's prose preface, he uses Parker's 1574 edition for the Anglo-Saxon text, printing his own English translation below. For Wright, Alfred's translations in general and this preface in particular represent "the purest specimens we possess of Anglo-Saxon prose." Presumably, by "pure," Wright means "early"; his privileging of Alfredian translations over later prose makes him a forerunner of Henry Sweet, who would subsequently normalize later texts to Alfred's Early West-Saxon dialect.[45]

In 1851, the magisterial treatment of Alfred's life by Reinhold Pauli appeared. Like Spelman's work in the seventeenth-century biography of the king, this biography also had political overtones. In his introduction, Pauli writes that he conceived his work in Oxford during the German political crisis of 1848, "zu einer Zeit, da deutsche herzen wie selten zuvor für die Erhaltung des Vaterlandes . . . erzitterten" ("at a time when German hearts trembled, as they had seldom done before, for the preservation of their Fatherland").[46] Pauli clearly sought in Alfred the heroic and liberal spirit that he wished for a greater Germany; his interest in Alfred seems to have been motivated by nationalism and by respect for the place "which Alfred occupies in the organic development of the history of the liberties of England." In his appendix to his work, Pauli prints Alfred's prose and metrical prefaces to the *Pastoral Care* along with the metrical epilogue under the heading "Vorrede, Eingangs-und Schlussverse zur Uebersetzung der Seelsorge Gregors des Grossen" ("Preface, Introductory and Closing Verses of the Translation of Gregory the Great's Pastoral Care").[47] Pauli prints the text from Hatton 20, thus becoming the first scholar to print a complete text from this manuscript.[48] He also recognizes Alfred's metrical preface and epilogue as verse and prints them that way—another first.

By the 1850s Anglo-Saxon studies had acquired basic handbooks and introductory texts, and Alfred's preface was included in two of these as an example of the earliest English prose. In his 1853 *Geschichte der englischen Sprache und Literatur,* the German scholar Ottomar Bensch includes Alfred's preface as an example of "das reinste Westsächsisch." Since Bensch takes his text from Wright's 1842 *Biographia Britannica*

Literaria, Parker's 1574 edition of Alfred appeared in yet another incarnation, this time printed in a column paralleled with Wright's translation. Similarly, the American Anglo-Saxonist Louis Klipstein had also republished Parker's text via Wright a few years earlier; in the second volume of his *Analecta Anglo-Saxonica,* a collection of readings in prose and verse, it appears as "King Alfred's Epistle to Bishop Wulfsige."[49]

Klipstein did not include a translation of Alfred's preface since he aimed his work at beginning readers of Anglo-Saxon. For the first time in its publication history, Alfred's text is accompanied by notes and a commentary. In this apparatus, Klipstein explains the title he has given to the work, saying, "We have so termed this production of Alfred's pen, although it is really given as the Preface, or rather Introduction to the Pastorale of Pope St. Gregory."[50] Given the nature of the text, Klipstein's title is right on target, yet he feels the need to apologize for his innovation, since the text had been canonized under the title "Alfred's Preface."

Like Turner before him, Klipstein reads Alfred's text as placing "the character and intellect of its royal author in a most favorable light" that displays his "true excellence of soul." Klipstein's commentary focuses mainly on grammatical issues, but in his comment on the phrase *On Angle-cynne freora manna,* which he translates as "in the Angle stock of free men" he reveals his political interest: "Observe the title which Alfred gives his subjects. The declaration, or sentiment, is one worthy of his name and character, and points to the original relation which the 'cyning' or king, bore to his people among the Teutonic nations, 'cyning' being none other than 'cyn-ing,' the son of the nation." Klipstein's comment picks up a thread that has run throughout Anglo-Saxon studies: the relation of Anglo-Saxon studies to claims of "Anglo-Saxon liberties," and hence, the uniquely superior nature of the Teutonic races who enshrined this principle from the earliest time.[51] In the "Introductory Ethnological Essay," included in the first volume of the *Analecta,* Klipstein espouses this notion of the inevitable progress of the Teutonic peoples because they are "possessed of a force of character naturally indomitable, of a spirit of enterprise latterly almost proverbial."[52] Klipstein, a southerner of German descent, footnotes his panegyric to the superiority of "Anglo-Saxon America" with a racialist justification for the settlement of Mexican territory, focusing on the "morally sublime . . . advance of the American people westward" and the concomitant "destiny of the African race to prepare the way in the march of civilization" by remaining in slavery.[53] Clearly, in his notes on the preface, Klipstein's racial politics underlie his praise of Alfred's role in promoting the education of Anglo-

Saxon "free men." Though Klipstein's *Analecta* was apparently a commercial failure, it did go through two editions, one in 1849 and one in 1856; furthermore, as the second such Anglo-Saxon reader in English after Benjamin Thorpe's *Analecta Anglo-Saxonica* of 1834, and as the first Anglo-Saxon reader published in America, it was probably used to teach Old English in the United States during the crucial years before the Civil War.[54]

Soon after its printing in Klipstein's ideologically charged reader, Alfred's preface appears in another politically significant context—the 1858 Jubilee Edition of *The Whole Works of King Alfred the Great*, dedicated to Queen Victoria and edited by J. A. Giles. To celebrate the thousandth anniversary of Alfred's birth, a meeting was held at Wantage in 1849, "attended by guests from every part of England, and from America—that hopeful mother of future Anglo-Saxons, as well as from Germany, that ancient cradle of our common race," at which it was resolved to issue "the valuable writings of the great king, whom Old England called her Hero and her Darling."[55] Despite its title, the jubilee edition offers only translations and selections from Alfred's work, rather than editions of the Anglo-Saxon works themselves. It was intended for popular consumption, to stir up "Anglo-Saxons, in America and Germany, as well as England" to appreciate "the burning words of him, whose life was only long enough to fulfil the work which was allotted him, who died worn out with the toils of saving his own generation from ruin, and yet has left these writings behind him to enlighten all succeeding generations."[56] Besides quoting Alfred's preface in its fulsome introduction, the jubilee edition includes a revised version of the late Reverend H. W. Norman's translation of the preface and parts of the *Pastoral Care*. Though he deems Alfred's prose and metrical prefaces "of the utmost interest and importance, both for history and philology," Giles's philological interest in them apparently did not extend so far that he cared to note which manuscript Norman had translated. Giles's earlier work on Alfred displays a similarly cavalier attitude toward manuscript sources; as an appendix to his 1848 *Life and Times of Alfred the Great*, Giles had printed Alfred's preface from Wise's 1822 edition (without any attribution to its editor or transcriber), followed by Sir John Spelman's translation of Parker's edition "with the phraseology slightly altered." Here, Giles's arbitrary pairing of a text based on one manuscript with a translation made from another shows how little he cared about philological accuracy.[57]

While Giles displays no interest in linguistic issues at all, Henry Sweet makes them the *raison d'être* of his 1871 edition of *King Alfred's West-Saxon Version of Gregory's Pastoral Care*. Claiming that "the interest of the work is mainly philological," Sweet declares Alfred's translation useful because "it affords data of the highest value for fixing the grammatical peculiarities of the West-Saxon dialect of the ninth century" and because "there is not another prose text in the language that offers so many rare words, many of which seem to occur nowhere else."[58] For generations, scholars had considered only Alfred's preface of sufficient interest to merit publication; even though Sweet is the first editor to present the entire text of both Alfred's preface to and his translation of the *Pastoral Care,* his introductory remarks make it clear that he has done so because he finds it a useful collection of linguistic data, not because he believes that it is interesting in itself or that it will contribute to an understanding of Alfredian culture.

In making his edition of the *Pastoral Care,* Sweet did not use all the available manuscript evidence. He prints Junius's transcript of Cotton Tiberius B.xi and the text of the Hatton manuscript on facing pages, with his translation below. Though he includes readings from the fire-damaged Cotton Otho B.ii, they are inconveniently located in an appendix. Finally, in the introduction to his edition he does not even describe the three Cambridge manuscripts.[59] He apparently intended to include an account of these manuscripts in an appendix, but he notes in his preface that he has been prevented from doing so by lack of time and access to the manuscripts, adding that "the omission is, however, not much to be regretted. These manuscripts, which are of late date—two of them at least being of the eleventh century, are of little or no value in elucidating the language of Alfred."[60] Sweet's disdain for the Cambridge manuscripts and his neglect of them in his edition have been sufficient to discourage much scholarly interest in them until quite recently. Though Sweet broke new ground in his discussions of early West-Saxon phonology, morphology, and syntax, his single-minded pursuit of early West-Saxon blinded him to the utility that these other, later manuscript witnesses might have for Anglo-Saxon scholars. As Dorothy Horgan's work on them has shown, by disregarding the Cambridge manuscripts, Sweet ignored valuable witnesses to later linguistic developments and scribal practices.[61] Sweet's cursory and incomplete discussion of the *Pastoral Care*'s complex manuscript transmission and its cultural milieu also exemplifies his tendency to isolate the scientific study of language from cultural history and to privilege the former—a tendency widespread in subsequent Anglo-Saxon scholarship.

Sweet's edition of Alfred's *Pastoral Care,* which is still the standard one, forms an appropriate stopping point for this study of the reception of Alfred's preface. Sweet's edition of the complete text of Alfred's prefaces and translation at last facilitated the discussion of the preface in its manuscript context. Despite this opportunity, however, most subsequent studies of Alfred's preface continue to treat it in isolation from the text it accompanies. A scholarly tradition that began with Parker in 1574 has been difficult to shake after three hundred years. Though Sweet's edition has not curbed scholars' tendency to decontextualize Alfred's preface, it has affected subsequent criticism in other ways. For example, as Shippey demonstrates, Sweet has influenced the punctuation and hence the interpretation of Alfred's preface in subsequent editions. Wrenn has shown the importance of Sweet's edition of the *Pastoral Care* in changing the way scholars thought about "standard" Old English. And Frantzen has discussed how Sweet's preface has set the tone for disparaging comments on the *Pastoral Care.*[62]

For better or for worse—and certainly until there is a new edition of the *Pastoral Care* based on all extant manuscripts—Sweet's century-old edition is an essential point of reference for Anglo-Saxonists working on Alfred's translations in general and on the *Pastoral Care* in particular. His text of the preface has become part of the "received wisdom" of Anglo-Saxon scholarship, supplanting Matthew Parker's edition, which for nearly three hundred years had been reprinted, retranslated, and recontextualized for the political, religious, and academic reasons discussed here. The reception history of Alfred's preface may serve as capsule history of Old English scholarship as a whole, as the text appears in the context of sixteenth-century religious controversies, seventeenth-century political propaganda, eighteenth-century encyclopedic scholarship, and nineteenth-century nationalist and racialist ideas. Its final incarnation in a late nineteenth-century scholarly edition may appear more "objective" than any of these, but as we have seen, Sweet's edition, too, has an ideological subtext of which contemporary scholars who use it would do well to be aware.

In examining the case history of the reception of Alfred's letter to his bishops, it is worth noting how frequently scholars tend to tread the track of the known, preferring to reprint and revise an established text rather than to go back to the manuscripts, rethink manuscript relationships, and re-edit. This tendency was perhaps understandable when the art of textual criticism was in its infancy; the willingness of later scholars to be content with the status quo—with the received wisdom—is less understandable. Ironically, when contemporary scholars discuss Alfred's preface without inquiring into the processes of its transmission or its treatment at the hands of textual critics, they do what Alfred himself warned against: by "refusing to follow the track" of their scholarly predecessors they lose some of the "wealth and the wisdom" of the past.

Notes

Some portions of this essay are based on my 1989 Princeton senior thesis, "The Beginnings of Old English Scholarship in the Sixteenth Century," which Hans Aarsleff, my advisor Seth Lerer, and William Stoneman of the Scheide Library read and commented on. I would like to thank them for their suggestions and to express my appreciation to Greg Hays and Thomas D. Hill of Cornell and Carl T. Berkhout of the University of Arizona for their comments on an earlier version of this essay.

1. T. A. Shippey, "Wealth and Wisdom in King Alfred's *Preface* to the Old English *Pastoral Care*," *English Historical Review* 94 (1979): 346.

2. See Allen J. Frantzen, *Desire for Origins: New Language, Old English and Teaching the Tradition* (New Brunswick, N.J.: Rutgers University Press, 1990), pp. 100–101, for a discussion of the way in which Anglo-Saxonists "study texts as if they contained the traces of Anglo-Saxons only, and had no part of the consciousness of the people who followed them."

3. Hans Robert Jauss, *Towards an Aesthetic of Reception,* Theory and History of Literature 2 (Minneapolis: University of Minnesota Press, 1982), p. 19.

4. Ibid.

5. Jerome J. McGann, "The Monks and the Giants," in *Textual Criticism and Literary Interpretation,* ed. Jerome J. McGann (Chicago: University of Chicago Press, 1985), p. 191.

6. For a bibliography on Alfred's preface, see Carl T. Berkhout, "Research on Early Old English Literary Prose, 1973–82," in *Studies in Earlier Old English Prose,* ed. Paul E. Szarmach (Albany: SUNY Press, 1986), p. 407. On Alfred's method of publishing, see Kenneth Sisam, "The Publication of Alfred's *Pastoral Care,*" in his *Studies in the History of Old English Literature* (Oxford: Clarendon Press, 1953), pp. 140–47. For discussions of the cultural context of Alfred's preface and translations, see Allen J. Frantzen, *King Alfred* (Boston: Twayne, 1986), pp. 22–42, which offers a reassessment of Alfred's work; Jennifer Morrish, "King Alfred's Letter as a Source on Learning in England in the Ninth Century," in *Studies in Earlier Old English Prose,* ed. Szarmach, pp. 87–107; R. H. C. Davis, "Alfred the Great: Propaganda and Truth," *History* n.s. 56 (1971): 169–83; and Dorothy Whitelock, "The Prose of Alfred's Reign," in *Continuations and Beginnings: Studies in Old English Literature,* ed. Eric Gerald Stanley (London:

Nelson, 1966), pp. 67–103. For a discussion of the version of Gregory's Latin text Alfred worked from, see Richard Clement, "King Alfred and the Latin Manuscripts of Gregory's Regula Pastoralis," *Journal of the Rocky Mountain Medieval and Renaissance Association* 6 (1985): 1–13. For a description of the Old English manscripts, see N. R. Ker, *A Catalogue of Manuscripts Containing Anglo-Saxon* (Oxford: Clarendon Press, 1957), nos. 19, 30, 87, 175, 195, and 324, and Ker, ed. *The Pastoral Care*, Early English Manuscripts in Facsimile 6 (Copenhagen: Rosenkilde and Bagger, 1956), pp. 11–26. Other discussions of the manuscripts and their relationships include Ingmar Carlson, ed., *The Pastoral Care, Edited from British Library MS. Cotton Otho B.ii*, Stockholm Studies in English 34 (Stockholm: Almqvist & Wiksell, 1975), pp. 12–37; Dorothy M. Horgan, "The Relationship between the O.E. MSS of King Alfred's Translation of Gregory's *Pastoral Care*," *Anglia* 91 (1973): 153–69; Horgan, "The Old English Pastoral Care: The Scribal Contribution," in *Studies in Earlier Old English Prose*, ed. Szarmach, pp. 109–27; Horgan, "The Lexical and Syntactic Variants Shared by Two of the Later Manuscripts of King Alfred's Translation of Gregory's *Cura Pastoralis*," *Anglo-Saxon England* 9 (1981, for 1980): 213–20; Karl Jost, "Zu den Handschriften der Cura Pastoralis," *Anglia* 37 (1913): 63–68; Suksan Kim, "A Collation of the Old English MS Hatton 20 of King Alfred's Pastoral Care," *Neuphilologische Mitteilungen* 81 (1980): 425–42; Francis P. Magoun, "King Alfred's Letter on Educational Policy According to the Cambridge Manuscripts," *Mediæval Studies* 11 (1949): 113–22; and Simeon Potter, "The Old English *Pastoral Care*," *Transactions of the Philological Society* (1947): 114–25.

7. See Bernard F. Huppé, "Alfred and Ælfric: A Study of Two Prefaces," in *The Old English Homily and Its Backgrounds*, ed. Paul E. Szarmach and Bernard F. Huppé (Albany: SUNY Press, 1978), pp. 119–37; Ker, ed., *The Pastoral Care*, p. 24.

8. Henry Sweet, *King Alfred's West-Saxon Version of Gregory's 'Pastoral Care,'* 2 vols., Early English Text Society o.s. 45 and 50 (London, 1871–72), p. xviii. Sweet, however, does not print these glosses in his edition.

9. Christine Franzen, *The Tremulous Hand of Worcester: A Study of Old English in the Thirteenth Century* (Oxford: Clarendon Press, 1991), pp. 59–63, 121–22. See also R. I. Page, "The Sixteenth-Century Reception of Alfred the Great's Letter to His Bishops," *Anglia* 110 (1992): 41–47, in which Page edits the Worcester scribe's glosses to the preface in Hatton 20 and CCCC 12.

10. On the persistence of the study of Old English in the Middle English period, see Angus Cameron, "Middle English in Old English Manuscripts," in *Chaucer and Middle English Studies in Honour of Rossell Hope Robbins*, ed. Beryl Rowland (London: Allen & Unwin, 1974) pp. 218–29. For the dissolution of monasteries and book collecting, see C. E. Wright, "The Dispersal of the Monastic Libraries and the Beginnings of Anglo-Saxon Studies," *Transactions of*

the Cambridge Bibliographical Society 1 (1949–63): 208–37, and Margaret Ashton, "English Ruins and English History: The Dissolution and the Sense of the Past," *Journal of the Warburg and Courtauld Institutes* 36 (1973): 231–55. On Parker, see Eleanor Adams, *Old English Scholarship in England from 1566–1800,* Yale Studies in English 55 (New Haven: Yale University Press, 1917), pp. 16–36.

11. R. I. Page, *Matthew Parker and His Books* (Kalamazoo, Mich.: Medieval Institute Publications, 1993), pp. 43–63, 87–107, and Page, "Sixteenth-Century Reception," pp. 36–64.

12. Page, *Matthew Parker and His Books,* pp. 102–3; Page, "Sixteenth-Century Reception," p. 48.

13. Page, *Matthew Parker and His Books,* pp. 103–4, discusses these translations briefly and reproduces the first page of the anonymous sixteenth-century translation as plate 63. He includes editions of these sixteenth-century translations in Page, "Sixteenth-Century Reception," pp. 59–64.

14. Page, "Sixteenth-Century Reception," pp. 38–39.

15. Matthew Parker, preface to *The Holie Bible Conteynyng the Olde Testament and the Newe* (London, 1568), fol. iir.

16. [John Caius, alias "Londinensi Authore"], *De Antiquitate Cantabrigiensis Academiæ Libri Duo* (London, 1568), p. 286. On the dispute, see Henry R. Plomer, "The 1574 Edition of Dr. John Caius's *De Antiquitate Cantabrigiensis Academiæ Libri duo,*" *Library,* 4th ser. 4 (1927): 254–55.

17. *Ælfredi Regis Res Gestæ* [ed. Matthew Parker], (London, 1574). On this book, see Suzanne Hagedorn, "Matthew Parker and Asser's *Ælfredi Regis Res Gestæ,*" *Princeton University Library Chronicle* 51 (1989): 74–90, and William Henry Stevenson, *Asser's Life of King Alfred* (Oxford: Clarendon, 1904), pp. xiv–xx. For a reproduction of the first page of Parker's edition of the preface, see Hagedorn, "Matthew Parker," p. 89 or Page, *Matthew Parker and His Books,* plate 62.

18. Francis P. Magoun, "Some Notes on King Alfred's Circular Letter on Educational Policy Addressed to his Bishops," *Mediæval Studies* 10 (1948): 93, 102–3.

19. In *Ælfredi Regis Res Gestæ,* Aiiiv, Alfred's letter is described as "præfatio præfixa." However, in the anonymous translation in MS CCCC 197a, the heading by Parker reads: "The Epistle of King Ælfred to———bishop." See the reproduction in Page, *Matthew Parker and His Books,* plate 63.

20. Bonaventura Vulcanius Brugensis, *De Literis & Lingua Getarum Sive Gothorum* (Leiden, 1597), pp. 73–86.

21. For biographical and bibliographical information on Vulcanius, see the *Biographie nationale, publiée par l'Académie Royale des Sciences, des Lettres et des Beaux Arts de Belgique* (Brussels, 1876), 5: 753–59.

22. "Ut studiosus Lector Saxonicam veterem cum Anglica & nostrate Teutonica lingua conferre possit." Vulcanius, *De Literis,* p. 72.

23. William Camden, *Anglica, Normannica, Hibernica, Cambrica, a veteribus scripta* (Frankfurt, 1603), pp. 25–28.

24. John Spelman, *Ælfredi Magni Anglorum Regis* [ed. Obadiah Walker], (Oxford, 1678), pp. 196–98.

25. Printed opposite Hatton 20 on the left-hand pages of Sweet's edition.

26. See Sisam, "The Publication of Alfred's *Pastoral Care,*" p. 142; Ker, ed., *The Pastoral Care,* p. 15.

27. Karl Jost, "Zu den Handschriften der Cura Pastoralis," pp. 63–68. See also the vitriolic exchange between Henry Sweet and H. R. Logeman on Junius's accuracy in the pages of the *Academy:* H. R. Logeman, "Junius's Transcripts of Old English Texts," *Academy* 38 (1890): 274–75, 343–44; Henry Sweet, "Junius's Transcripts of Old English Texts," *Academy* 38 (1890): 319, 366.

28. For biographical information, see the *Dictionary of National Biography* 18: 741–42, s.v. Spelman, and see Philip Bliss, ed., *Athenæ Oxoniensis* (London, 1817), 3:62–63.

29. On Walker see *DNB,* 20:536.

30. Andrew Clark, ed., *The Life and Times of Anthony Wood, Antiquary, of Oxford 1632–1695, Described by Himself* (Oxford, 1892), p. 449.

31. John Spelman, *The Life of King Alfred the Great,* ed. Thomas Hearne (Oxford, 1709), p. 225.

32. Ibid., p. 143.

33. See Walker's letter, quoted in *DNB,* 20:536.

34. See Eric Gerald Stanley, "The Glorification of Alfred King of Wessex (from the publication of Sir John Spelman's Life, 1678 and 1709, to the publication of Reinhold Pauli's, 1851)" in Stanley, *A Collection of Papers with Emphasis on Old English* (Toronto: Pontifical Institute of Medieval Studies, 1987), pp. 410–42.

35. See J. A. W. Bennett, "Hickes's 'Thesaurus': A Study in Oxford Book-Production," *Essays and Studies* n.s. 1 (1948): 28–44.

36. For the description of Cotton Tiberius B.xi see Humfrey Wanley, *Catalogus Historicus,* book 2 or vol. 3 of George Hickes, *Linguarum Veterum Septentrionalium Thesaurus* (London, 1705) 3: 217; on the attribution of the manuscript to Alfred's headquarters, see Sisam, "The Publication of Alfred's *Pastoral Care,*" p. 142.

37. Francis Wise, ed., *Annales Rerum Gestarum Ælfredi Magni* (Oxford, 1722), pp. 81–91.

38. Stevenson, *Asser's Life of King Alfred,* p. xxx.

39. Sharon Turner, *The History of the Anglo-Saxons,* 4 vols. (London, 1799–1805 and seven later editions). I quote from the fourth edition of 1823.

40. *DNB,* 19:1283.

41. Turner, *History of the Anglo-Saxons,* 2:17.

42. Ibid., 2:20.

43. *DNB* 19:1284.

44. Ibid., 21:1045–48.

45. It should be noted that Sweet's "normalization" of later Old English texts (such as those of Ælfric) to Early West-Saxon was intended to aid beginning students of Old English. However, as C. L. Wrenn notes, Sweet's ideas later became influential in grammarians' adoption of Early West-Saxon as "standard" Old English. See C. L. Wrenn, "'Standard' Old English," *Transactions of the Philological Society* (1933): 65–88.

46. Reinhold Pauli, *König Aelfred und seine Stelle in der Geschichte Englands* (Berlin, 1851); translation from Reinhold Pauli, *The Life of Alfred the Great,* trans. B. Thorpe (London, 1857), p. ix.

47. Pauli, *König Aelfred,* p. 313. Thomas Wright's English translation of the German scholar's work in 1852 follows Pauli in publishing this appendix, though Benjamin Thorpe's 1857 translation omits it.

48. Wanley had, however, printed excerpts from Hatton in his 1705 *Catalogus.*

49. Louis F. Klipstein, *Analecta Anglo-Saxonica: Selections in Prose and Verse from the Anglo-Saxon Literature,* 2 vols. (New York, 1856), 2:442–45.

50. For this and other quotations from Klipstein's notes below, see Klipstein, *Analecta Anglo-Saxonica,* 2:406–7.

51. See Frantzen, *Desire for Origins,* pp. 206–7, and Reginald Horsman, *Race and Manifest Destiny: The Origins of American Racial Anglo-Saxonism* (Cambridge: Harvard University Press, 1981), pp. 9–77.

52. Klipstein, *Analecta Anglo-Saxonica,* 1:96.

53. See Horsman, *Race and Manifest Destiny,* pp. 208–71, on Anglo-Saxonist racial rhetoric and the Mexican war.

54. For the financial failure of the *Analecta,* see J. B. Henneman, "Two Pioneers in the Historical Study of English—Thomas Jefferson and Louis F. Klipstein," *PMLA* 8 (1893): xliii–ix; on Klipstein and American teaching of Anglo-Saxon, see C. R. Thompson, "The Study of Anglo-Saxon in America," *Essays and Studies* 18 (1936): 241–53; for the chronology of Old English readers, see Richard Wülker, *Grundriss zur Geschichte der Angelsächsischen Literatur* (Leipzig, 1885), pp. 101–5.

55. J. A. Giles, ed., *The Whole Works of King Alfred the Great,* 2 vols. (London, 1858), 1:ix–x.

56. Ibid., 1:xvi.

57. I have worked from Giles's second edition of 1854, though according to Magoun, the pagination is identical in both editions. See J. A. Giles, *Life and Times of Alfred the Great* (Oxford, 1854), pp. 29–34.

58. Sweet, *King Alfred's West-Saxon Version,* pp. xvii, v–vi.

59. See the discussion of Sweet's edition in Carlson, ed., *The Pastoral Care,* pp. 21–22.

60. Sweet, *King Alfred's West-Saxon Version,* p. xi.

61. See Horgan, "The Lexical and Syntactic Variants" and "The Old English Pastoral Care."

62. See Shippey, "Wealth and Wisdom in King Alfred's *Preface,*" pp. 346–47; C. L. Wrenn, "Henry Sweet," *Transactions of the Philological Society* (1946): 180–81; and Wrenn, "'Standard' Old English," pp. 74–82, as well as Frantzen, *King Alfred,* pp. 40–41.

Part Two

Nineteenth- and Early Twentieth-Century Anglo-Saxonism

An Anglo-Saxon Chieftain, A.D. 449.

An Anglo-Saxon Chieftain, A.D. 1849.
Illustrations from *The Anglo-Saxon* 1:3 (London, 1849).
Reproduced with permission of the Newberry Library, Chicago.

5. Nineteenth-Century Scandinavia and the Birth of Anglo-Saxon Studies

Robert E. Bjork

I N 1941, Kemp Malone expressed the opinion that "though all Beowulfians ought to be at home in the Danish language, some of them are not."[1] In 1817, the Dane Rasmus Rask observed that Anglo-Saxon, a tongue that the most astute scholars have considered to be the source of Danish, "ought certainly not to be indifferent to any Dane or Swede aspiring to a thorough knowledge of his native language."[2] And yet earlier, in 1679, the Swede Olaus Rudbeck, mentioning Anglo-Saxon not at all in his *Atland, eller Manheim* (Atlantis or the Home of Mankind), asseverated that all languages demonstrably descend from a Swedish original and that Sweden—that is, Atlantis—is the birthplace of European culture.[3] Between Malone's matter-of-fact sigh and Rudbeck's intractable Gothic patriotism lies my subject, the slightly Romantic, slightly empirical world of Scandinavian Anglo-Saxonism from the eighteenth century to the end of the nineteenth.[4]

My purpose in exploring that subject is twofold: to sketch a history of the early Scandinavian involvement in Anglo-Saxon studies, a study that has not been sketched before, and to shed some light thereby on the cultural geography of Anglo-Saxonism and Anglo-Saxon scholarship during the rise of nationalism in Europe as well as on the current ramifications of that geography. Although the work of Danes, not Englishmen, for example, introduced the new, scientific philology into England in 1830, few scholars know that;[5] the Danes' contributions to the birth of Anglo-Saxon studies were quickly swept aside as British

national interests moved scholars briskly into a field previously thought
barren. The Danes' work, in fact, was muted in one case and stolen in the
other, and Benjamin Thorpe was the culprit both times. He deliberately
omitted Rask's provocative dedicatory epistle, which I discuss here, from
his 1830 translation of *A Grammar of the Anglo-Saxon Tongue,* and
(with the London Society of Antiquaries as a co-conspirator) he stole the
ambitious ideas of N. F. S. Grundtvig from Grundtvig's 1830 prospectus
for the publication of a large number of central Anglo-Saxon texts. He
thus eradicated Grundtvig's name from the project and rendered Anglo-
Saxonism distinctly, stubbornly British.[6]

Before focusing on Rask, Grundtvig, or any other Scandinavian scholar,
however, I must first take a brief detour into the history of the period.
The road to Scandinavian Anglo-Saxonism winds through certain complex and tumultuous political realities—especially Napoleonic ones between 1795 and 1815—as well as reactions to those realities by both
poets and historians. Following that road helps give some sense as to why
"the idea of Anglo-Saxon England" for Scandinavians at the time was in
part that the British Isles, Anglo-Saxon or otherwise, held hostage things
Danish, Swedish, and Norwegian, things that ought somehow to be
retrieved.

During the earliest period, the cradle of Scandinavian Anglo-Saxonism,
the political climate in Scandinavia—like the weather—tended toward
flux.[7] Before Napoleon, for example, Sweden was plagued by recurrent
internal strife and imperiled by a Danish-Russian alliance leading to a
war with Russia in 1789. After the advent of Napoleon, all of Scandinavia
was in jeopardy, either because of him and his allies or because of his
enemies. Denmark was threatened by England (which was then allied to
Sweden); it successfully repelled an English naval attack in 1801 but
suffered grievously from another onslaught six years later. In 1807,
Copenhagen was besieged once more as a result of the British belief that
Denmark would help Napoleon exclude all British goods from import to
Europe. Grímur Jónsson Thorkelin, who had ventured to England from
1785 to 1791 for the express nationalistic purpose of bringing home as
many Scandinavian documents as he could find, claimed that he would
have published his edition and translation of *Beowulf* in 1807 instead of
1815 had not "divum antiqva domus sævo ter incluta bello Havnia"
("the city of Copenhagen, ancient home of the gods, thrice renowned in
cruel war") sunk in flames, as he paraphrases the *Aeneid* in his preface to

his 1815 edition. His scholarship, wrote Thorkelin, sank along with Copenhagen, and only love of country and the support of his patron allowed him to bring it back again.[8]

Sweden meanwhile had more of its own troubles. England was its only ally; it was at odds with Denmark-Norway (a well-established tradition but this time because of Denmark's alliance with Russia); Russia invaded Finland in 1808; and the Swedes lost that country, which had been theirs for six hundred years, by 1809. Then followed revolution, the abdication of King Gustav IV Adolf, the new constitution (which lasted until the 1970s), and a new truce with Denmark. Everything was in turmoil. Obviously some fears about Sweden's future arose among those who cared about it.

Norway, too, was in a precarious position, especially after Denmark's aligning itself with Napoleon after the 1807 British attack on Copenhagen. Norway disapproved of Danish foreign policy, but because it was under Danish rule at the time, that did not lessen the oppressive effect that the British hunger blockade on the Danes had on the Norwegians. When Jean Baptiste Jules Bernadotte, Napoleon's marshal to Sweden, became the successor to the Swedish throne and then took part in the allied victory over Napoleon, Denmark gave up Norway through the treaty of Kiel in 1814. The Norwegians, though, were disgruntled about this act since they had not been directly involved in it. They developed a new set of laws as a consequence and had hardly begun reveling in their newfound freedom and solidarity when the country put itself under the rule of Bernadotte. Bernadotte, however, approved the new constitution anyway, thus preserving Norwegian freedoms.

The reaction to all this political tumult and uncertainty and to the rampant expansionism of Napoleon was, of course, nationalism, the glorification of the fatherland. While nationalism was first manifest in such acts as establishing new constitutions, it found its most forceful and compelling articulation in imaginative literature.[9] Although Finland itself plays no direct role in Scandinavian Anglo-Saxonism, what took place there epitomizes a more general Scandinavian response. The separation of Finland from Sweden in 1808–9 and its incorporation into Russia as an autonomous grand duchy caused patriotic scholars such as Elias Lönnrot to search the length and breadth of the country for a shared history, language, and culture. The desire for a revived national literature produced the *Kalevala* in 1835 (expanded in 1849), the massive collection of oral poetry that has become the national folk epic of Finland. Folklore studies in turn can justifiably claim a great deal of responsibility for helping Finland achieve nationhood.[10]

In Denmark Adam Oehlenschläger and N. F. S. Grundtvig responded to the two British sieges by reaching back into the Viking age for inspiration. Oehlenschläger (then deemed by the Swedish author Esaias Tegnér as the "Nordic prince of poets" and now recognized as the renewer of Danish literature)[11] penned three poisoned poems against the British in which, for instance, he says that "Oldtids Aand og Oldtids Ære" (the past's spirit and the past's glory) are rekindled by the Danish deeds of the present, and Thor actually awakens to inspire the Danish and Norwegian warriors with the fire of ancient heroism.[12] Grundtvig in his "Drapa om Villemoes" (The Heroic Poem of Villemoes, 1808) has Valhalla opening to welcome the brave naval officer Peter Villemoes, slain like a dauntless Viking by the British.[13]

The Swedes responded with the same righteous fury (and fear) to the loss of Finland as the Danes did to the assaults from England. Pehr Henrik Ling, for example, wrote about the loss in an allegorical poem (1810) in which the Viking king Gylfe (Sweden) sits on a burial mound mourning his dead love, Aura (Finland).[14] Esaias Tegnér wrote his anti-Russian "Svea" (subtitled "Pro patria") in response to that situation as well. In that poem the poet's glorious Viking forefathers rise from their graves to applaud Swedish soldiers who recapture Finland. In such writers as Ling and Tegnér, Swedish nationalism was being redirected and rejuvenated. It actually began in a flamboyant way in the Middle Ages, as I show in this essay, and in the Renaissance with independence from Denmark. From a linguistic point of view, it was institutionalized in 1786 when the Swedish Academy was established to preserve the purity of the national language and to compile a historical dictionary, the only analogues of which are those in English, French, German, and Italian.

The Norwegians, too, joined in the Scandinavian turn toward nationalism as a response to the uncertainty of the period. Wanting the freedom and independence they had not possessed since the Middle Ages, they clung above all to *Heimskringla*—the book about ancient Norwegian kings and glory that took a place next to the Bible in most Norwegian homes—even as they penned new poems about their heritage.[15]

Amid the striking literary reactions to political chaos and threat come the somewhat more restrained reactions of historians and philologists. Less fired by the flames of hyperborean Apollo (Thorkelin's phrase) than poets, perhaps, they nevertheless manifest the same kind of patriotic feeling. There is a long tradition of appropriative, nationalistic historical writing in Scandinavia, including Saxo Grammaticus's *Gesta Danorum* (ca. 1208), which compares the history of Denmark favorably with the history of Rome.[16] Saxo is followed by somewhat less restrained reflections on the past such as the Swede Ericus Olai's *Chronica regni Gothorum* (late fifteenth century), which promotes the thesis that the Swedes (Geats) descend from the Goths of antiquity, and the Swede Johannes Magnus's *Historia de omnibus gothorum suedonumque regibus* (History of All the Kings of the Goths and Swedes, 1554), which elaborates Isidore of Seville's idea that the Swedes descend directly from Gog and Magog of the Old Testament.[17] The Dane Hans Svaning's *Refutatio calumniarum cuiusdam Ioannis Magni* (Refutation of the False Claims of One Johannes Magnus, 1561), on the other hand, seeks to prove that the Goths originated in Denmark, not Sweden, and that only Danes therefore can claim to descend from them. And similarly Erasmus Laetus's *Res Danicæ* (1574) tries to show that the Danes have roots in the Cimbrian and Gothic past, the Swedes only in the Gothic.[18] After moving through the slightly maniacal speculations of Olaus Rudbeck, the tradition of historical writing settles into the more empirically based, but still nationalistic, studies of the Age of Reason.

Philologists—and here I reach my true subject—embed national spirit first in the titles of many of their works on Anglo-Saxon language and literature. Thorkelin's title—*De Danorum rebus gestis seculi III & IV: Poëma Danicum dialecto Anglo-Saxonica* (Of Events Concerning the Danes in the Third and Fourth Centuries: A Danish Poem in the Anglo-Saxon Dialect)—is a prime example. So, too, are the various titles of works by Grundtvig. In 1819, he titled his selection of translations from *Beowulf* "Stykker af Skjöldung-Kvadet eller Bjovulfs Minde" (Fragments of the Scylding Song or Beowulf's Memorial), but he is subtler on other occasions.[19] He labeled his important 1817 review of Thorkelin "Om Bjovulfs Drape" or "Concerning the [implied Old Norse or northern European] Heroic Poem of Beowulf"[20] and titled his 1820 translation *Bjowulfs Drape* but appended a subtitle: "Et Gothisk Helte-Digt fra forrige Aartusinde af Angelsaxisk paa Danske Rim" (A Gothic Heroic Poem from the Previous Millenium rendered from Anglo-Saxon into Danish Rhyme).[21] He then transmutes the subtitle in his 1841 review of Thorkelin, Kemble, Leo, and Ettmüller to reaffirm the poem's northern European provenance: "Bjovulfs Drape eller det Oldnordiske Heltedigt"

(The Heroic Poem of Beowulf or the Old Nordic [northern European] Heroic Poem).[22]

The change in Grundtvig's subtitle clearly reflects the cultural geography of scholarship, not the geography of the poem or the poem's provenance. As *Beowulf* speedily gained stature as a major early Germanic text, more peoples tried laying claim to it. Kemble, of course, considered the poem English, but Grundtvig was undoubtedly reacting more against Leo's explicitly appropriating the poem as German. Leo, who naturally also viewed Anglo-Saxon as a German (not Danish) dialect,[23] would be the first of five German scholars to think *Beowulf* was "dasz älteste *deutsche* . . . Heldengedicht,"[24] and Grundtvig had a reputation, by his own account, "for being almost as bitter an enemy of the Germans as of the Romans" for their tendency to want to make everything, such as poems and the Scandinavian languages, German.[25]

But Grundtvig had another nationalistic reason for altering the subtitle in his 1841 review. He hoped that *Beowulf* would "instantly attract the attention of all Nordic, and especially Danish, scholars, and, as soon as it became readable in the mother tongue [i.e., in Grundtvig's Danish translation], be found in all homes and become a reader for all children, yes, become for Scandinavia in a small way what the *Iliad* and the *Odyssey* were for the Greeks."[26] Grundtvig concludes by stating that indifference to "such a treasure trove" is "truly a crystal-clear testimony to how horribly unnatural we have become in placing Latin above our mother tongue."[27]

Titles do or can imply nationalistic sentiment, but philological studies, grammars, prefaces to collections of texts, and random comments interspersed throughout the literature frequently make the nationalism explicit. In pre-Napoleonic Scandinavia, we find the love of country seen as early as the Middle Ages bubble to the surface in works embracing Anglo-Saxon language or literature. Three examples from 1751, 1772, and 1787 will suffice here. In the earliest yoking of Danish and Anglo-Saxon I have found so far, "Prøve af Danske Ord og Talemaader, af det Engel-Saxiske Sprog forklarede" (Sampling of Danish Words and Expressions Clarified by the Anglo-Saxon Language, 1751), Hans Gram gives shape to an idea that will influence many subsequent Danish scholars. He maintains that language is an integral part of a nation's history. One needs it not only to "understand those documents that pertain thereto, but also to be able to decide about the origin of its people and inhabitants or its relationship to other nations."[28] Icelandic has been accepted as Old

Danish (128), he writes, but there is a language older than Icelandic that can help us understand modern Danish even better: Anglo-Saxon, a tongue that "on the one hand our old forefathers from southern Jutland and on the other their neighboring Saxons, whom people have since called Holsteiners [i.e., Danes], brought with them to Britain."[29] The 117 Danish words and phrases from *aand* (spirit) to *øl* (ale) Gram examines "have been [in use] among the ancient Saxons and Jutlanders long before they come to appear in any Icelandic text."[30]

Jacob Langebek, the compiler of a massive collection of documents having anything at all to do with Denmark, Norway, and provinces— *Scriptores rerum Danicarum medii ævi* (Danish Historians of the Middle Ages)—is unequivocal both in his title and in his preface about what moved him to his enterprise. "Glory and love of my country, both of which seem wholly at risk in whatever part of our land you turn, have given me stimulus."[31] Langebek's patriotism, as keen as Gram's, seems to have roots running deeper into Danish history than the fifteenth century, when Holstein became a Danish duchy. He comes close to apologizing for some small items "written in the inferior Saxon tongue" that have crept into his work,[32] a disdain that may hark back to ninth-century nationalism and the building of the Dannevirke. The walls in southern Denmark were raised, according to an entry for 808 in the Frankish annals, *Annales regni Francorum,* to protect the kingdom from the Saxons.[33] In a real sense, Anglo-Saxon scholarship in the eighteenth century was a kind of Dannevirke protecting and preserving national linguistic and literary boundaries against the Germans. The fortification grew stronger in the nineteenth century.

Erasmus Nyerup is my last eighteenth-century example. His preface to Peter Frederik Suhm's *Symbolæ ad Literaturam Teutonicam Antiquorem* (Contributions to Ancient Teutonic Literature) echoes Hans Gram and makes nationalism a clear motivator for studying Anglo-Saxon. It is absolutely certain, he writes, that the origin of Danish should not be sought solely in the Icelandic dialect:

> It appears that three languages once held sway in the northern and western regions of Europe, sprung from one and the same mother and differing among themselves solely by dialect: Franco-Theotiscan [Old Frisian and Old Low German?], Anglo-Saxon, and Gothic. The name Gothic signifies that language from which in the course of time flowed Danish, Swedish, Norwegian, and Icelandic. Both

the other dialects, Anglo-Saxon and Franco-Theotiscan, prove of
remarkable use for scrutinizing and studying the antiquity and
origins of our language, and Anglo-Saxon, polished and cultivated
with great learning from the most ancient times, supplies written
memorials that are numerous, distinguished, and more ancient than
the Icelandic.[34]

Note here and in Gram that the simplifications of the *Stammbaum* model
for the development of the Germanic languages (i.e., dividing the language group into branches) serve an unconscious ideological purpose.
The ancient Franco-Theotiscan and Anglo-Saxon (now called West Germanic) branches both explain and legitimate the younger Gothic (North
Germanic) branch. Scandinavian Anglo-Saxonism thus grows as the
philological Dannevirke rises.

In post-Napoleonic Scandinavia we find even more intense expressions of love for the fatherland stretching from 1815 to 1885. The
sophistication of that love varies from scholar to scholar and does not,
alas, seem to climb chronologically toward higher and higher peaks.
Frederik Hammerich, for example, writing in 1873, claims that for
hundreds of years, the English have resented the fact that their cultural
life began with the Scandinavians, and that has made them "blind to their
rich heritage."[35] Thorkelin, writing at the beginning of the century in
1815, expresses a different kind of simplicity (or petulance?) as well as a
dependence on the work of Hans Gram. Obviously having formulated
his ideas long before Napoleon caused him so much grief, he says this
about the language and origin of *Beowulf*:

> By Hercules! I am astounded that Hickes attributed to the Anglo-
> Saxons a song that poured forth from the Danish bard, fired by the
> flame of hyperborean Apollo. . . . Obviously he does not remember
> that the language spoken by the English before William I had been
> common to three peoples of the north—all called by one name,
> "Danes"—who spoke slightly different dialects of the same tongue.
> This fact is as clear as the light of day, even if no other authority
> could be found for it. For our epic plainly teaches that the Anglo-
> Saxon idiom is actually Danish, a language cultivated and kept pure
> even to this day by the inhabitants of Iceland, who dwell almost
> beyond the path of the sun.[36]

The clear light of Thorkelin's day would have had a different luster in Germany, where the Anglo-Saxon idiom was actually German. "The German language," wrote Count Friedrich Leopold zu Stolberg, "became the language of England, and remained fairly pure."[37]

Two other Scandinavian scholars, both editing the same texts by Ælfric, one writing in Latin in 1835, the other in Danish in 1853, offer the standard Hans-Gramian justifications for studying Anglo-Saxon but add a couple of twists. Ludvig Müller begins his *Collectanea Anglo-Saxonica* with the bold statement that "No obsolete Germanic dialect is more distinguished today than Anglo-Saxon."[38] But, he argues, Anglo-Saxon and Icelandic poetry represent the whole range of Nordic literature, a literature revealing a race not inferior in its thinking, feeling, and writing to that of the Romans. Furthermore, Anglo-Saxon sheds great light on Danish and German and that alone justifies its retrieval from oblivion. "I, being a Dane," he states, "have concluded that a language so closely related to ours should be cultivated."[39]

George Stephens, being an Englishman turned Dane, agrees.[40] In his *Tvende Old-Engelske Digte med Oversættelser og Tillæg* (Two Old English Poems with Translations and Supplements, 1853), he generates both a more complicated edition than Müller's and a more convoluted brand of nationalism. He dedicates the book to Grundtvig, "Great as Priest, Poet, Patriot, Greatest as the Unwearied Champion of the Northern Mother-Tongue," and reprints Müller's texts as poetry (Ælfric's "Letter of Christ to Abgarus" from *Lives of the Saints* and his homily on the third Sunday in Lent). Together with these texts are translations of the letter in English, Danish, and Old Norse (by Gísli Brynjlfsson) as well as versions in original Old Norse, Old Swedish, Middle High German, German, and Dutch.

Including such a panoply of languages is meant to affirm international brotherhood: one of the most important developments in recent times, Stephens feels, is the growing spirit of community among Denmark, Norway, Sweden, and England, partially because of mutual recognition of common roots. The work of philologists reinforces that idea, according to Stephens: "The English are now eagerly studying the Nordic languages in order to understand their own, and Danes learn with satisfaction that sumptuous Old English (i.e., Anglo-Saxon) in a sense may be called a West Danish dialect from the fifth and sixth centuries within which the peculiarities that now distinguish the Scandinavian languages (passive form in sk or s, enclitic definite article, etc.) had developed to a certain extent."[41]

Linguists, claims Stephens, recognize that the sound system of English has preserved more Old Norse features than has Danish and that many Old Norse words and expressions "extinct in Denmark are in lively use among the common people of England."[42] Small wonder, then, that the old water route between Denmark and England—"det stolte Vikinge-Stræde" (the proud Viking Street)—has been traversed once more. Old English, "de Danskes Modersmaal" (the Danish mother tongue), has such great simplicity, such striking usefulness, that it understandably came to supplant first Latin and then French as the universal language. Stephens concludes: "That such an illustrious future was decided by Providence for a branch of the Nordic people, whose cradle was west Denmark (northern and southern Jutland) and Norway . . . is a thought that cannot help but rouse every Northman, each and every Danish man."[43] A false syllogism worthy of Rudbeck seems to run beneath this argument. Modern English is for Stephens the universal language; it descended from Old English, which is really West Danish; modern Danish also descended from West Danish, which is really Danish; therefore modern Danish is the universal language. Stolberg would have found this equation ludicrous unless the word "German" were substituted for the word "Danish" in it.

By far the most sophisticated statements of Scandinavian Anglo-Saxonism seem to come at the beginning and end of the nineteenth century. In his dedicatory letter to Johan Bülow (patron also of Thorkelin and Grundtvig) for *Angelsaksisk Sproglære, tilligemed en kort Læsebog* (1817; translated as *A Grammar of the Anglo-Saxon Tongue, with a Praxis*, 1830), Rasmus Rask reveals a nationalistic bias that probably has its philosophic roots in the works of such Storm and Stress writers as Johann Gottfried Herder, who emphasized the importance of concentrating on language and poetry in order to recover a nation's culturally distinct, glorious past.[44] But Rask's nationalism also participates in the pan-Scandinavian penchant in imaginative literature for setting heathen cult and Christian faith in opposition.[45] In this pairing, heathenism frequently has the upper hand; Christianity sometimes does as in Grundtvig after 1810;[46] and sometimes the two balance each other as in Grundtvig's "Maskeradeballet i Danmark 1808" (The Masquerade Ball in Denmark, 1808), where he states that Odin and Christ are "begge Sønner af Alfader" (both sons of the All-Father).[47]

Rask's sympathies seem to fall with the heathens. Writing to Bülow, Rask quotes first from Christen Andersen Lund's "Lunden ved Jægerspriis" (The Grove at Jægerspriis, 1788), a poem celebrating the spirit of the Nordic heroic past that was forgotten after the advent of Christianity. Both poem and poet, now utterly forgotten, were well enough known at the time that neither needed to be identified by Rask and the poem could be excerpted in a standard school reader.[48] "More than eight hundred years have elapsed," Rask begins, since the time

da gamle Norden vendte bort sit Öje
med hellig Gru fra Fædres Hvilehöje,
og Munkens Messe dövede den Sang
der fordum höjt om Nordens Kjæmpe klang.[49]

when Old Scandinavia turned its eye with righteous horror from the Father's lofty place of rest, and the priest's mass muffled the song which once was raised about the Nordic warrior.

It was then, Rask states, that the country was thrown into disarray, its customs transformed, its language corrupted; that was when national power began to falter. Although the country sank into barbarism and thralldom, it was saved by the Reformation and the resultant birth of scholarship, which allowed Danes to turn to ancient books "to purify and adorn our language as well as zealously seek its original sources."[50] Seeking the sources of Danish justifies Rask's project. "Our modern mother tongue as well as our ancient history can gain so much light from Anglo-Saxon that it is well worth dragging it from the darkness and describing it in Danish."[51] For Rask, it seems, Anglo-Saxon language and literature were the loftiest expressions, in a pure Herderian sense, of the Danish soul. To recover them was to recover Danish national identity.

Rask's *A Grammar of the Anglo-Saxon Tongue* is known to just about all Anglo-Saxonists, but his highly charged, polemical dedicatory epistle has not been until now. Thorpe published his English translation of the grammar in 1830 but did not include the epistle. He did, however, include Rask's lengthy introduction, which, among other things, establishes the importance of studying Anglo-Saxon for Scandinavians, so Rask's nationalism was not entirely effaced. That effacement took place later as the impulse to claim Anglo-Saxon as specifically English seems to have taken full control. From the third edition of 1879, Thorpe eliminates Rask's introduction as well, explaining the alteration thus: "The Grammar, as originally published, was obnoxious to at least one objection, which, in the present edition, will not be found—it was, perhaps, too Scandinavian, owing, no doubt, to the very natural bias of its author."[52] Thorpe's own bias caused him to suppress Rask's valuable letter and expunge his introduction, to steal Grundtvig's ideas for a library of Anglo-Saxon texts, and to become a prime mover in the mounting English antipathy to Scandinavian Anglo-Saxonism.[53]

Frederik Rönning, writing on "Den oldengelske digtning" (Old English Poetry) at the end of the century, reflects a more modest kind of nationalism than Rask and a more balanced view of paganism and Christianity. Because, says Rönning, the language and literature of the northern peoples are distinct from those of other geographic areas— Herder seems in the background here—"the study of Old English poetry will therefore always be of great value for us Northern dwellers." In Old English literature we have "an important source for the illumination of our own ancient past."[54] Beowulf, for example, "in its original form arose in Scandinavia, probably in southern Sweden" and manifests distinctly Nordic characteristics. Beowulf's fighting Grendel without weapons is one of these; the poem's verse form itself is another.[55] In Christian literature, where "den hvide Krist" (the white Christ) is described in terms previously reserved for "den stærke Thor" (the powerful Thor), Rönning sees his Nordic heritage. The Nordic (as opposed to the generally Germanic) view of life as a battle manifests itself in both Christ and his apostles. "Christ is the great hero, who bursts the gates of hell, and his apostles are the loyal warriors who surround their chieftain."[56] All these distinctive features of Anglo-Saxon, Rönning argues, demand that it be learned by Scandinavians. Clearly Müller and Stephens, Rask and Rönning illustrate how varied, but essentially the same, Scandinavian Anglo-Saxonism can be.

Scandinavian Anglo-Saxonism is nonetheless remarkable for its vigor as well as its relative obscurity. Should readers stumble on Scandinavian contributions to Anglo-Saxon scholarship now, a comment by R. W. Chambers could well typify their response. Looking back on Frederik Rönning's 1883 Beovulfs-kvadet: En literær-historisk undersøgelse (The Heroic Poem of Beowulf: A Literary-Historical Study), Chambers pointed out that it contained a view of Beowulf that was fifty years old but only then (in 1921) had come to be generally accepted.[57]

The relative neglect of Scandinavian scholarship is, of course, understandable and inevitable because, in the first place, fewer scholars than Malone would have liked can read the modern Scandinavian languages and, in the second, the nationalistic bias in Anglo-Saxon studies shifted decidedly away from Scandinavia (and Germany) to England and North America, beginning in 1830. To be sure, the Danes were present at the birth of Anglo-Saxon studies—they even induced labor—but they were immediately driven from the room. Today we pay some homage to the prominent names (Thorkelin, Grundtvig, Rask), thanks in large part to several scholars who have recognized the importance of the Scandinavian involvement in Anglo-Saxon studies. We would have less of *Beowulf* without Thorkelin's transcriptions, as Kevin Kiernan has shown, and would have seen the poem only much later had it not been for Thorkelin and Grundtvig.[58] And our knowledge of Old English grammar and that of such antiquarians as Thorpe and Kemble would have progressed much more slowly had it not been for Rask, as Hans Aarsleff has demonstrated.[59] But we have been unaware of many other Scandinavian names, and much less have we paid homage to them. Once ejected from the delivery room of Anglo-Saxon studies, however, the Scandinavians developed their own brand of Anglo-Saxonism in a different direction and at a different pace from that of the English. In particular, they achieved an early aesthetic appreciation for Old English poetry that scholars still have not discovered, despite occasional inroads into the field of Scandinavian Anglo-Saxonism by a handful of them.[60] Rönning's book is one good example. I will close with one more.[61]

Ludvig Schrøder's contribution to our understanding of *Beowulf* in his 1875 study *Om Bjovulfs-drapen: Efter en række foredrag på folkehöjskolen i Askov* (The Heroic Poem of Beowulf: From a Series of Lectures at the Folk High School in Askov) has gone unnoticed. Chambers alludes to Schrøder in a footnote; Andreas Haarder alludes in a footnote to Chambers's footnote; and Stanley B. Greenfield and Fred C. Robinson in their bibliography list him with a cryptic allusion to Chambers's note.[62] Yet all deal only with Schrøder's treatment of the Unferth-Hrothgar relationship. The Danish family feud forming the backdrop of *Beowulf*, Chambers claims, was first fully described by Schrøder.[63]

Schrøder's symbolic reading of the poem, however, seems to me much more significant than his pedestrian observation about Unferth, whom Schrøder thinks should not be trusted because of his questionable character. Despite Schrøder's dependence on Grundtvig, his reading is more elaborate and detailed and convincing than that of his great predecessor, who, according to such scholars as Malone, George Clark, and S. A. J. Bradley, anticipates Tolkien's 1936 symbolic interpretation of the poem.[64] In 1820, for example, Grundtvig says that the poem bodies forth the hostile relationship between truth and falsehood "partly in history, and partly in nature" and that "the stories correspond to this as shadow pictures, in that Grendel functions as the evil spirit of time, the dragon as the evil spirit of nature."[65] In 1861, Grundtvig says that the dragon signifies Roman domination of Danes.[66] As Haarder cautions, however, in Grundtvig's symbolic reading "we are not anywhere near the holistic interpretation advanced by Tolkien, because Grundtvig makes a point of distinguishing between on the one hand *Beowulf,* the work of art, and on the other, the poem in which the totality receives a deeper significance" that is mythical.[67] With Schrøder, though, we are closer to Tolkien's view. Had critics been aware of Schrøder, in fact, 1875 instead of 1936 might have become the traditional turning point in the history of *Beowulf* criticism, and subsequent scholarship might have become a footnote to Schrøder.

Schrøder's interpretation is fairly comprehensive. "It is certain," he writes, "that there is a connection between the completion of Heorot and the coming of the troll."[68] He reviews secular and Christian history and finds that the building of such magnificent edifices usually coincides with the decline of a society: the Egyptian pyramids are an example, as are the heathen temples in Athens and Solomon's temple, which Solomon built in Jerusalem when the glory of Israel was past. The Church of Hagia Sophia was erected in Constantinople as the power of the Greek church waned and the great monument waited for the Turks, "like another Grendel to swallow it."[69] And when Leo X built St. Peter's in Rome, he sold indulgences to help subsidize it, and that was one of the great causes for the Luther's Reformation.[70] Heorot is a similar edifice, and Grendel's descending on it has unmistakable meaning.

Grendel—and this idea actually comes from Grundtvig[71]—symbolizes sloth or lethargy, which represents the decline of society and which casts sleeping spells over those who inhabit the great hall. Grendel has bereft the Danes not only of Heorot and greatness but also of the giant sword with its inscription about the flood and the previous owner's name. That sword represents great deeds past, a symbol of honor captured by sloth;[72] Beowulf can return it to Hrothgar, and tries to, but the blade itself melts in Grendel's blood. This, says Schrøder, means that a time of remarkable achievement will not return to the Danes as a permanent fruit of Beowulf's great deed.[73]

The dragon's role in the poem parallels that of Grendel, and his treasure hoard has symbolic value paralleling that of the giant sword.

> If the troll broods over the sword, so the dragon broods over the gold. But if the sword is for the Nordic warrior race the natural reflection of their illustrious feats, the gold is the expression in imagery for happiness and joy which can flower under the protection of peace. As the troll Grendel casts sleep on the Danes, the dragon Starkheart casts fire on the Goths. If there is a connection between the sword's being stolen and sleep's ruling, there is also a connection between the gold's being the dragon's booty and fire's ruling. The fire may signify evil strife; we still talk, after all, about anger flaring up, about the fire of battle, and about the flame of discord. It is anger and dissension that destroy peace and drive away joy, just as it is sloth that brings achievements to an end.[74]

Schrøder's interpretation is a big step toward Tolkien and a great advance over Grundtvig, who says in 1861 that there is no connection between Beowulf's fights with Grendel and Grendel's mother and the dragon.[75] Just as the sword represents the memory of great things past, the treasure hoard represents the happiness and peace that is so essential to continuation of society. However, "as little as the sword won for the Danes during his fight with the troll, so little does the gold win for the Goths during his fight with the firedrake."[76] The dragon, hoarding peace and happiness and spewing the fire of rage and feud, has apocalyptic overtones; Beowulf dies fighting it "like Thor after his victory over the Midgard serpent."[77]

Schrøder's reading is holistic, Tolkienesque, and frequently compelling, although occasionally quaint and fanciful as well. And it exemplifies Scandinavian Anglo-Saxonism, although it seems not to concern itself with nationalism. It emerged, after all, in the context of Grundtvig's educational program in the folk high schools that Grundtvig founded in Denmark, and Beowulf was being used by Schrøder as the nationalistic reader Grundtvig had hoped it would be. Schrøder concludes his book by affirming its Grundtvigian purpose. Although Grundtvig's goal of inspiring Scandinavians to embrace Beowulf was still far from being realized, Schrøder sought it, too, and hoped that "my talk and my writing will contribute a little to that purpose."[78]

Beowulf never did become the unifying and unified epic of Scandinavia; Anglo-Saxon studies as a whole withered there in the twentieth century; and the Scandinavian involvement in Anglo-Saxon studies has gained only scant recognition, despite more than three hundred book and article contributions to it in the languages of the north.[79] What may have transpired in the first two instances is that as the cultural geography of scholarship—wide-ranging and appropriative in the eighteenth and early nineteenth centuries—retreated to the geographical boundaries of Scandinavia, Anglo-Saxon studies lost their appeal or relevance. What happened in the third instance, however, is surely simple neglect. Excusable as that neglect may be, it is not, I believe, desirable. As we become increasingly aware of the political and ideological dimensions of scholarship in any age, we also come to see that the birth of a discipline in one culture is not synonymous with its birth in another. Studying that phenomenon is vital. It serves as a corrective to mistaken notions about progress in a field, and it helps us better understand why we find ourselves where we do. As modern Anglo-Saxonists, for example, we may venerate Tolkien too much and appreciate too little the effect that nationalistic motives have had on us. The history of Scandinavian Anglo-Saxonism amply demonstrates both points.

Notes

1. Kemp Malone, "Grundtvig as *Beowulf* Critic," *Review of English Studies* 66 (1941): 130.

2. Rasmus Rask, *Grammar of the Anglo-Saxon Tongue, with a Praxis,* trans. Benjamin Thorpe (Copenhagen, 1830), p. v.

3. James Larson, "The Reformation and Sweden's Century as a Great Power: 1523–1718," in *A History of Swedish Literature,* ed. Lars G. Warme (Lincoln and London: University of Nebraska Press, 1996), pp. 92–93.

4. I am greatly indebted to Taylor Corse for checking my translations from the Latin, to Vivian Greene-Gantzberg for helping me track down the Lund reference in Rask's *Angelsaksisk Sproglære,* and to Allen J. Frantzen, Stephen O. Glosecki, John D. Niles, Marijane Osborn, Sven H. Rossel, and two anonymous reviewers for offering invaluable suggestions for improving this essay. All translations unless otherwise noted are my own. All remaining errors are mine as well.

5. Hans Aarsleff, *The Study of Language in England 1780–1860* (Princeton, 1967; rpt. Minneapolis: University of Minnesota Press, 1983), p. 166.

6. Ibid., pp. 187–89. Grundtvig's 15-page prospectus is titled *Bibliotheca Anglo-Saxonica* and subtitled: "Prospectus and Proposals of a Subscription for the Publication of the most valuable Anglo-Saxon Manuscripts, illustrative of the early Poetry and Literature of our Language: Most of which have never yet been printed." Thorpe's prospectus, published in 1831, is titled *Prospectus of a Series of Publications of Anglo-Saxon and Early English Literary Remains* and was

offered to the public "under the Superintendence of a Committee of the Society of Antiquaries of London."

7. The following sketch of Scandinavian history is based on Jöran Mjöberg, *Drömmen om sagatiden,* 2 vols. (Stockholm: Natur och Kultur, 1967), 1:207–39. See also T. K. Derry, *A History of Scandinavia: Norway, Sweden, Denmark, Finland, and Iceland* (Minneapolis: University of Minnesota Press, 1979).

8. Robert E. Bjork, "Grímur Jónsson Thorkelin's Preface to the First Edition of *Beowulf,* 1815," *Scandinavian Studies* 68 (1996): 290–320. Latin original of Preface with facing-page translation by Taylor Corse and Robert E. Bjork, pp. 298–317.

9. For an account in English of this phenomenon, see Jöran Mjöberg, "Romanticism and Revival," in *The Northern World: The History and Heritage of Northern Europe, A.D. 400–1100,* ed. David M. Wilson (New York: Harry N. Abrams, 1980), pp. 207–38.

10. See William A. Wilson, *Folklore and Nationalism in Modern Finland* (Bloomington and London: Indiana University Press, 1976).

11. Sven H. Rossel, "From Romanticism to Realism," in *A History of Danish Literature,* ed. Sven H. Rossel (Lincoln and London: University of Nebraska Press, 1992), pp. 187–91, and "Oehlenschläger, Adam," in *Dictionary of Scandinavian Literature,* ed. Virpi Zuck (New York, Westport, Conn., and London: Greenwood Press, 1990), pp. 446–49.

12. Quoted in Mjöberg, *Drömmen,* 1:209.

13. Ibid., 1:211.

14. Ibid., 1:216.

15. Ibid., 1:224.

16. David W. Colbert, "The Middle Ages," in *A History of Danish Literature,* ed. Rossel, pp. 11–18.

17. Kurt Johannesson, *The Renaissance of the Goths in Sixteenth-Century Sweden,* trans. and ed. James Larson (Berkeley and Los Angeles: University of California Press, 1991), p. 85 (Olai), xviii (Magnus).

18. Karen Skovgaard-Petersen, "The Literary Feud between Denmark and Sweden in the Sixteenth and Seventeenth Centuries and the Development of Danish Historical Scholarship," in *Renaissance Culture in Context: Theory and Practice,* ed. Jean R. Brink and William F. Gentrup (Aldershot, Eng.: Scolar Press, 1993), p. 115.

19. *Danne-Virke* 4 (1819): 234–62.

20. N. S. F. Grundtvig, "Om Bjovulfs Drape eller det af Hr. Etatsraad Thorkelin 1815 udgivne angelsachsiske Digt," *Danne-Virke* 2 (1817): 207–89.

21. In his introduction to his translation, Grundtvig solidified Nordic provenance by stating that "har jeg Ret, da er Digtet ogsaa unægtelig høit, ja en Thors-Drape, hvortil selv ei Island kan opvise Mage" (if I'm correct, then the poem is also undeniably lofty, yes, a heroic poem of Thor, to which not even Iceland itself can produce an equal), p. l.

22. N. S. F. Grundtvig, *Brage og Idun* 4 (1841): 481–538.

23. E. G. Stanley, *The Search for Anglo-Saxon Paganism* (Cambridge and Totowa, N.J.: Boydell & Brewer, 1975), pp. 5–7.

24. Heinrich Leo, *Bëówulf, dasz älteste deutsche, in angelsächsischer Mundart erhaltene, Heldengedicht* (Halle, 1839). Andreas Haarder, *Beowulf: The Appeal of a Poem* (Copenhagen: Akademisk Forlag, 1975), p. 20, n. 10, lists the other four scholars: J. P. E. Gerverus (1848), Karl Simrock (1859), P. Hoffmann (1893), and G. Paysen Petersen (1904).

25. Edward Broadbridge and Niels Lyhne Jensen, trans., *A Grundtvig Anthology: Selections from the Writings of N. F. S. Grundtvig,* ed. Niels Lyhne Jensen et al. (Cambridge: James Clarke & Co., 1984), p. 99.

26. Grundtvig, "Bjovulfs Drape," p. 482: "Strax tiltrække sig alle Nordiske og da især Danske *Lærdes* Opmærksomhed, og, saasnart det blev læseligt paa Modersmaalet, findes i alle Huse og blive Læsebog for alle Börn, ja, blive for Norden, efter fattig Leilighed, hvad *Iliaden* og *Odysseen* var for *Grækerne.*" A nationalistic preference for Old Norse over Latin continued throughout the century in Scandinavia. August Strindberg in 1872, for example, suggested replacing Latin instruction with Old Norse in schools (Mjöberg, *Drömmen,* 2:21).

27. Grundtvig, "Bjovulfs Drape," p. 482: "Saadant et *Dannefee* er ret et soleklart Vidnesbyrd om, hvor rædsom *unaturlige* vi er blevne ved at sætte *Latinen* over *Modersmaalet.*"

28. Hans Gramm, ["Sampling . . ."], *Det Københavnske Selskabs Skrifter* 5 (1751): 127–208, quotation from p. 127: "Forstaae de Skrifter, som dertil hører, men endogsaa til at kunde dømme om dets Folkes og Indbyggeres Herkomst, eller dets Slegtskab med andre Nationer."

29. Ibid., p. 129: "Til deels vore gamle Forfædre fra Synder-Jylland, till deels deres Naboer Saxerne, som man siden har kaldet Holster, bragte over med sig til Britannien."

30. Ibid., p. 30: "Har været [i Brug] hos de ældgamle Saxer og Iyder, længe førend de ere komme i noget Islandsk Skrift at staae."

31. Jacob Langebek, *Scriptores rerum Danicarum medii ævi* (1772), vol. 1 (rpt. Nendeln, Liechtenstein: Kraus Reprint, 1969), p. iv: "Gloria & amor patriæ meæ, qvi uterqve, in qvamcunqve etiam partem systema nostrum vertas, periclitari admodum videtur, mihi stimulos addidit."

32. Ibid., p. vi: "In lingva Saxonica inferiori scripta."

33. P. V. Glob, *Denmark: An Archaeological History from the Stone Age to the Vikings,* trans. Joan Bulman (Ithaca: Cornell University Press, 1971), p. 275.

34. Erasmus Nyerup, preface to Peter Frederik Suhm, *Symbolæ ad Literaturam Teutonicam Antiquorem* (Copenhagen, 1787), pp. v–vi: "Plane et unice ex Islandica dialecto peti non debere, nec posse. Obtinuere scilicet olim in septentrionalibus et occidentalibus Europæ regionibus tres fere, ut videtur, lingvæ, ab una eademqve matre prognatæ, et sola dialecto inter se discrepantes, Franco-theotisca,

Anglosaxonica, et Gothica. Gothico nomine fas est insignire illam, ex qva tractu temporis fluxere Danica, Svevica, Norvegica, Islandica. Ambas reliqvas dialectos, Anglosaxonicam et Franco-theotiscam, insignem in antiqvitatibus et originibus lingvæ nostræ perscrutandis excolendisqve præstare utilitatem, inde intelligitur, qvod illa, ab antiqvissimis inde temporibus magno studio exculta et expolita, monumenta suppeditet, ut longe multa et egregia, ita Islandicis antiqviora."

35. Frederik Hammerich, *De episk-kristelige oldkvad hos de gotiske folk* (Copenhagen, 1873), p. 3: "Det er en gennem hundreder af år næret fordom, at Englands kulturliv begynder med Normannerne, som har gjort Engelskmænd blinde for den rige fædrenearv."

36. Bjork, "Thorkelin's Preface," pp. 302–3: "Igitur hercle miror Hickesium Anglosaxonibus tribuisse carmen, qvod vates Danus Appolinis hyperborei igne calefactus fudit. . . . Eqvidem non bene meminit lingvam, qva ante Wilhelmum I. utebantur Angli, fuisse communem tribus septentrionis populis, qvi vocati uno nomine Dani, omnes ore eodem dialectice solummodo differente loqvebantur. Hujus si vel aliunde auctoritas nulla peti posset, plena sane hic in aprico cubat. Epos etenim hoc, qvale id nunc habemus, evidenter docet, idioma Anglosaxonicum esse revera Danicum, qvod Islandi extra solis vias fere jacentes hodiedum servant purum, et studiose colunt."

37. Quoted in Stanley, *Search,* p. 5.

38. Ludvig Müller, *Collectanea Anglo-Saxonica maximam partem nunc primum edita et vocabulario illustrata* (Copenhagen, 1835), p. iii: "Nulla dialectus Germanica hodie obsoleta insignior est quam Anglo-Saxonica."

39. Ibid., p. iv: "Natione Danus linguam colendam existimavi nostræ affinem."

40. On Stephens, see Andrew Wawn, "George Stephens, Cheapinghaven, and Old Northern Antiquity," *Studies in Medievalism* 7 (1995): 63–104.

41. George Stephens, *Tvende Old-Engelske Digte med Oversættelser og Tillæg* (Copenhagen, 1853), p. 1: "Englænderen begynder nu ivrigt at studere de nordiske Folkesprog for at kunne forstaae sit eget, og Danskeren lærer med Velbehag, at det rige Old-Engelske (Angel-Saxiske) i en vis Forstand maa kaldes en Vest-Dansk Mundart fra det 4de og 5te Aarhundrede, inden de Egenheder, som nu udmærke de skandinaviske Sprog (Passiv-Formen paa sk eller s, Post-Artikeln m. fl.) havde udviklet sig i nogen Grad."

42. Ibid.: "Uddöde i Danmark, ere i frisk Brug iblandt Englands Almue."

43. Ibid., p. 2: "At denne glimrende Fremtid af Forsynet er bestemt en nordisk Folkestamme, hvis Vugge var Vest-Danmark (Nörre-og Sönder-Jylland) og Norge . . . er en Tanke, som ikke kan andet end röre hver Nordbo, hver dansk Mand."

44. See Wilson, *Folklore,* pp. 28–31.

45. See Mjöberg, *Drömmen,* 1:107–207.

46. Ibid., 1:155–62.

47. Ibid., 1:112. For a continuation of this theme—somewhat modified—in the twentieth century, see my translation of Jan Fridegård's trilogy of novels about the Vikings from the slaves' point of view: *Land of Wooden Gods, People*

of the Dawn, and *Sacrificial Smoke* (Lincoln and London: University of Nebraska Press, 1989, 1990, 1991, respectively). Basing his story on Rimbert's ninth-century *Vita Anskarii,* Fridegård does pit Christianity against paganism, but he primarily shows both Christianity and paganism in active opposition to the rights of the Swedish proletariat.

48. Knud Lyne Rahbek, *Dansk Læsebog og Exempelsamling til de lærde Skolers Brug,* 2 vols. (Copenhagen, 1818), 1:184–86.

49. Rasmus Rask, *Angelsaksisk Sproglære, tilligemed en kort Læsebog* (Stockholm, 1817), p. i.

50. Ibid., pp. ii, iv (quotation): "At rense og pryde vort Sprog, samt opsöge med Iver dets Kilder i deres förste Udspring."

51. Ibid., pp. iv–v: "Vort nuværende Modersmaal saavel som vor gamle Historie kan ogsaa af Angelsaksisken vinde saa meget Lys, at denne vel fortjente at fremdrages af Mörket og skildres paa Dansk."

52. Benjamin Thorpe, preface to Rask, *Grammar of the Anglo-Saxon Tongue, with a Praxis,* 3d ed. (Copenhagen, 1879), pp. iii–iv.

53. J. M. Kemble likewise reveals his bias in the following statement at the beginning of his 1840 study of Anglo-Saxon runes: "These preliminary remarks will not be without service in assisting to explain why my interpretations of certain Anglo-Saxon Runic monuments differ *toto coelo* from those of the learned Danes, who have been so obliging as to attempt to decypher them for us; and to save them this trouble in the future, is partly the intention of this paper; especially as there seems to have been a sort of tacit understanding in this country, that the labour and the honour might just as well be left to them; in the propriety of which view it is difficult to concur" (*Anglo-Saxon Runes* [1840; rpt. Pinner, Middlesex: Anglo-Saxon Books, 1991], pp. 9–10).

54. Frederik Rönning, "Den oldengelskke digtning," *Historisk Månedsskrift for Folkelig og Kirkelig Oplysning* 4 (1885): 1–36, quoted text from p. 2: "Studiet af den oldengelske digtning vil derfor altid være af stor betydning for os Nordboer" and "En vigtig kilde til oplysning om vor egen oldtid."

55. Ibid., p. 2 (quotation): "I sin oprindelige skikkelse er opstået i Norden, og rimeligvis i Sydsverrig," and pp. 8–9.

56. Ibid., p. 5: "Kristus er den store helt, der sp! ænger Helvedes porte, og hans apostler er de trofaste kæmper, der slår kreds om deres høvding."

57. R. W. Chambers, *Beowulf: An Introduction to the Study of the Poem with a Discussion of the Stories of Offa and Finn* (1921), 3d ed., with a supplement by C. L. Wrenn (Cambridge: Cambridge University Press, 1959), p. 400.

58. Kevin Kiernan, *The Thorkelin Transcripts of Beowulf* (Copenhagen: Rosenkilde og Bagger, 1986).

59. Aarsleff, *The Study of Language in England,* pp. 182–85.

60. Most of the work done on Scandinavian scholarship has focused on Grundtvig. See Franklin Cooley, "Grundtvig's First Translation of *Beowulf,*" *Scandinavian Studies* 16 (1941): 234–38; Haarder, *Beowulf,* and his "Grundtvig

and the Old Norse Cultural Heritage," in *N. F. S. Grundtvig, Tradition and Renewal,* ed. Christian Thodberg and Anders Pontoppidan Thyssen, trans. from the Danish by Edward Broadbridge (Copenhagen: Det Danske Selskab, 1983), pp. 72–86 (on Grundtvig's 1820 translation of *Beowulf*); Kemp Malone, "Grundtvig as *Beowulf* Critic," *Review of English Studies* 17 (1941): 129–38, and "Grundtvig's Philosophy of History," *Journal of the History of Ideas* 1 (1940): 210–11; Bent Noack, "Grundtvig and Anglo-Saxon Poetry," and S. A. J. Bradley, "'The First New-European Literature': N. F. S. Grundtvig's Reception of Anglo-Saxon Literature," in *Heritage and Prophecy: Grundtvig and the English-Speaking World,* ed. A. M. Allchin et al. (Aarhus: Aarhus University Press, 1993), pp. 33–44 and 45–72, respectively; Fred C. Robinson, *The Tomb of Beowulf and Other Essays on Old English* (Oxford: Blackwell, 1993), pp. 299–303 (on Grundtvig's Old English poem about Beowulf preceding his 1861 edition of the poem); and David J. Savage, "Grundtvig: A Stimulus to Old English Scholarship," in *Philologica: The Malone Anniversary Studies,* ed. Thomas A. Birby and Henry B. Woolf (Baltimore: Johns Hopkins University Press, 1949), pp. 275–80. Three other essays broaden or shift the focus: Franklin Cooley, "Early Danish Criticism of *Beowulf,*" *English Literary History* 7 (1940): 45–67 (on Thorkelin, Grundtvig, and Rask); Frederik Gadde, "Viktor Rydberg and some *Beowulf* Questions," *Studia Neophilologica* 15 (1943): 71–90; and Gösta Langenfelt, "Swedish Explorers into Anglo-Saxon," *Scandinavian Studies and Notes* 9 (1926): 25–30 (on late nineteenth- and early twentieth-century scholars such as Axel Erdmann, Erik Björkman, and Eilert Ekwall). See also Allen J. Frantzen's *Desire for Origins: New Language, Old English, and Teaching the Tradition* (New Brunswick, N.J.: Rutgers University Press, 1990) for intermittent commentary on Grundtvig and Rask, and Aarsleff, *The Study of Language in England,* for observations on Grundtvig, Rask, and Thorkelin.

61. For more on the early aesthetic insights of the Scandinavians, see my chapter on "Digressions and Episodes" in *A Beowulf Handbook,* ed. Robert E. Bjork and John D. Niles (Lincoln: University of Nebraska Press, and Exeter: University of Exeter Press, 1997), especially pp. 196–99.

62. Chambers, *Introduction,* p. 30; Haarder, *Beowulf,* p. 97, n. 18; Stanley B. Greenfield and Fred C. Robinson, *A Bibliography of Publications on Old English Literature to the End of 1972* (Toronto: University of Toronto Press, 1980), item 2715.

63. Chambers, *Introduction,* pp. 30–31.

64. Malone, "Grundtvig as *Beowulf* Critic," p. 135; George Clark, *Beowulf* (Boston: Twayne, 1990), p. 11; Bradley, "First New-European Literature," p. 57.

65. Haarder, *Beowulf,* p. 75, n. 38.

66. Ibid., pp. 83–84, n. 62.

67. Ibid., pp. 75–76.

68. Ludvig Schrøder, *Om Bjovulfs-drapen: Efter en række foredrag på folke-höjskolen i Askov* (Copenhagen, 1875), p. 50: "Det kan ikke fejle at der er en

sammenhæng imellem Hjorteborgens fuldendelse og troldens komme."

69. Ibid., p. 51: "Som en anden Grændel for at sluge den."

70. Ibid.

71. Haarder, *Beowulf,* pp. 82–83.

72. Schrøder, *Bjovulfs-drapen,* p. 38.

73. Ibid., p. 41.

74. Ibid., p. 43: "Når trolden ruger over *sværdet,* så ruger dragen over *guldet.* Men er sværdet for Nordens kæmpefolk det naturlige billede på de lysende *bedrifter,* så er guldet på billedsproget udtrykket for *lykken* og *glæden,* der kun blomstrer i fredens skjöd. Når trolden Grændel spyer *søvn* på de danske, da spyer dragen Stærkhjort *ild* på Gotherne. Er der sammenhæng imellem dette, at sværdet er røvet, og det, at søvnen råder, så er der tilvisse også sammenhæng imellem det, at guldet er dragens bytte, og det, at ilden råder. Ilden må betyde den onde kiv; vi taler jo også endnu om, at vreden blusser op, om kampens ild og om tvedragts-luen. Det er vreden og splidagtigheden, som forstyrrer freden og fordriver glæden, som det er sløvheden, der bringer bedrifterne til at ophører."

75. Haarder, *Beowulf,* p. 73, n. 33.

76. Schrøder, *Bjovulfs-drapen,* p. 47: "Så lidt som sværdet vandtes for de danske ved hans kamp mod trolden, så lidt vandtes guldet for Gotherne ved hans kamp mod ilddragen."

77. Ibid., p. 46: "Som Thor efter sejren over Midgårdsormen."

78. Ibid., p. 94: "Skulde min tale og min skrift derom gjærne bidrage lidet til."

79. The Greenfield/Robinson *Bibliography* is extremely thorough in its cover-age of Scandinavian scholarship. The only omissions I have noted thus far are five books by the Swede Carl Otto Fast: *Beowulf, germanernas äldsta epos* (Stockholm: Kurt Lindberg, 1929); *Västgöta-Dal. Daner och Anglo-sachsare* (Stockholm: Kurt Lindberg, 1930); *Götaland, den forngermanska diktningens landskap* (Göteborg: Kurt Lindberg, 1933); *Svenska rikets ursprung* (Göteborg: Aktiebolaget Götatryckeri, 1944); and *Vänerbygdens sägner* (Stockholm: Kihlström & Setreus, 1950), especially pp. 35–39.

6. Mid-Nineteenth-Century American Anglo-Saxonism

The Question of Language

J. R. Hall

URING THE LAST three-quarters of the nineteenth century America displayed a progressive interest in Anglo-Saxon history, culture, and language.[1] In 1825, study of the Anglo-Saxon language was available only at the newly founded University of Virginia— and available there only because Thomas Jefferson, whose interest in the language dated back to 1762, insisted that it be taught at the school he founded.[2] By 1899, however, one could study the language at some three dozen schools throughout the country, and the subject was more readily available in the United States than anywhere else in the world.[3] Two main factors account for nineteenth-century America's progressive interest in the Anglo-Saxon language. First, the century witnessed an intense and immense advance in scholarship in nearly all areas; the study of Anglo-Saxon was part of that large movement. Second, many Americans understood the Anglo-Saxon linguistic and historical tradition to be a vital part of America's cultural heritage.

Thomas Jefferson insisted that the Anglo-Saxon language be taught at the University of Virginia because he was convinced the Anglo-Saxon era was, politically, a golden age. The original Anglo-Saxon civilization, he believed, was based on natural rights, popular government, and free institutions—in short, it was a prototype of the American democratic experiment. On June 5, 1824, Jefferson wrote to Major John Cartwright,

"As the histories and laws left us in [Anglo-Saxon] type and dialect, must be the text-books of the reading of the learners, they will imbibe with the language their free principles of government."[4] For Jefferson, making a course in Anglo-Saxon available at the University of Virginia was not a merely academic decision; it was a political act. To teach Anglo-Saxon was to teach more than how the Anglo-Saxons spoke; it was to teach how the Anglo-Saxons thought and to encourage students to absorb their animating political ideas and ideals.

The view that the Anglo-Saxons were democratic forerunners of freedom-loving Americans, a view held by other Founding Fathers as well as Jefferson, seems to me as charming as it is mythic. According to Reginald Horsman, however, it contained in it the seeds of something less pleasant. By the 1840s, many Americans, prompted by current European thought and by their own experience with slaves, American Indians, Mexicans, and certain groups of European immigrants, conceived of the Anglo-Saxon race itself as superior and of themselves as derived from that race and possessing a mission to bring to the rest of the world the fruits of what they understood to originate among the Anglo-Saxons.[5] By midcentury the term *Anglo-Saxon* had been extended to refer to the English-speaking world as a whole,[6] and Anglo-Saxonism—a political movement exalting the later English-speaking tradition as well as the Anglo-Saxons, their language, and their entire culture—had become a national issue.

Thousands of Americans had studied the Anglo-Saxon language by 1899, but how many actually knew something of it at mid-century? Few.[7] In the 1840s the language was taught at only four schools: the University of Virginia, Amherst College, Randolph-Macon College, and the University of Alabama. At the last three schools, Anglo-Saxon was available for only a few years. It was introduced at Amherst by the self-taught William C. Fowler, Noah Webster's son-in-law, about 1840 but died out in 1843, when Fowler resigned his position.[8] Similarly, Edward D. Sims, who had graduated A.B. from the University of North Carolina in 1824 and A.M. in 1827 and later studied in Germany, taught the language at Randolph-Macon from 1839 to 1842, then at the University of Alabama until his death in 1845.[9] It was many years before Anglo-Saxon was reintroduced at Amherst, Randolph-Macon, or the University of Alabama.

Against this background I would like to focus on the thought of two notable Americans at mid-century—Charles Anderson, a passionate opponent of Anglo-Saxonism, and John Seely Hart, a passionate proponent of Anglo-Saxon—to show that Anderson's ignorance of the language led him to distort his argument against Anglo-Saxonism and that Hart's sophisticated knowledge of the language did not protect him from drawing an unwarranted conclusion on the value of studying it. After giving a biographical sketch of Anderson, I outline his argument against Anglo-Saxonism, then discuss in detail his views on Anglo-Saxon. Later, I give a sketch of Hart and discuss his very different views on the language.

Charles Anderson was born on June 1, 1814, at his father's estate near Louisville, "Soldier's Retreat," so called apparently because his father, Richard Clough Anderson, had been a soldier in the Revolutionary army.[10] After the war, Colonel Anderson went west as a surveyor of territory that would later become the states of Kentucky and Ohio. His first wife, Elizabeth Clark, was the sister of General George Rogers Clark. Richard Anderson's second wife, and Charles's mother, was Sarah Marshall, a relative of Chief Justice John Marshall. Visitors to Soldier's Retreat in Charles Anderson's youth included President James Monroe and General Andrew Jackson.

In 1829, at the age of fifteen, Charles Anderson entered Miami University, a school literally cut out of the forest five years earlier at Oxford, Ohio. After graduating in 1833, he studied law, being admitted to the bar in 1835; the same year he married Eliza J. Brown, daughter of a Dayton merchant. In 1843, while living in Dayton, Anderson served as prosecuting attorney for Montgomery County and the next year was elected to the Ohio Senate, where he "established himself as a champion of Negro rights," laboring hard (but fruitlessly) for the repeal of Ohio's "Black Laws."[11] For reasons of health, in 1844 he set out on a long journey to points east: Cuba, the Azores, Spain, France, Italy, Turkey, Austria (where he took the "water cure"), and England. Back home, he resumed the practice of law in Dayton until 1848, when he joined a law firm in Cincinnati.

A year later—perhaps because his travels abroad had given him an appreciation of different cultures—he took on Anglo-Saxonism. From Cincinnati he journeyed half the state, to Gambier, Ohio, to deliver an address before the Philomathesian Society at Kenyon College on August 8, "The Anglo Saxons: Their Origin, History, Character, Identity and Connection with the English and American People; and Their Destiny." On December 20 he delivered the address again before the New England Society of Cincinnati. Running to forty-eight pages and "altogether unchanged from its original form" (2), the address was published in Cincinnati in 1850 at the request of the Philomathesian Society.[12]

Near the beginning of the address Anderson remarks:

> It has scarcely escaped the observation of any one present, how
> decided and how universal is the belief amongst the North Ameri-
> cans and Englishmen of this age, that there is, in what they choose
> to call (for what reasons I know not,) the "*Anglo Saxon*" Race,
> some extraordinary power, or capability of accomplishing greater
> things, than in any other family of men. Some writers and speakers
> describe this power, or mystery, by its results, and referring it to a
> higher agency, call it a "Destiny." Now, this idea of any "Destiny,"
> or of any inborn or primitive superiority appertaining to ours, or to
> any other division of the human race, constitutes, in my judgment,
> a double error, to which it is desired to ask your attention. (4)

Finding the claim of superiority universal among nations and ages,
Anderson judges it "quite an excusable and generally a harmless form of
monomania"—save when descent claimed from "some horrific, blood-
quaffing Baron, or some black-whiskered felon" serves as "a pretext for
claiming a 'manifest Destiny,' by divine right, to perpetuate similar
crimes and villainies, now and here" (6). He derides the notion that
English will soon be the only language spoken in the Western Hemi-
sphere, apart from Canada, when there are villages "within gun-shot of
St. Louis" where English is not spoken at all (8).

The fact that Tacitus does not mention the Saxons, says Anderson,
suggests they were a tribe "too deeply hidden in the dark recesses of
oblivion for any grappling hook of history ever to reach them" (12).
Adopting a derogatory view of the Anglo-Saxons that goes back, ultimately, to Gildas in the mid-sixth century, Anderson calls the Angles and
Saxons who turned against Vortigern after serving him as mercenaries "a
mere handfull of hardy and desperate Barbarian banditti, without letters,
arts, property, moral or social institutions, or any other possession to
make their own homes worth living at" (14).[13] After he discusses the
relationship between the Anglo-Saxon language and modern English—a
question I address later—Anderson makes a surprising admission, given
the words of scorn he earlier leveled against claims of national superiority. Taking together the achievements of all English-speaking nations, he
must acknowledge, he says, "an actual greatness, perhaps decided superiority, in these British families of men" (25). These British families of men,
however, may not at all boast of a pure bloodline: "this race is the

product of the Britons, Romans, Picts, Scots, Kelts or Celts, Angles, Jutes, Saxons, (and many other Germanic tribes,) Danes, Normans, Swedes, Irish, French, East Indians, Negroes and all the other tribes under the sun, who have visited them, or been visited by them, in commerce, love or war. It is perhaps the most mixed, mongrel and heterogeneous stock of people on earth." Anticipating in his own terms certain claims of the present day that excellence can be achieved through ethnic diversity, Anderson concludes, "I attribute a superiority of constitution *to that very variety of mixture*" (25, Anderson's emphasis).[14]

The great virtue of the British race, Anderson asserts, lies in "common sense": "the application of a sound and healthy judgment to the practical and daily affairs of life. It is the employment of a well balanced mind, for the accomplishment of practical, visible and tangible realities and results, and especially to the acquisition and the stable security of property." This is something but not everything. Other races—the Germans, French, Spanish, and Italians, for example—have pursued values arguably "more conducive to a higher happiness, and more consonant with true wisdom" (26).

Anderson now returns to the question of causality. He denies that the greatness of the British race is to be ascribed to "divine appointment or destiny" (28). The Bible names only the Jews as the chosen people, and the New Testament makes it clear that all people are "God's children" (29). Arguing that different races were produced by different external circumstances, he denies that "the English, or the British, or any other race of men are, in blood or bone, primitively better than, or different from, the rest of mankind" (37). Finally, he considers at length the judgment of history on the several peoples who have claimed to be superior in race or destiny—the Egyptians, Israelites, Assyrians, Babylonians, Medes, Persians, Macedonians, Carthaginians, Romans, Turks, Mohammedans, French, and Spanish—and urges America to abandon the path that will lead to ruin and instead to find its way into the future "without any overweening and self-satisfied confidence in our own inevitable and endless supremacy" (47).

Anderson's essay is rich in learning. There is one area, however, in which his learning is deficient. He has, he admits, no knowledge of Anglo-Saxon, a language he dismisses as mere "jargon": "Some . . . claim, that we are now speaking and writing the 'Anglo Saxon' language. For one, I utterly disclaim any knowledge whatever of that language. Nor do I believe I have ever seen a person, who could read or speak a single line or sentence of that jargon, or even knew its alphabet, since it became sufficiently civilized to claim the possession of one. And if I could attain sufficient scholarship in its letters, to read the 'Anglo Saxon' version of the Lord's prayer, I am sure not a soul here would understand a word of our lesson" (20). Anderson's belief that he had never met a person able to speak or read a single sentence in Anglo-Saxon is plausible. To my knowledge, Anglo-Saxon was not taught in Ohio until James M. Hart— who first learned the language from his father, John Seely Hart—introduced it at the University of Cincinnati in 1876, about twenty years after Anderson left town.[15]

Anderson's lack of any real experience in Anglo-Saxon is indicated by his conviction that the characters in its alphabet are abstruse. Although there was a long tradition of printing the language in characters imitating the Anglo-Saxon hand, by Anderson's time Anglo-Saxon was commonly printed in roman type except for three letters: æ, ash; ð, eth; and þ, thorn.[16] Ash, representing the low front vowel sound in modern English "ash," Anderson may have known from its occasional use in Latin texts. Eth and thorn (interchangeable in Anglo-Saxon) represent either the voiced or voiceless interdental fricative, depending on phonological context. Today we indicate both sounds by the digraph th, as in modern English "them" (voiced) or "thin" (voiceless).

Had Anderson read the Lord's Prayer (Matt. 6:9–13) in Benjamin Thorpe's *Ða Halgan Godspel on Englisc: The Anglo-Saxon Version of the Holy Gospels,* printed in roman and published seven years before Anderson delivered his lecture, he might have recognized not simply almost all the letters but many of the words, despite the unfamiliar spelling:

> Fæder úre, þu þe eart on heofenum, Si þin nama gehalgod. To-
> becume þin ríce. Geweorðe þin willa on eorþan, swa swa on
> heofenum. Urne dæghwamlican hlaf syle us to-dæg. And forgyf ús
> úre gyltas, swa swa we forgifað úrum gyltendum. And ne gelæd þu
> us on costnunge, ac alys us of yfele: Soðlice.[17]

With a bit of linguistic imagination Anderson might have seen "Father our" in *Fæder úre;* "thou . . . art in heaven" in *þu . . . eart on heofenum;* "thine name" in *þin nama;* "thine will on earth . . . in heaven" in *þin willa on eorþan . . . on heofenum;* "our . . . loaf" in *urne . . . hlaf;* "us today" in *us to-dæg;* "and forgive us our guilts" in *and forgyf ús úre gyltas;* "we forgive" in *we forgifað;* "and nay lead thou us" in *and ne gelæd þu us;* and "loose us of evil" in *alys us of yfele.*[18] Although it is difficult to agree with Thomas Jefferson that but "few weeks of attention" are required to learn the language,[19] it is true that, for speakers of English, Anglo-Saxon is easier to learn than Latin or Greek.

After saying that no one in his audience is likely to understand a single word of the Lord's Prayer in Anglo-Saxon, Anderson anticipates a possible objection: "It will be replied to this, however, that the calling our mother tongue the 'Anglo Saxon' language, is a figure of speech. It is only naming it after its chief root—the offspring for its parent. I am very sorry to deprive affectation of her last pretext. But truth demands it" (20). Anglo-Saxon, Anderson asserts, is not the "main root" of modern English. "It does not even hold a secondary rank in that relation. There are some 2800 foreign words, which are the roots of the entire present English language. Of these some 1700 are actually Latin; 629 are Greek, and only 341 are of Saxon origin." We can precisely determine which roots derive from Latin and Greek, says Anderson, because they were "authentic tongues," whereas Saxon was "imperfect and indefinite in its pretensions," and many words ascribed to it "belonged really to the generic family of Teutonic or Gothic tongues" (21).

To categorize "Saxon" words among "foreign" influences on English is like calling the United States Constitution a document foreign to United States civil polity. Three decades before Anderson delivered his lecture, Jefferson accurately defined the relative value of Anglo-Saxon, Latin, and Greek for the English language. In explaining the role of Anglo-Saxon in the future curriculum at the University of Virginia, he observed: "We have placed it among the modern languages, because it is in fact that which we speak, in the earliest form in which we have knowledge of it. It has been undergoing, with time, those gradual changes which all languages, ancient and modern, have experienced; and even now needs only to be printed in the modern character and orthography to be intelligible, in a considerable degree, to an English reader. It has this value, too, above the Greek and Latin, that while it gives the radix of the mass of our language, they explain its innovations only."[20]

Although I cannot comfortably endorse Jefferson's assertion that Anglo-Saxon is "in fact that which we speak," his point that the language provides the "radix" of modern English is incontrovertible. Modern English has lost most Anglo-Saxon inflections—inflections weakening even in late Anglo-Saxon—and modern English word order is less flex-

ible than that of Anglo-Saxon, but the syntax of modern English, together with the noun, pronoun, and verb systems, and function words, is
closer to Anglo-Saxon than to Latin or Greek or any other language
apart from later stages of English.[21]

It is true that Anderson appears to be concerned with the vocabulary
of modern English rather than its structure, an area in which Latin and
Greek do have considerable influence. According to A. Hood Roberts,
however, 83 percent of the thousand most frequent words in modern
English come from Anglo-Saxon, as against less than two percent from
Latin and much less than one percent from Greek.[22] Conversely, according to Frederic G. Cassidy and Richard N. Ringler, 55 percent of the
thousand most frequent words in Anglo-Saxon poetry survive in modern
English, and of the hundred most frequent words in Anglo-Saxon poetry,
76 percent remain in use.[23]

To my mind Anderson is nonetheless correct to scoff at those who
urged users of English to shun words not derived from Anglo-Saxon:

> Amongst other eminent reformers of this class, Lord Brougham has
> quite distinguished himself, in an address in the university of Glasgow.
> This gentleman presents to the world, one of those melancholy
> examples of a mind of very various and extraordinary abilities,
> whose influence is greatly impaired by a morbid preference of
> notoriety to fame. He is, alas! a sublime humbug. Presenting in his
> own style a marked example of a highly Grecian and Latinized
> composition, and being vain enough to think himself a model of
> every excellence, he as gravely advises the rising generation, to
> exclude all words which are derivatives from those classic lan-
> guages, as if without them the English would suffice to go to market
> with, or, as if he wrote with the simplicity of Addison, Southey or
> Daniel Webster. (21–22)[24]

To support his view, Anderson quotes an unnamed writer who argues
that an English limited to words of Anglo-Saxon origin would be poor
indeed. Consider, says the writer, "the immeasurable, sea-like arena upon
which Shakspeare careers—co-infinite with life itself—yes, and with
something more than life. What is the choice of diction? Is it Saxon
exclusively or by preference? So far from that, the Latinity is *intense*—
not indeed in his construction, but in his choice of words" (22).

Anderson also enlists the support of John Milton, who explicitly disparaged attempts to archaize seventeenth-century English. "Milton," says Anderson, "had drank too often and too deeply from 'the well of English undefiled,' to consent that by any experimental tricks of chemical philology, it should be decomposed and again reduced to its most meagre, though a simple and useful element" (23).[25] Although Anderson's reference to Milton is much to the point, Milton's own reliance on Anglo-Saxon words can hardly be called "meagre." In 1807, more than forty years before Anderson's address, James Ingram undertook an exercise in Milton's diction. "In order to prove how much even Milton himself is indebted for the majestic simplicity of his verse to the Saxon materials therein," Ingram says, "I have ventured to give a translation of the first sixteen lines of the Paradise Lost into that language; a kind of exercise, which, together with that of modernizing ancient documents, might be recommended to all Saxon students as both amusing and instructive."[26] Discounting the eight proper nouns, there are 114 words in *Paradise Lost,* lines 1–16. Of these, Ingram found only twelve not of Anglo-Saxon origin. Although Ingram should have found nineteen such words, the fact remains that Milton's diction is heavily Anglo-Saxon.[27]

In challenging Anglo-Saxonism, Anderson made several strong points, but most of his attack on the language itself missed the mark. The irony is that he did not need to bring the Anglo-Saxon language into discussion at all; rebutting Anglo-Saxonism as a political doctrine would have been sufficient. Once he decided to broach the subject of the language, however, he owed it to his audience to have learned some of it. It is true he would have had to learn it on his own, but he could have managed that. Others had. Some of them, like Thomas Jefferson, are names to conjure with: Noah Webster, Henry Wadsworth Longfellow, Henry David Thoreau, and Walt Whitman. Two others—Henry Wheaton and George P. Marsh— although little known today, were internationally acclaimed for their work in law and diplomacy. Others enjoyed at least a regional reputation, including William G. Medlicott, a Massachusetts businessman and book collector, who began the Anglo-Saxon part of his collection in the 1840s; and Louis F. Klipstein, of Santee, South Carolina, the first American to publish books of Anglo-Saxon scholarship, 1846–49. Others were academics. The first three men to teach Anglo-Saxon at the University of Virginia—Georg Blaettermann, 1825–40; Charles Kraitsir, 1841–43; and Maximilian Schele De Vere, 1844–95—were self-taught, as was William C. Fowler, who, as earlier noted, taught Anglo-Saxon at Amherst College, 1840–43.[28] Finally, John Seely Hart, educator, editor, and writer, also learned the language on his own. I would like to focus on Hart because he delivered a lecture on Anglo-Saxon just four years after the publication of Anderson's address—and fell into a very different sort of error.

John Seely Hart was born January 28, 1810 in Stockbridge, Massachusetts, the son of Isaac and Abigail (Stone) Hart and an eighth-generation descendant of Deacon Stephen Hart, who emigrated to Massachusetts Bay about 1632.[29] When John Hart was two years old, his family moved to Pennsylvania, settling on the Lackawanna River near where the city of Scranton now stands. Here he lived in a log house in a forest clearing—and in grinding poverty. Later in life Hart described his boyhood as "one continued sorrow."[30] In 1823 his family moved to Laurel Run, two miles south of Wilkes-Barre, where he received his first formal schooling. Four years later he enrolled in the sophomore class of the College of New Jersey (later Princeton), graduating in 1830 as valedictorian.

After serving a year as principal at Natchez Academy, Natchez, Mississippi, Hart returned east to attend Princeton Theological Seminary, from which he graduated in 1834. The same year he served as adjunct professor of ancient languages in the College of New Jersey, a position he held until 1836, when, after marrying Amelia C. Morford, he resigned his professorship and purchased and ran Edgehill School, in Princeton. In 1842 he was appointed principal of Central High School of Philadelphia, a post he held more than sixteen years. "He found this institution in a state of feebleness and placed it on a solid foundation of discipline, accomplishments and popular confidence—making it a representative American institution."[31] Under Hart's leadership the school attained more than local fame. In 1845, for example, two Englishmen of the Society of Friends studied the school and praised it in their report on American education, and in 1847 President James K. Polk visited Central High to address the students.

Hart's Central High School offered an array of subjects that would have done credit to a college.[32] For the present purpose the most notable subject taught was Anglo-Saxon, available at the school from 1850 until mid-1854, when it was dropped by the Board of Controllers. "The reason for this action on the part of the Controllers," remarks Franklin Spencer Edmonds, "will be understood by the student of local history, who will recall that the period of Know-Nothing agitation was not an auspicious time for the advocacy of the study of foreign languages."[33]

Anglo-Saxon as foreign to America: the roots of America's language as un-American. Small wonder Hart went to extremes in extolling the value of Anglo-Saxon in his paper, "On the Study of the Anglo-Saxon Language; or, the Relations of the English Language to the Teutonic and Classic Branches of the Indo-European Family of Languages," read before the fourth meeting of the American Association for the Advancement of Education at the Smithsonian on December 27, 1854.[34]

Hart begins with the study of Sanskrit by Sir William Jones, discusses Indo-European and its derivative language families, illustrates the consonant shift we today call Grimm's Law, and outlines the early history of England, including the settlement of the Celts in Britain, their subjugation by the Romans, and the invasion of the Jutes, Angles, and Saxons (33–45). Hart does not wax romantic when he considers the invaders' "bloody work" upon the Celts: "I know of but one instance in history of an extermination so complete, and that is, of the Indian race who originally occupied this country, and whose fate presents a curious parallel to that of the ancient Britons" (46). Yet in practically the same breath he indulges in romantic hyperbole: "We, Englishmen and Americans, are lineal descendants from the Saxons, and our language, it can not be too often repeated, is the Saxon language. The English language, whose history we are now sketching, though it has received large admixtures from various sources, is in the main the same that was spoken by Hengist and Horsa, and by their countrymen along the southern shores of the Baltic, before their arrival in England in the fifth century" (46). It is odd that Hart should claim that Englishmen and Americans are "lineal descendants from the Saxons" when he shortly goes on to discuss the Danish invasions of the ninth and tenth centuries and the Norman Conquest of the eleventh, expressly noting that "a mingling of race" resulted from the settlement of the Normans in England (47). Hart does not directly acknowledge what Anderson knew well: that both English and American blood is so mixed as to render the Saxon element nebulous.

It is perhaps best to classify Hart's claim that the English language is "in the main the same that was spoken by Hengist and Horsa" as a forgivable exaggeration akin to Anderson's claim that Hengist and Horsa and their followers were "a mere handfull of hardy and desperate Barbarian banditti, without letters, arts, property, moral or social institutions, or any other possession to make their own homes worth living at." Both claims are rhetorically adroit; neither claim will bear much scrutiny. In any case Hart is well aware that the Norman Conquest had a profound impact on English, making it a "mixed language," whose chief element remains Anglo-Saxon. "But it has another element, amounting to more than one third of the whole, the introduction of which is to be attributed to the Norman conquest" (48). Hart also knows, as well as any modern scholar, that the Conquest was important not simply for the many words brought into English at the time but for softening up the language for further loans, especially Latin and Greek words introduced by scholars. "The wall of partition between native words and foreign words having been broken down by the Norman conquest, scholars have completed what warriors, traders, and artists began. Hence the strange anomaly, that with us, learned men have been the chief corruptors of the language" (50).[35] Hart asserts that, despite all the loans, the lexicon of everyday English is essentially Anglo-Saxon: "taking the average of different writers, and excluding works of science in which sometimes the words are almost entirely Latin and Greek, I suppose that the Saxon and the Latin words on any page of ordinary English will be found as five, perhaps, as six, to one" (52).[36] According to my calculations, based on Roberts, *A Statistical Linguistic Analysis of American English,* of the thousand most frequent words in English, those of Anglo-Saxon origin outnumber those of Latin and French origin by 6.3 to one.[37] More than a century before Roberts fired up his computer, Hart was almost dead on target.

After distinguishing two classes of Latin loan words in English—those coming directly from Latin and those entering through modern romance languages—Hart observes, "It is the common opinion, that the language has deteriorated in consequence of this multitude of foreign admixtures. Some purists in style have gone so far as to recommend and attempt an entire disuse of words of Latin origin, to put them upon the ban of public odium, and to stigmatize them as intruders and foreigners." Without committing himself to the purist position, Hart argues that "many writers have carried to a ridiculous extent their partiality for Latin vocables. No writer, perhaps, has made himself more notorious in this respect than Dr. Johnson" (53). In contrast is "the English translation of the Bible," by which Hart apparently refers to the King James version.

> You will find sometimes, in whole pages, scarcely one word in ten, that is not pure Saxon. In the Lord's Prayer, for instance, the only Latin words are *debts, debtors, deliver, temptation,* and *glory.* Among the writers who come nearest to the translators of the

English Bible in the purity of their English, are Shakespeare and Addison. If in any of these writers, we were to substitute for the Saxon words the corresponding Latin synonyms, we would instantly perceive a falling off in expressiveness. "Our Father, who art in Heaven," for instance, translated into Johnsonese, would become such vapid trash as this,—"Paternal Being, who existest in the celestial regions!" (53)

Hart is correct that the English version of the Lord's Prayer is predominantly Anglo-Saxon.[38] To my ear he is also correct to ridicule a Johnsonese rendering of the prayer, and it is plausible to believe Anderson would have agreed with him. It is difficult, however, to agree with Hart's adducing Shakespeare as a writer notable for the "purity" of his English. Closer to the truth is Anderson's unnamed critic, who asserts that, in Shakespeare's diction, "the Latinity is *intense*."

Hart goes on to deplore the heavy use of Latin and especially Greek terms in the sciences—which, with reason, he considers "undoubtedly a hindrance to the communication of knowledge"—then remarks, "The actual number of foreign words in the language, great as this is, is not the worst feature of the case. A still greater evil is the national tendency to adopt others as fast as they are wanted, without reluctance and apparently without limit, instead of producing them by a process of home-manufacture" (54). Speakers of other languages, Hart affirms, mold words from their native resources to express new concepts or name new objects. Speakers of English, however, are only too eager to borrow foreign words. "Such is the fashion; and fashion in language, as in most other things, is supreme. The writer of a treatise for every-day use, who, instead of calling it a 'Manual,' should call it a 'Handbook,' which is honest English, would be regarded as an innovator and a pedant, and his book would be very quietly consigned to the 'tomb of the Capulets'" (55). Sixteen years after delivering his lecture, Hart published a composition handbook, calling it *A Manual of Composition and Rhetoric;* eighteen years after delivering his lecture, he published two literature handbooks, calling one *A Manual of English Literature* and the other *A Manual of American Literature.*[39]

"But let us not be among the croakers," says Hart. "Bad as the case is, it is not entirely hopeless. The introduction of the study of the Anglo-Saxon, as a part of a course of liberal education, will help to check the Latinizing tendency of scholars and writers" (55–56). He concedes there are advantages to the myriad loan words in English. One is that "we have thereby become, beyond all nations, rich in synonyms"; another is that synonyms of different origin—for example, "maternal" and "motherly"—often present a distinction of meaning "so delicate and evanescent as scarcely to be defined, and yet perceptible to a cultivated taste, and beautiful in proportion to its delicacy." Hart does not wish "to join the ranks of those who would dismiss with a rude rebuff" loans from Latin or modern romance languages. Rather, he says, "let us give to the Latin element such a portion of study as will enable us to understand both its meaning and the laws of its formation" (56).[40] What Hart deplores is that, although "nearly all educated persons are acquainted with either Latin or French . . . not one educated person in a thousand is acquainted with the original Anglo-Saxon" (57). This despite the fact that, as he explains in detail, modern English inherits from Anglo-Saxon its inflectional suffixes, its function words, most of its rhetorically powerful words, and the majority of its most frequent words—"cogent reasons for giving to the study of the Anglo-Saxon that distinct and prominent position in our course of liberal education, which has never yet been assigned to it" (60).

Hart's paper, delivered before the 1854 meeting of the American Association for the Advancement of Education, provoked pointed discussion (60–66). Speaker after speaker objected to Hart's argument that the flow of loan words into the language must be halted. Two discussants, Bishop Alonzo Potter and the Reverend John Proudfit, made points that, in the larger context, are powerfully ironic.[41] Dismayed by Hart's characterization of classical loans as "intruders," Potter asked him to consider "whether the capacity of the English language to appropriate and naturalize foreign words, is not a most praiseworthy feature of our language; whether it is not that feature of the language which promises to fit it, and to fit the nations which speak it, preëminently to become the missionaries of the globe; whether, if the language had obstinately refused, as the German has, to appropriate to itself words from other languages, it would have been as well fitted, either for its destiny in the future, or for its destiny in the past" (60). Anderson had objected to glorifying Anglo-Saxon as part of a "manifest Destiny" for Anglo-Saxon nations in serving as missionaries to the world; here Potter objects to glorifying Anglo-Saxon because it would hinder such a mission.

In another response to Hart's paper, Proudfit commented that although he might favor limiting immigration, he would not like to turn out all immigrants. "So he could not go to the length of linguistic Know-Nothingism, and he did not believe Prof. Hart would have the *heart* to do it. (Laughter.) He [Proudfit] believes that the introduction of these foreign terms had vastly enriched and strengthened our language" (62). Know-Nothingism had influenced the dropping of Anglo-Saxon from Hart's high school a few months earlier; now Proudfit implicitly levels a similar charge against Hart himself. If Hart felt a twinge of irony, it went unrecorded. He did remind the audience, however, that he had not urged the banishment of loan words now part of English. He had called the words "intruders," he said, "because they have been so styled by others. What I meant to insist upon was that educated men should give a tone to our language by cultivating the original element, so that Latin may not be the only element that is in the minds of educated men. . . . I merely wish to interpose some barrier against this flood-tide of introducing foreign words" (63).

Potter, Proudfit, and other discussants urged Hart to soften the language in which he treated loan words in English. For good and for ill, Hart refused: for good because otherwise it would have served little purpose to have printed the discussion of the lecture, and we would not know the strong reactions the lecture elicited; for ill because Hart's intolerant position on loan words distracted attention from his central point, on the value of introducing the study of Anglo-Saxon into high school or college curricula. The irony is that Hart did not need to make any argument about loans. It would have been sufficient to have shown, as he did, that Anglo-Saxon is the historical basis for modern English and deserves study in its own right. The weakness in Hart's paper, then, is comparable to the weakness shown by Anderson, who needlessly and misleadingly disparaged the Anglo-Saxon language in making an otherwise strong argument for political toleration.

I know of no evidence that Hart knew Anderson's lecture, but one can speculate on what Hart's reaction to it might have been. He would not have rejoiced in Anderson's negative view of Anglo-Saxon. It does not follow, however, that Hart would have rejected Anderson's political argument. Although in the discussion of Hart's paper the question of whether English-speaking nations might become (in Bishop Potter's words) "missionaries of the globe" came up three times, Hart did not take occasion to embrace the idea. More important, there is nothing in his paper to suggest that he held the political beliefs Anderson abhorred.

And what might Anderson have thought of Hart's essay? He would

have disdained Hart's wish to stop the flow of loan words into the
language. However, it is far from clear that Anderson, once he read Hart
on the importance of Anglo-Saxon to modern English, would have
objected to teaching Anglo-Saxon in high schools or colleges. The minutes of the Board of Trustees of Miami University for August 7, 1850,
preserve a report by Anderson, a member of the board and chairman of a
committee charged with studying a possible role for English literature at
the school. "The committee has long been perswaded," says the report,
"that a radical defect exists in the course of instruction, in every College
in the United States, so far as this committee is advised." The radical
defect is the failure of colleges to instruct students in the literature of
"their mother tongue." Among the authors the report specifies for study
is Chaucer.[42] It is not a long step from wanting students to understand
and appreciate Chaucer to wanting them to understand and appreciate
the phase of the language largely underlying Chaucer's English, Anglo-
Saxon. At Hart's Central High School, students in their junior and senior
years took a course devoted to "History of English Language and Literature and Anglo-Saxon."[43] Anderson would have approved of the first
two parts of the course; had he come to recognize Anglo-Saxon as the
historical basis of modern English, he might have approved of the third
part as well.

Immediately before the report of the committee on English literature
in the Board of Trustees minutes for August 7, 1850, is the report of the
committee on honorary degrees. The committee found that "John S. Hart
of Philadelphia is worthy of receiving the Degree of Doctor of Laws."
The board accepted the recommendation, and the following day—the
same day on which Anderson, on behalf of the Board of Trustees,
delivered an address on the installation of a new president of Miami
University—the school conferred an honorary doctorate on Hart.[44] I do
not know if Hart traveled to Ohio to receive the degree or if he and
Anderson otherwise met. It does no harm to imagine that they did. They
could have learned something from each other. We can learn from them
both, from the weaknesses in their lectures as well as the strengths.

Notes

I dedicate this essay to James F. Doubleday, University of Rio Grande, who was
my dissertation director at the University of Notre Dame and who has given me
the benefit of his advice and the pleasure of his friendship for many years.

1. Although I prefer *Old English* to *Anglo-Saxon* in reference to the language spoken by the Anglo-Saxons, here I use *Anglo-Saxon* because that is the term usually employed by nineteenth-century American scholars and, more important, because the term directly links the study of the language to the larger subject of Anglo-Saxonism. The question of terminology was discussed early by George P. Marsh (who prefers *Anglo-Saxon* to *Old English*), *Lectures on the English Language* (New York: C. Scribner, 1867), pp. 47–48. The first recorded use of the term *Old English* as equivalent to *Anglo-Saxon* is attributed to Henry Sweet, ed., *King Alfred's West-Saxon Version of Gregory's Pastoral Care*, Early English Text Society 45 (London: Oxford University Press, 1871), vol. 1, p. v, n. 2. See the *Oxford English Dictionary*, 2d ed., s.v. "English," B. *sb.*, 1. b; and E. G. Stanley, "Old English = 'Anglo-Saxon'. . . ," *Notes and Queries* 42 (1995): 169. On the strong preference for *Anglo-Saxon* to *Old English* in nineteenth-century America, see Arthur G. Kennedy, "Progress in the Teaching of Early English," *Studies in English Philology: A Miscellany in Honor of Frederick Klaeber*, ed. Kemp Malone and Martin B. Ruud (Minneapolis: University of Minnesota Press, 1929), pp. 473–76.

2. See Stanley R. Hauer, "Thomas Jefferson and the Anglo-Saxon Language," *PMLA* 98 (1983): 879, 887. On Jefferson's Anglo-Saxonism, see also Reginald Horsman, *Race and Manifest Destiny: The Origins of American Racial Anglo-Saxonism* (Cambridge: Harvard University Press, 1981), pp. 18–24; and Allen J. Frantzen, *Desire for Origins: New Language, Old English, and Teaching the Tradition* (New Brunswick, N.J.: Rutgers University Press, 1990), pp. 15–19, 203–7.

3. See my essay "Nineteenth-Century America and the Study of Anglo-Saxon: An Introduction," *The Preservation and Transmission of Anglo-Saxon Culture: Selected Papers from the 1991 Meeting of the International Society of Anglo-Saxonists,* ed. Paul E. Szarmach and Joel Rosenthal (Kalamazoo, Mich.: Medieval Institute Publications); the book is forthcoming as *Studies in Medieval Culture* 40 (1997).

4. For the letter see *The Writings of Thomas Jefferson*, Monticello Edition, ed. Andrew A. Lipscomb and Albert Ellery Bergh, 20 vols. (Washington, D.C.: Thomas Jefferson Memorial Association, 1904–5), 16:51. Part of the passage was earlier quoted by Hauer, "Thomas Jefferson," p. 880. John Cartwright (1740–1824) was a British naval officer and political reformer. See the *Dictionary of National Biography* (hereafter *DNB*) 3:1133–34.

5. See Horsman, *Race and Manifest Destiny*, pp. 1–6, for a summary of his main findings.

6. See the *OED*, 2d ed., s.v. "Anglo-Saxon," III.a. *sb.* and b. *adj.*; and s.v. "Anglo-Saxondom." See also Kemp Malone, "Anglo-Saxon: A Semantic Study," *Review of English Studies* 5 (1929): 182–84.

7. Later I name a dozen men who, in the 1830s and 1840s, learned Anglo-Saxon on their own. My point here is that Anglo-Saxon was not readily available to the public at large.

8. On Fowler see Francis A. March (a student of Fowler's), "Recollections of Language Teaching," *PMLA* 8 (1893): xix–xx; *Appletons' Cyclopædia of American Biography* 2:518; *The National Cyclopædia of American Biography* (hereafter *NCAB*) 5:311; and Morgan Callaway, Jr., "The Historic Study of the Mother-Tongue in the United States: A Survey of the Past," University of Texas *Studies in English* 5 (1925): 27. Fowler retired from teaching at Amherst to write, among other things, *English Grammar* (New York: Harper and Brothers, 1850). See James Wilson Bright, "An Address in Commemoration of Francis Andrew March, 1825–1911," *PMLA* 29 (1914): cxix.

9. On Sims see *NCAB* 7:131; A. A. Kern, "A Pioneer in Anglo-Saxon," *Sewanee Review* 11 (1903): 337–44; and Callaway, "Historic Study," pp. 12–13.

10. On Anderson see Joseph P. Smith, ed., *History of the Republican Party in Ohio and Memoirs of Its Representative Supporters,* 2 vols. (Chicago: Lewis Publishing Co., 1898), 1:165; Dwight L. Smith, "Charles Anderson, 1865–1866," *The Governors of Ohio* (Columbus: Ohio Historical Society, 1954), pp. 86–88 (with portrait); "Anderson, Charles, 1865–66," *Biographical Directory of the Governors of the United States 1789–1978,* 4 vols. (Westport, Conn.: Mackler Books, 1978), 3:1210–11; and especially Walter Havighurst, "The Education of Charles Anderson," *Men of Old Miami, 1809–1873* (New York: Putnam's, 1974), pp. 49–63. In my essay I outline Anderson's life only to 1849, when he argued against Anglo-Saxonism. The rest of his life was eventful. He moved to Texas in 1859, was imprisoned for defending the Union cause, escaped to Mexico, was sent by President Lincoln to England to speak on behalf of the Union, returned to the United States to fight for the North in the Civil War, was elected lieutenant governor of Ohio in 1863, and succeeded to the governorship upon Governor John Brough's death in 1865. Thirty years later Anderson died in Kuttawa, Kentucky, a village he founded (and which still stands).

11. D. Smith, "Charles Anderson," p. 87. The issue of civil rights for blacks was politically complex. Anderson worked to eliminate the discriminatory "Black Laws" in 1844 but twenty years later argued against immediately enfranchising black men in Ohio. See George H. Porter, *Ohio Politics during the Civil War Period,* Columbia University Studies in the Social Sciences (formerly Studies in History, Economics and Public Law) 105 (1911; rpt. New York: AMS Press, 1968), pp. 206, 219.

12. The title on the title page (as distinct from the title on the cover) is *An Address on Anglo-Saxon Destiny: Delivered before the Philomathesian Society, of Kenyon College, Ohio, August 8th, 1849: and Repeated before the New England Society of Cincinnati; December 20th, 1849* (Cincinnati, 1850). Citation of Anderson's lecture is by page number and is incorporated into the body of this chapter. For another summary of the lecture, see Horsman, *Race and Manifest Destiny,* pp. 266–69.

13. In *Liber querulus de excidio Britanniae,* Gildas characterized the Anglo-Saxons as ruthless barbarians without redeeming virtues, but he portrayed his

fellow Britons in almost equally unflattering terms. However, some later writers, e.g., Richard Harvey in his *Philadelphus* (1593), simply lionized the Britons and demonized the Anglo-Saxons. See T. D. Kendrick, *British Antiquity* (London: Methuen, 1950), p. 116. In contrast to Gildas, Anderson belittles the Anglo-Saxons without also belittling the Britons; in contrast to Harvey, he belittles the Saxons without also glorifying the Britons.

14. In his satiric poem *The True-born Englishman* (1701), Daniel Defoe, like Anderson, also catalogues the many different peoples who have settled and intermarried in England over the centuries but reaches a very different conclusion: "From this Amphibious Ill-born Mob began / That vain ill-natured thing, an Englishman." See Hugh A. MacDougall, *Racial Myth in English History: Trojans, Teutons, and Anglo-Saxons* (Montreal: Harvest House; Hanover, N.H.: University Press of New England, 1982), p. 76.

15. On James M. Hart (1839–1916) see the *Dictionary of American Biography* (hereafter *DAB*) 4.2:357–58.

16. I suspect that the only Anglo-Saxon texts Anderson knew are those printed by Samuel Johnson in "The History of the English Language," *A Dictionary of the English Language,* 2 vols. (London: Knapton, 1755), 1:sigs. D–E, from the first page of which Anderson quotes (p. 20). Johnson's selections from Anglo-Saxon (which do not include the Lord's Prayer) are printed in Anglo-Saxon type. Besides upper and lower case ash, eth, and thorn, the only letters that might require explanation are *d, g, h* (upper case), *r, s, w* (wynn), þ (standing for ðæt or þæt, "that"), and 7 (Tironian nota, standing for *ond* or *and*). Jefferson considered Anglo-Saxon type "rugged, uncouth, and appalling to an eye accustomed to the roundness and symmetry of the Roman character": *An Essay Towards Facilitating Instruction in the Anglo-Saxon and Modern Dialects of the English Language for the Use of the University of Virginia* (1851), rpt. in *The Writings of Thomas Jefferson* (see note 4), 18:359–411 (p. 367). On the change from type imitating Anglo-Saxon minuscule to roman type, see Hans Aarsleff, *The Study of Language in England, 1780–1860,* 2d ed. (Minneapolis: University of Minnesota Press, 1983), pp. 183–206, and Peter S. Baker, "Time for a Revival of Old English Types?" *Old English Newsletter* 27.1 (1993), appendix B.

17. Benjamin Thorpe, ed., *Ða Halgan Godspel on Englisc: The Anglo-Saxon Version of the Holy Gospels* (London: J. F. G. and J. Rivington, 1842), p. 11. Had Anderson read the passage in Louis F. Klipstein's American reprint of Thorpe's edition, *Tha Halgan Godspel on Englisc: The Anglo-Saxon Version of the Holy Gospels* (New York: Wiley and Putnam, 1846), p. 11, he would not have needed to know ash, for which Klipstein substitutes *ae,* or eth or thorn, for which Klipstein substitutes *th* (placing periods under *th* where *th* represents thorn in Thorpe's text). In the same year Anderson gave his lecture, Klipstein edited the first Anglo-Saxon reader published in America, *Analecta Anglo-Saxonica. Selections, in Prose and Verse, from the Anglo-Saxon Literature: with an Introductory Ethnological Essay, and Notes, Critical and Explanatory,* 2 vols. (New York:

Putnam, 1849). Klipstein's version of the Pater Noster is found in 1:163, where *ae* is again substituted for ash and *th* for eth or thorn. Thorpe's attempt to indicate long vowels (signaled by an accent mark) is woefully incomplete. In his reprint of Thorpe and especially in the Pater Noster of his *Analecta,* Klipstein, to his credit, repaired many of Thorpe's omissions.

18. For an excellent discussion of the Anglo-Saxon Lord's Prayer geared to beginning students, see L. M. Myers and Richard L. Hoffman, *The Roots of Modern English,* 2d ed. (Boston: Little, Brown, 1979), pp. 73–78. Also useful is Albert S. Cook, "The Evolution of the Lord's Prayer in English," *American Journal of Philology* 12 (1891): 59–66. I am grateful to Phillip Pulsiano for bringing Cook's article to my attention.

19. "Report of the Commissioners Appointed to Fix the Site of the University of Virginia, &c.," appendix J in Roy J. Honeywell, *The Educational Work of Thomas Jefferson* (1931; rpt. New York: Russell and Russell, 1964), p. 255. Honeywell observes, "This report was written by Jefferson before the meeting and adopted by the commissioners [in August 1818] with only minor changes" (p. 248). The longer passage of which the quotation is part was earlier given by Hauer, "Thomas Jefferson," p. 883.

20. "Report of the Commissioners," in Honeywell, *Educational Work,* p. 255.

21. As Bruce Mitchell observes, "The syntactical differences between Old English and Modern English are minor compared to the syntactical similarities." See "The Englishness of Old English," in *From Anglo-Saxon to Early Modern English: Studies Presented to E. G. Stanley,* ed. Malcolm Godden, Douglas Grey, and Terry Hoad (Oxford: Clarendon Press, 1994), p. 171. Mitchell regards this point as so crucial that he repeats it word for word on the next page.

22. *A Statistical Linguistic Analysis of American English,* Janua Linguarum, Series Practica 8 (The Hague: Mouton, 1965), pp. 36–37, 69. In the next nine deciles (groups of a thousand) of the most frequent words in modern English, the proportion of Anglo-Saxon words drops off considerably, ranging from a high of 34 percent in the second decile to a low of 23 percent in the seventh decile. "Despite the secondary position of Anglo-Saxon in nine deciles," Roberts remarks (p. 38), "its high frequencies in the first largely determine the [etymological] composition of the whole," which comes out to 78 percent in favor of Anglo-Saxon. We cannot expect Anderson to have learned what Roberts took great pains to establish a century later. However, had Anderson consulted a book available in America, Joseph Bosworth's *A Compendious Anglo-Saxon and English Dictionary* (London: John Russell Smith, 1848), p. iv, he would have read that "more than five-eighths" of the words in English are of Anglo-Saxon origin. (Note that Bosworth's finding is plausible for only the common vocabulary of English.)

23. *Bright's Old English Grammar and Reader,* 3d ed., 2d corr. printing (New York: Holt, 1971), p. 4. For the statistics, Cassidy and Ringler cite John F. Madden and Francis P. Magoun Jr., *A Grouped Frequency Word-List of Anglo-*

Saxon Poetry (Cambridge: Harvard University, Department of English, 1960). To judge by the 1967 printing of the *Word-List,* however, Madden and Magoun include no such statistics; Cassidy and Ringler's figures must be their own, based on the *Word-List.*

24. Henry Peter Brougham (1778–1868) was a writer, lawyer, legal reformer, abolitionist, politician, lord rector of Glasgow University (1825), educational reformer, and lord chancellor (1830). See *DNB* 2:1356–66.

25. The phrase "the well of English undefiled" comes not from Milton but from Spenser, *The Faerie Queene,* bk. IV, can. II, stan. 32, l. 8. Anderson may have borrowed the phrase from Johnson, who used it in the preface to his 1755 dictionary (in which the phrase is also cited without attribution, and in which Spenser's "undefyled" is also spelled "undefiled" but "well" is given in the plural). See E. L. McAdam, Jr., and George Milne, eds., *Samuel Johnson's Dictionary: A Modern Selection* (New York: Pantheon, 1964), p. 18. Anderson seems unaware that his use of the phrase—in view of its original context—is ironic: Spenser calls Chaucer "the well of English undefiled" as part of his rhetorical strategy to influence the English language of his day to return to its roots; Anderson uses "the well of English undefiled" as part of his rhetorical strategy to ridicule such a return.

26. James Ingram, *An Inaugural Lecture on the Utility of Anglo-Saxon Literature; to Which Is Added the Geography of Europe by King Alfred, Including His Account of the Discovery of the North Cape in the Ninth Century* (Oxford: Oxford University Press, 1807), p. 47.

27. The seven non-Anglo-Saxon words Ingram overlooked are *till* and *seat* (both Old Norse) and *taste, restore, regain, aid,* and *unattempted* (French). To these words one might add *call,* usually considered an Old Norse borrowing. For the argument that the word is Anglo-Saxon, however, see E. G. Stanley, "Old English '-calla,' 'ceallian,'" *Medieval Literature and Civilization: Studies in Memory of G. N. Garmonsway,* ed. D. A. Pearsall and R. A. Waldron (London: Athlone Press, 1969), pp. 94–99. Fred C. Robinson, "The Afterlife of Old English: A Brief History of Composition in Old English after the Close of the Anglo-Saxon Period," in *The Tomb of Beowulf and Other Essays on Old English* (Oxford: Blackwell, 1993), p. 298, describes Ingram's knowledge of Anglo-Saxon as "abysmal" and his translation as "feeble." Although Ingram himself calls his rendering a "translation," it is more precisely a transverbation. Ingram does not really attempt to compose an Anglo-Saxon verse version of *Paradise Lost,* lines 1–16: for modern words derived from Anglo-Saxon he simply substitutes the original Anglo-Saxon forms (e.g., *mannes* for "man's"), and for modern words not derived from Anglo-Saxon he simply substitutes Anglo-Saxon equivalents (e.g., *wæstmes* for "fruit").

28. For Webster through Schele De Vere, see the essay cited in note 3 above.

29. On Hart see Henry A. Boardman, *A Discourse Commemorative of the Character and Life of John Seely Hart, LL.D.* (Philadelphia: Eldredge and Brother,

1878); "John Seely Hart, LL.D.," *Necrological Reports and Annual Proceedings of the Alumni Association of Princeton Theological Seminary,* vol. 1, 1875–89 (Princeton: C. S. Robinson and Co., 1891), pp. 29–30; Franklin Spencer Edmonds, *History of the Central High School of Philadelphia* (Philadelphia: Lippincott, 1902), pp. 98–157, 165–66, 328 (with portrait after p. 102); and *DAB* 4.2:359–60. Here I sketch Hart's life down to his assuming the headship of Philadelphia Central High School. Later, Hart became one of the most influential writers in the country promoting the Sunday-school movement, directed the New Jersey State Normal School (1863–71), and served as a professor of English at Princeton (1872–74). He died in 1877. Hart was a prolific author throughout his life, with a dozen books to his credit.

30. Edmonds, *History of the Central High School,* p. 98.

31. *Necrological Reports,* p. 29.

32. See Edmonds, *History of the Central High School,* appendix G, "I.— Course of Study, 1852 (Hart)" (following p. 386). Concerning the school's offering Latin, Greek, French, German, Spanish, and Anglo-Saxon, Edmonds notes, "It has been suggested that this record is not surpassed by any college of the period" (p. 133).

33. Ibid, p. 132. Edmonds notes that two years later the board cut German and French, and it was all Hart could do to preserve the teaching of Latin (p. 148). The Know Nothings, as they were popularly called, formally began in 1849 as a secret fraternal organization, the Order of the Star Spangled Banner, predecessor to the American Party. Dedicated to resisting the influence of immigrants and Roman Catholics, the Know Nothings achieved stunning but short-lived political success in the mid-1850s. In the June 1854 mayoral election in Philadelphia, the Whig and Know Nothing candidate, Robert T. Conrad, won almost 60 percent of the vote against the Democratic candidate, Richard Vaux. For an account of Know Nothing influence in Pennsylvania politics, see Tyler Anbinder, *Nativism and Slavery: The Northern Know Nothings and the Politics of the 1850s* (New York and Oxford: Oxford University Press, 1992), pp. 53–68.

34. The paper was published in the *American Journal of Education* 1 (1856): 33–60. A report on the association's fourth meeting is printed in the same issue on pp. 9–16.

35. Hart's hidden axiom is that the earliest stage of a language is "pure" and any movement from that is "corruption." So far as we can tell historically, however, Anglo-Saxon was never pure. While the Angles and Saxons were still on the Continent, they had already incorporated many Latin loan words (some of which Latin had borrowed from Greek) into their language, including such basic words as *stræt* "road, street," *sæcc* "sack," *candel* "candle," *butere* "butter," *win* "wine," *cupp(e)* "cup," *ynce* "inch," and *plante* "plant." After the Anglo-Saxons settled in Britain, they borrowed many more Latin words as well as many words from Celtic, Scandinavian, and French. See Mary S. Serjeantson, *A History of Foreign Words in English* (London: Routledge and Kegan Paul, 1961), pp. 11–

74, 271–92. Ironically, the greatest, most powerfully worded statement of the doctrine Hart invokes—that language change is roughly tantamount to corruption—was advanced by a scholar whose Latinate style Hart deplored, Samuel Johnson, in the preface to his dictionary. Johnson says, in part, "Life may be lengthened by care, though death cannot be ultimately defeated: tongues, like governments, have a natural tendency to degeneration; we have long preserved our constitution, let us make some struggles for our language." See McAdam and Milne, eds., *Samuel Johnson's Dictionary,* p. 27.

36. Hart includes among "Latin words" words that came into English via French.

37. Roberts, *A Statistical Linguistic Analysis,* p. 69, reports the relative frequency of Anglo-Saxon words in the first decile as 82.8 percent; French, 11.4 percent; and Latin, 1.8 percent (figures rounded to the nearest tenth). See also the graph, p. 37.

38. As the version of the Lord's Prayer to which Hart refers contains the doxology (as indicated by his citation of "glory"), he should have included "power" (Latin via French) among the non-Anglo-Saxon words. That the diction of the prayer is predominantly Anglo-Saxon was pointed out long before Hart. In a flier advertising his Anglo-Saxon dictionary in progress (first published in 1838), Joseph Bosworth quotes George Hickes (1642–1715) on the question: "The great septentrional scholar, Dr. Hickes, observed 'that of *fifty-eight words* of which the Lord's Prayer is composed, not more than *three* are of Gallo-Norman introduction. The remaining *fifty-five* are immediately and originally derivable from the Anglo-Saxon.'" A copy of the flier, "Prospectus of A Dictionary of the Anglo-Saxon Language . . . ," is preserved in the Bodleian Library as Bodleian MS Eng. Lett. b. 4, folios 5–6. (Bosworth used blank space on this copy to write a letter, dated May 7, 1833, Rotterdam, to John M. Kemble, the first English editor of *Beowulf.*) Although it is unclear which version of the prayer Hickes analyzed, presumably he should have found four so called Gallo-Norman words: "debts," "debtors," "deliver," and "temptation"; perhaps he regarded "debts" and "debtors" as a single borrowing.

39. Although Hart's *Manual of American Literature* was not innovative in the wording of its title, it was innovative in its content. According to Susan Koppelman, ed., *Old Maids: Short Stories by Nineteenth-Century U.S. Women Writers* (London: Routledge and Kegan Paul, 1984), p. 8, Hart's *Manual* was "the first American literature textbook." I am grateful to my wife, Joan Wylie Hall, for the reference.

40. For Hart this was no idle principle. At Central High School during his tenure, freshmen were required to take five classes a week throughout the year devoted to "the Latin Element of the English language." See Edmonds, *History of the Central High School,* appendix G, "I.—Course of Study, 1852 (Hart)" (following p. 386). On Hart's insistence that Latin be taught at the school, see note 33 above.

41. Alonzo Potter (1800–65), for a time a professor and vice president of Union College, was ordained Protestant Episcopal bishop of the diocese of Pennsylvania in 1845 and was active in the field of education as well as in religion. See *NCAB* 3:470–71; and *DAB* 8.1:124–25. Rev. John Proudfit, D.D., was a professor at Rutgers College. See the *American Journal of Education* 1 (1856): 8–10.

42. "Journal of the Proceedings of the President and Trustees of the Miami University. From the Twelfth day of April One thousand eight hundred & Forty Two Untill the ninth day of November One thousand eight hundred and Fifty two," pp. 420–22. I am grateful to C. Martin Miller, Department of Special Collections, Miami University, for providing copies of pages from the journal (still in manuscript) and a copy of p. 27 in the school catalogue of 1851 (note 44 below).

43. See Edmonds, *History of the Central High School,* appendix G, "I.— Course of Study, 1852 (Hart)" (following p. 386).

44. Hart's degree is listed as one of only three honorary LL.D.s granted to date in *Eighth Triennial Catalogue of the Officers and Graduates of Miami University. 1851* (Cincinnati: Miami University, 1851), p. 27.

7. Byrhtnoth in Dixie

The Emergence of Anglo-Saxon Studies in the Postbellum South

Gregory A. VanHoosier-Carey

I N AN 1894 article published in the *Sewanee Review,* J. B. Henneman, professor of English at the University of Tennessee, provides a historical account of Anglo-Saxon studies. What makes this account especially interesting is that the article, "The Study of English in the South," situates the discipline in a Southern rather than an American context. For Henneman, the pedagogical and scholarly methods that comprise Anglo-Saxon studies are an integral part of Southern history and culture, a history and culture separated from the larger rubric of "American" by the Civil War and Reconstruction. He claims, for example, that "within the two or three years immediately following the War" Southern institutions "were demanding instinctively and almost simultaneously" university courses in Old English. He goes on to state that "everywhere it [Old English] was a movement essentially of native growth, . . . a product answering to local needs, as those needs had become intensified through the interruptions and derangements of the War."[1]

Henneman's descriptions are certainly curious, but I believe that there is more here than an eccentric narrative. Words such as *instinctive, simultaneous,* and *native growth* imply that Henneman views Anglo-Saxon studies as an "organic" aspect of Southern society. He suggests that Southerners' interest in the Anglo-Saxon language somehow connected them with their Anglo-Saxon forerunners. In short, the article discursively links together Southerners, Old English, education, and the Civil War and naturalizes these connections by implying that they were ethnically and culturally determined.

Henneman's historical account exemplifies how an academic discipline such as Anglo-Saxon studies can perform important cultural and political work by authorizing the worldview of its practitioners. The study of Anglo-Saxon in the postbellum South was greatly influenced by the social and political residue of Civil War defeat. The institutional motivations behind the choice of subject matter, the methodological axioms, and the scholarly and pedagogical practices that comprised it had more to do with responding to the crises in Southern society than with some disinterested love for England's past.

This claim is consistent with Allen Frantzen's argument in *Desire for Origins*. Because the process of scholarly examination itself alters and shapes its subject, Anglo-Saxon texts can be only one-half of the discipline's focus; the other half is necessarily "the ideas and attitudes of readers" that have "accumulated around" these texts. Frantzen states that "the scholarship of each generation adheres to the subject and becomes part of the subject that the next generation then studies."[2] For these reasons, he suggests that Anglo-Saxonists should acknowledge the role they play in forming the discipline and should focus their scholarly attention on the discourse surrounding and engaging these texts rather than merely on the texts themselves. Such an approach would reveal the dynamic nature of these texts and would allow readers to see them as something more than static documents; it would permit readers to view them as "textual events" that, although originally produced in their Anglo-Saxon context, have been undergoing a continual process of reproduction through their interaction with subsequent cultural contexts.[3]

In this study I employ this discursive approach to explain the cultural reproduction of the concept "Anglo-Saxon" as it occurred in the postbellum South. In particular I discuss how the body of texts and disciplinary interests that comprised Anglo-Saxon studies in 1865 resonated with the social and cultural concerns of Southern intellectuals after the Confederate defeat. The "idea" of Anglo-Saxon England formed by the scholarship of earlier American Anglo-Saxonists interacted with postbellum Southern thought and subsequently affected Southern culture as well as the further development of Anglo-Saxon studies. This interaction produced a new set of "textual events" in the form of scholarship, grammars, and readers that were then passed on to the next generation of

Anglo-Saxonists, shaping their particular conception and practice of Anglo-Saxon studies as well as their political attitudes.

Ideological associations involving Anglo-Saxon language and culture did not suddenly appear in the South after the war; Anglo-Saxonism had played an important role in the formation of national identity in antebellum America.[4] As both Stanley Hauer and Reginald Horsman note, many principal figures involved in the American Revolution and the early republic traced the origins of American democracy to the Anglo-Saxons.[5] The most vocal proponent of this theory was Thomas Jefferson, who developed an intricate cultural narrative from his readings on Anglo-Saxon language and culture. Jefferson believed that the Germanic tribes in Europe (or, as he called them, the Teutonic tribes) were the first to conceive of democracy. The Anglo-Saxons then transported these democratic principles, along with the egalitarian, agrarian economy on which they rested, to England where they refined them into a foundation of government characterized by an elective king, annual parliaments, and trial by jury.[6] Jefferson saw an analogy between this cultural narrative and the events contributing to the formation of the United States. Like Saxons who had migrated from their continental homelands to Britain, the American colonists had traveled to a new land and there transformed the loose democratic elements of their political legacy into a more developed system of social and political institutions.[7] Hence, Jefferson maintained that the heroes of Anglo-Saxon history and legend could serve as authoritative examples of the socially responsible behavior necessary to the success of the new republic.

Jefferson believed in using the university curriculum to inculcate democratic beliefs. He held that one of the principal duties of an American university was to instill in students the social habits and cultural knowledge that would encourage participation in the social and political life of their community, state, and nation. For this reason, Jefferson felt the study of Anglo-Saxon was essential to the educational mission of the University of Virginia and made sure the institution included it as part of its course of study. Although Jefferson thought Latin and Greek should still remain a central part of the curriculum, he believed the insight they provided was limited to "embellishments" of English language and thought, mere "engraftments on its idiomatic stem."[8] In contrast, he felt that a course in Anglo-Saxon would provide insight into "the radix of the mass of our language" and with it "a full understanding of our ancient common law."[9] In other words, Jefferson believed that the Anglo-Saxon language was vital to American education because it alone modeled Anglo-Saxon cultural practices.

For Jefferson, the Anglo-Saxon form of the English language contained all of the Anglo-Saxon cultural characteristics that had given birth to democracy and common law centuries before. He believed that these original democratic elements could be transferred to the modern student through the study of Anglo-Saxon language. After absorbing these elements, the student could then trace the changes in English from that period to the present day and, thereby, gain a corresponding understanding of the development of English social, political, and legal customs up to the American Revolution.[10] Studying this early English grammar and vocabulary as well as its subsequent changes would provide insight into the relationship between Anglo-Saxon cultural institutions and their descendants. Jefferson felt that this was the perfect training for an American citizen.

Jefferson's narrative was not just a curious way to advocate the study of Anglo-Saxon but instead a politically motivated justification of America's institutions and a map for America's future. He interpreted America's connection with Anglo-Saxon culture as a portent of future American power and success. As Frantzen argues, Jefferson's plan to feature Hengist and Horsa, the Anglo-Saxon conquerors of Britain, on the national seal "picture[s] the ambitions of early settlers for westward expansion" and thereby reveals a desire for conquest and American empire.[11] The connection between this desire and the Anglo-Saxons remained an important emblem in American culture throughout the nineteenth century. Horsman argues that the aspirations underlying Jefferson's Anglo-Saxonism shaped American racial ideology and, in turn, prompted land acquisition campaigns such as the annexation of Texas and the Mexican War.[12]

While I agree with this interpretation of Jefferson's narrative, the designs and effects discussed by Frantzen and Horsman reflect only one of many historical trajectories emanating from Jefferson's encounters with Anglo-Saxon texts. American empire presupposes a unified American nation with a shared national identity, notions no longer held by most Southerners after 1861. In order to understand the ideological uses that Southerners made of Anglo-Saxon texts and textual events like Jefferson's, one must use such points of reference as those emphasized in Henneman's essay. Jefferson's interpretations of Anglo-Saxon texts resulted in a proliferation of textual events, providing what Frantzen has called "many different and simultaneous plots enacted, as it were, on the same stage at the same time."[13] Southern Anglo-Saxon studies represents one of these different plots, one that contrasts with yet still intersects the plots that Frantzen and Horsman examine. Southern readings of Anglo-Saxon texts included Jefferson's links between Anglo-Saxon language, education, and national identity; however, as Southern nationalism gained momentum, national identity also gradually took on a Southern orientation.

Subsequent Southern scholars refined Jefferson's notions of Anglo-Saxon to meet Southern concerns; they portrayed Old English not only as a reservoir of democratic values but also as a means of protection against tyranny. One such scholar, Maximilian Schele De Vere, professor of modern languages at the University of Virginia from 1844 until the mid-1890s, invoked the resilience of the Anglo-Saxon language in the aftermath of the Norman invasion as the perfect example of this protective quality. In *Outlines of Comparative Philology,* Schele De Vere argues that the strength of the Anglo-Saxons lay in the speech of the commoners, "who clearly perceived and expressed the fundamental truths of civil liberty" through their language. He asserts that, throughout history, the language of the Anglo-Saxon race preserved the people in the face of adversity; when the Anglo-Saxon people faced political and religious oppression, they found "in the forgotten and neglected dialects of distant provinces [Saxon Germany] assistance as powerful as it was unexpected."[14] Given the defensiveness of contemporary Southerners about local institutions such as slavery, Schele De Vere's statement appears to address regional problems while describing Anglo-Saxon culture; in other words, the description serves as a vehicle for local cultural work.

Schele De Vere goes on to relate the story of the Norman Conquest, portraying the Saxons as defenders of a democratic society and the Normans as conquerors who robbed them of their political freedom. In doing so, he conflates human resistance with linguistic resistance. He claims that the tenacity of the Anglo-Saxon language allowed the Saxons not only to endure the Normans but also to "conquer" them linguistically: "The Normans had conquered the land and the race, but they struggled in vain against the language that conquered them in its turn, and, by its spirit, converted them into Englishmen."[15]

Although such comparisons between Southerners and the Anglo-Saxons would become commonplace after the Confederate defeat in 1865, they were relatively rare before then. Many antebellum Southerners were fascinated with the cultural struggle following the Norman Conquest, made popular by the novels of Sir Walter Scott; however, they tended to identify themselves with the aristocratic Normans rather than the defiant Saxons. As Eugene Genovese notes, antebellum Southern society with its proslavery ideology had no modern models. Southerners, therefore, turned to the aristocracy, chivalry, and paternalism of medieval France and post-Conquest Britain for a tradition.[16] The analogy between plantation culture and feudalism validated Southern culture by suggesting to Southerners that their values and institutions had historical precedent. Wealthy Southerners could imagine themselves as civilized conquerors whose vast holdings of land and slaves made them aristocratic, rather than perceiving themselves as what, for the most part, they really were—pioneers surrounded by the crudities of frontier life. In addition, the analogy allowed Southern slaveholders to counter Northern accusations that slavery was abnormal and inhumane. Since slavery in the form of serfdom had contributed to the formation of European civilization, they could argue that slavery was not an anomaly but a tradition, a way of life that promised to enlighten those of African descent and to provide a social structure to prevent them from slipping back into savagery.

Southern defeat, however, destroyed the relevance of this analogy and the social model it provided. It transformed Southerners from would-be conquerors to vanquished subjects almost overnight. The consequences of this defeat—the abolition of slavery, military occupation, the arrival of carpetbaggers, and disfranchisement—brought economic devastation and social disruption. Without a social and economic infrastructure that "fit" with the analogy, the cultural comparison between Southerners and Normans no longer seemed applicable.

What Southerners experienced in the first couple of years after the war was alienation from their society. Just as the war had deprived them of their material possessions, it also had shattered the sense of reasonableness underlying their cultural symbolism. The immense distance between the illusions of antebellum cultural analogies and the realities of postbellum Southern life made even everyday tasks difficult. Within this new social order, Schele De Vere's interpretation of the Norman Conquest made Anglo-Saxon studies appealing to postbellum Southern intellectuals. With the defeat of the Southern nationalist movement in the American Civil War and the subsequent occupation of the former Southern states by the Union army, Southerners found themselves in a position they believed to be similar to that faced by the Anglo-Saxons after the Norman Conquest.

Southern intellectuals afraid of both political oppression and the potential loss of their Southern cultural values and institutions found solace in
Schele De Vere's views; they began to believe that knowledge of the
Anglo-Saxon language would safeguard the culture and political rights of
Southerners against the dangers posed by federal Reconstruction in the
same way that it had preserved Anglo-Saxon culture and its democratic
tradition from the Norman conquerors.

This new analogy emerged through a fusion of Schele De Vere's views
and Southern attitudes toward education that emerged during the war. In
an 1863 article entitled "Education after the War," written at the height
of the Confederacy's military success, Professor Edward Joynes of William and Mary College, one of Schele De Vere's former students, advocates a revolution in Southern education comparable with the war for
political independence; he argues that the South needs to look ahead and
prepare educational methods and materials that will secure the liberty of
the new nation after the war. Joynes links education with Southern
nationalism by associating educational independence with national independence. In so doing, he transforms the classroom into another "battle-
field" on which war with the North could be fought.

Joynes maintained that the new educational tools must be free of
Northern taint; they must have a distinctly Southern foundation to
nurture successfully "the wise, the conservative, the conscientious citizen" who would serve as the South's "bulwark of liberty and peace."[17]
According to him, the common ground on which this new educational
program should be built was discipline, both intellectual and moral.
Instead of relying on the "short cuts to knowledge in the North's empirical methods of instruction," Southern education would develop the
faculties of both mind and will. This type of learning would provide the
discipline needed to properly inculcate Southern values in future generations. Joynes closes his article by calling on all Southern educators to
devise "such textbooks and such modes of teaching as shall realize this
idea"; by claiming that these endeavors are "not less of patriotic than of
professional duty," Joynes blurs the lines between politics and pedagogy
as well as between nationalism and curriculum.[18]

Despite the Confederate defeat, the associations between Southern
identity and education remained an important part of Southern discourse. Many Southerners advocated distinctly Southern educational
means and methods but not for the reasons Joynes had given; the goal of
this regional education had shifted from engendering support for a new

nation to erecting pedagogical barricades to defend traditional values. Southerners looking for a distinctly Southern educational tradition again found inspiration in Anglo-Saxon language and culture. The status of Old English as an institutionalized course in the South's premier university and Jefferson's belief in the capability of the language to instill democratic impulses resonated with the Southern desire for a curricular rampart. For this reason, Anglo-Saxon studies rapidly became an important component in the Southern curriculum.

Between 1865 and 1870 a number of articles discussing Anglo-Saxon language and its power to bolster cultural norms appeared in Southern journals and Northern journals frequently read by Southerners. One of the earliest of these articles, "Language: Its Sources, Changes, and Philosophy" (1866), presented the importance of one's "mother tongue" in the formation of thought and dispositions. The anonymous author offers a number of points that support the associations between Anglo-Saxon, education, and Southern identity. For one, he explicitly connects the study of the language with the development of behavioral dispositions. He argues that each generation of speakers transmits "to its progeny, not merely the vocabulary of expression, the modes of inflection, and the forms of syntax, but the habits of thought and feeling which are crystallized in its idioms, and the associations which cluster around the words of which it is composed."[19] This point clarifies exactly how Anglo-Saxon could act as a cultural bulwark in Southern society; an educational program devoted to Anglo-Saxon could potentially pass on the essential "habits of thought and feeling" needed to defend Southern traditions. The author of the article confirms the promise of such an educational endeavor by identifying "the mother tongue" as the cultural force that "constitutes the intellectual and moral atmosphere" of a society (28).

Another anonymous article, "German Works on English" (1867), is significant because it stresses the Anglo-Saxons' successful efforts to preserve their language, and thereby the democratic spirit, in the face of conquest and subjugation. The author explicitly connects these efforts to nineteenth-century America by claiming that modern Americans are "Teutons and Saxons—the representatives of skill, endurance, duty, and independence" and, therefore, that their character can "find expression only in Saxon terms." Given this important cultural and linguistic connection, the author advocates widespread study of Old English language and literature; he argues that such study would provide "a lesson in liberty" since it would "bring our sons face to face with generations of

their forefathers, let them . . . feel, for example, as the fathers, brothers
and sons of those who fell on the battle of Hastings felt on the eve of that
fatal day."[20] Southerners reading this essay only two years after the end of
the Civil War certainly would have found it resonant with their immedi-
ate cultural situation.[21]

A third article, "Anglo-Saxon Learning" (1868), builds on the suggestions hinted at above; in particular, it lays out an account of the Norman
Conquest in which the English language plays a central role. The author
asserts that "those institutions on which the Anglo-Saxon race most
prides itself" as well as "those personal characteristics which distinguish
us from other races" originated in Anglo-Saxon England. He suggests
that the Norman conquerors ultimately "exchanged their adopted French
for the language of the nation they conquered."[22] Essentially, this is a
reiteration of Schele De Vere's narrative of the Norman Conquest as he
had presented it in *Outlines of Comparative Philology* fifteen years
before; however, postbellum political circumstances made it much easier
for Southerners to identify culturally with this narrative. They could now
easily incorporate it into their discursive nexus by envisioning the educational "battleground" that existed between them and the North in terms
of the Norman Conquest. The result was a cultural analogy that aligned
Southerners with the Anglo-Saxons and Northerners with the Normans.

The promise of a future linguistic victory implicit in this analogy
provided comfort to Southerners who believed their region had been
unjustly conquered by antidemocratic forces. It suggested that although
Southerners, like the Saxons, had lost the political and military struggle,
they were destined to prevail in the linguistic and cultural "battles" that
would ultimately decide the fate of the American people. In short, the
analogy provided Southern academics with a purpose; it would be their
job to preserve the American democratic heritage, a heritage that they
believed was inextricably connected to Southern customs and dispositions. By teaching university courses on Anglo-Saxon, these academics
could continue the battle against the North while simultaneously instill-
ing Southern customs and dispositions in future generations of Americans. Southern collegiate classrooms, therefore, became sites of linguistic
and cultural conservation.

Much Southern philological scholarship in the years after the war
focused on further solidifying the associative links between Southerners
and the Anglo-Saxons. A number of Southern scholars concentrated on
distinguishing dialects and other aspects of speech that were "distinctly

Southern" and demonstrating that they were older and therefore closer to the original Anglo-Saxon than were the characteristics of Northern speech. One such work is Schele De Vere's *Americanisms,* in which he discusses how the unique aspects of the American experience have revealed themselves in the dialects and idioms of American speech. He suggests that two such experiences, the Civil War and increased immigration, were changing American industry, politics, and thought and would once again alter American English.[23] Schele De Vere claims that these cultural changes would eventually erode "the old English terms preserved in the South" that "Southern conservatism" had maintained "while at home and all around her everything changed."[24] Such comments imply that Southern Anglo-Saxonists believed Southern dialects retained elements of English that had died out in the rest of the world in the seventeenth century, and that the changes the Civil War had brought to the South endangered these older forms of speech. Once they disappeared, according to the Jeffersonian formula, American democratic institutions would also be threatened.

A similar study by Sylvester Primer of the College of Charleston, South Carolina, reinforces this notion. In an article on his local dialect, Primer voices his concern that Northern progressivism posed a linguistic threat to the postbellum South: "During the last twenty years the conservatism of the old South has been gradually retiring before the new and progressive spirit, and the pronunciation has undergone a more rapid change than ever before in its history. . . . At the present day we are in a transitional state of more than ordinary import, since the constant laws of phonetic change, ever in operation under all circumstances, have been accelerated."[25] Implicit within this "new and progressive spirit" are the forces of Reconstruction, which brought increasing numbers of immigrants, "standard" Northern pronunciation, and "floods of cheap books" to the South, eroding the older Southern dialects as well as the region's culture (200–203). Primer suggested that if this influence continued, Southerners would need to make a massive educational effort to preserve their traditional speech.

One of the main reasons for the pervasiveness of the analogy linking the Saxons with Southerners and the Normans with Northerners was its flexibility; it was able to accommodate the wide range of attitudes that Southerners had about the North in the years following the war. For those "unreconstructed" Southerners who still held animosity toward the North, the implicit promise of linguistic and cultural "victory" meant that the dream of a Southern nation was still possible. In their discussions of English language and culture, such Southerners stressed those parts of the narrative that emphasized Norman injustices toward the Anglo-Saxon people and the Saxon commoners' rejection of Norman language and customs. They viewed the uncompromising stance of the Anglo-Saxons as leading ultimately to gains in social and political power, and they adopted this stance as a model for dealing with the North. In contrast, those who advocated political reconciliation and economic cooperation with the North had a different interpretation of this fated victory. They focused on the "amalgamation" of the Norman and Anglo-Saxon languages and cultures that gave rise to modern English. These Southerners acknowledged the linguistic and cultural contributions that the Normans made to English society but held that Anglo-Saxon language and dispositions provided the foundation for English speech and customs.

Most Southerners' attitudes were situated somewhere between these two positions; they wanted to remain true to the Confederate cause, but at the same time they once again wanted to align themselves with the United States. The analogy between the postbellum South and post-Conquest England mediated between these two contradictory allegiances; the slippage between these interpretations allowed Southerners to identify themselves simultaneously as both Americans and Southerners. A good example of this slippage occurs in an 1877 speech given by former Confederate Major John W. Daniel before the Literary Societies of the University of Virginia. In this speech, entitled "Conquered Nations," Daniel connects the South's defeat in the Civil War to the Norman Conquest of the Anglo-Saxons in order to show that the fate of the South had also been the fate of the Saxons.[26] He accomplished this by merging a narrative account of the Conquest with his account of Reconstruction, and thereby associating Northerners with the Normans and Southerners with the Saxons. As David Culbreth, a member of the audience, notes, Daniel presented "a vivid picture of the doings of 'Norman carpetbaggers'" and "show[ed] at the same time how this state of things developed the 'English Kuklux.'"[27] By describing Norman rule in terms of carpetbaggers and Klansmen, Daniel appeals to those Southerners who still resisted reunification. However, he also appeals to those Southerners in favor of cooperation through his conciliatory attitude; he goes on to relate "the benefits which the Normans brought to the English, and how Norman and Saxon blood gradually blended together until conquered England came to the front as conqueror.'"[28] He ends his speech by advocating a merging of North and South like the merging of Normans and Saxons, claiming that such a combination would preserve elements of both cultures while it forged a stronger hybrid people.

This example demonstrates that the Southern discourse of Anglo-Saxonism was not politically neutral. As in every other historical context in which Anglo-Saxon language and culture have been objects of scholarly interest, the study of Anglo-Saxon was advocated and pursued in the postbellum South because it was capable of performing important cultural work. Anglo-Saxon studies spread quickly throughout Southern universities after the war because Southern intellectuals saw in here an area of scholarship that they felt was directly applicable to their own cultural situation.[29]

In addition to helping Southern intellectuals negotiate their regional and national allegiances, Anglo-Saxon studies served as an arena in which they could work out social anxieties created by the emancipation of African-American slaves. Before the war, the social spheres of slaves and masters had been intimately tied together despite the widely held belief that African-Americans were racially inferior. This interwoven social structure was possible because there was a clear understanding of social "place" among both white and black Southerners. The abolition of slavery, however, destroyed the legal framework that held together this rigid social hierarchy; the result was fear among white Southerners that the traditional boundaries between the racial groups would be crossed and that social chaos would result.

Once again the notion that the Anglo-Saxon language contained the roots of Southern habits and institutions served as a means of social adaptation to the effects of the war. Anglo-Saxonists used their discipline to support the notion that the speech of African-Americans lacked some of the important Anglo-Saxon characteristics found in the speech of white Southerners. A good example of this bias occurs in nineteenth-century American poet Sidney Lanier's discussion of rhythm in his *Science of English Verse* (1880). According to Lanier, who held the post of lecturer in English at Johns Hopkins University, rhythm is the primary constant that connects modern English to its Anglo-Saxon roots in both everyday speech and poetic verse. Lanier refers to the distinctive rhythm "natural" to English as "3-rhythm," since almost all English poetry is divided into rhythmic units or feet that contain three beats or their equivalent.[30] He contrasts 3-rhythm, which he describes as "bold" and "manly," with 4-rhythm, which he claims produces a comic effect. What is interesting about this contrast is that Lanier explicitly describes 3-

rhythm as a quality universal to the Anglo-Saxon race while he associates 4-rhythm with popular dance music in black minstrel shows. Through this opposition, Lanier sets up a rationale for metrical segregation analogous to the rationale for social segregation that was gaining supporters in the South at this time. The theory accomplishes this division by portraying 3-rhythm as a "noble" meter that is "natural" to English and therefore to the Anglo-Saxon race and opposing that natural meter to an alien one that, although familiar to English speakers, has foreign origins.[31] The suggestion is that foreign linguistic elements cannot blend into the English language without distorting their own nature and producing extreme effects in the ears of English listeners.

Lanier claims that unlike that of white English speakers who have ancestral ties to the Anglo-Saxon "forefathers," the language of Southern African Americans is built upon "the most primitive form of rhythm-producing apparatus" (214). Given this description, it should be no surprise that he also views African Americans' use of speech-tones as "primitive"; in fact, he sees their speech as the perfect example of an early moment in linguistic/poetic evolution.[32] Their speech-tone is supposedly more closely tied to a musical, sing-song quality that is "not bearable" to "the more cultivated ear" (215). Once again Lanier's theory provides an endorsement for social segregation, this time on the basis that the melody of African-American speech is primitive. The conflation of language, culture, and race at the core of Anglo-Saxon studies allowed Southerners to view language as another characteristic of race. In short, the discipline encouraged a fear of "linguistic miscegenation." Lanier's analysis implies that racial integration could lead to the introduction of "inferior" African-American speech practices into English and that these foreign practices would then undermine the Anglo-Saxon foundation of the language.

Lanier's *Science of English Verse* and similar scholarly works are based on a confusion of linguistic and racial notions that stretches back to the origins of philology. The early practice of organizing languages into "families" tended to skew the boundaries between biological and cultural traits by encouraging the belief that an essential correspondence existed between inherited physical features and learned customs such as language. In addition, the connections between philology, colonialism, and nationalism in Europe invited linguistic science to address the question of the superiority and inferiority of ethnic groups. In the postbellum South, this conflation blended with fears of cultural anarchy, moral decline, and miscegenation and encouraged Anglo-Saxonists to employ philological methods to rationalize racial discrimination.

The development of distinctive attitudes toward Anglo-Saxon studies in the postbellum South provides an interesting chapter in the discipline's history and an excellent example of the ideological use made of Anglo-Saxon texts. The language and culture of Anglo-Saxon England was more than an academic subject in the postbellum South; it also furnished Southern intellectuals with a narrative to meet the cultural crises of their day. They saw themselves as a defeated nation whose language and culture were threatened by multiple invading forces. On one front they viewed the growing urban and industrial civilization of their Northern conquerors as a potent challenge to their traditional agrarian customs. On the other, they saw the millions of African-Americans freed from slavery as a danger to their social hierarchy and racial purity. Thus it is no wonder that Southern intellectuals would transform Anglo-Saxon studies from an obscure course offering into an important part of the curriculum. The discipline enabled Southerners to reinterpret the disorienting events of the Civil War and Reconstruction as a comprehensible narrative that both legitimized Southern defeat and promised eventual Southern victory.

Notes

I am grateful to Mary Blockley, Melinda Menzer, and Kim VanHoosier-Carey for their suggestions on earlier versions of this paper.

1. John B. Henneman, "The Study of English in the South," *Sewanee Review* 2 (1894): 188.

2. Allen J. Frantzen, *Desire for Origins: New Language, Old English, and Teaching the Tradition* (New Brunswick, N.J.: Rutgers University Press, 1990), p. 125.

3. Ibid., p. 126.

4. I have borrowed the term *Anglo-Saxonism* from Frantzen and historian Reginald Horsman to refer to "the use of Anglo-Saxon culture and texts for ideologically motivated and political ends" (Frantzen, *Desire for Origins*, p. xi).

5. Stanley R. Hauer, "Thomas Jefferson and the Anglo-Saxon Language," *PMLA* 98 (1983): 880; Reginald Horsman, *Race and Manifest Destiny: The Origins of Racial Anglo-Saxonism* (Cambridge: Harvard University Press, 1981), p. 18.

6. Hauer, "Thomas Jefferson," p. 880; Horsman, *Race and Manifest Destiny*, pp. 21, 24.

7. Horsman, *Race and Manifest Destiny*, p. 22.

8. Thomas Jefferson, "An Essay Towards Facilitating Instruction in the Anglo-Saxon and Modern Dialects of the English Language," in *The Writings of Thomas Jefferson,* ed. Andrew A. Libscomb and Albert Ellery Baugh, 20 vols. (Washington, D.C.: Thomas Jefferson Memorial Association, 1903), 18:166.

9. Nathaniel Francis Cabell, *Early History of the University of Virginia as Contained in the Letters of Thomas Jefferson and Joseph C. Cabell* (Richmond: J. W. Randolph, 1856), pp. 440–41.

10. Ibid.

11. Frantzen, *Desire for Origins,* pp. 15–17.

12. Horsman, *Race and Manifest Destiny,* pp. 208–16.

13. Frantzen, *Desire for Origins,* p. 106.

14. Maximilian Schele De Vere, *Outlines of Comparative Philology* (New York: George P. Putnam, 1853), p. 81.

15. Ibid., p. 121.

16. Eugene Genovese, "The Southern Slaveholders' View of the Middle Ages," in *Medievalism in American Culture,* ed. Bernard Rosenthal and Paul E. Szarmach (Binghamton, N.Y.: Center for Medieval and Early Renaissance Studies, 1989), pp. 32–33.

17. Edward S. Joynes, "Education After the War," *Southern Literary Messenger* 37 (1863): 488–89.

18. Ibid., pp. 489–90.

19. "Language: Its Sources, Changes, and Philosophy," *De Bow's Review* 32 (1866): 26.

20. "German Works on English," *Round Table* (1867): 324.

21. This is particularly true considering that the article that precedes this one is a letter written by a Southerner in which he attempts to describe to Northerners what it is like to live under "the barbarous despotism" of the Radical Republicans.

22. "Anglo-Saxon Learning," *Round Table* (1868): 119.

23. Maximilian Schele De Vere, *Americanisms* (New York: C. Scribner & Co., 1872), p. 4.

24. Ibid., pp. 5, 427.

25. Sylvester Primer, "Charleston Provincialisms," *American Journal of Philology* 9 (1888): 199.

26. John Warwick Daniel, "Conquered Nations," in *Speeches and Orations of John Warwick Daniel,* ed. Edward M. Daniel (Lynchburg, Va.: J. P. Bell, 1911), p. 156.

27. David M. R. Culbreth, *The University of Virginia: Memories of Her Students and Professors* (New York: Neale Publishing, 1908), pp. 361–62.

28. Daniel, "Conquered Nations," pp. 146–49; Culbreth, *The University of Virginia,* p. 362.

29. The data that Henneman provides in "The Study of English in the South" reveals a rapid proliferation of Anglo-Saxon studies in Southern universities

following the Civil War. At the start of the war in 1861, there was only one Southern university offering courses in Old English; between 1865 and 1870, this number increased to five. By 1894, there were at least twenty-three universities offering course work in this field.

30. Sidney Lanier, *The Science of English Verse*, vol. 2 of *The Centennial Edition of the Works of Sidney Lanier*, ed. Paull F. Baum (Baltimore: Johns Hopkins University Press, 1945), p. 110. By "equivalent," Lanier means that the beats in each foot, regardless of their number, must together equal three counts.

31. Elsewhere in this work, Lanier claims that *The Battle of Maldon* "counts with perfect confidence upon the sense of rhythm which is well-nigh universal in our race" (ibid., p. 113).

32. Lanier believes that the Anglo-Saxons also went through this 4-rhythm stage, but their "natural" use of the more complex 3-rhythm allowed them to evolve out of it. Lanier implies here that the "primitive rhythm" of Southern African Americans will not allow them to evolve past this stage.

8. Historical Novels to Teach Anglo-Saxonism

Velma Bourgeois Richmond

T HE EDWARDIAN PERIOD is widely regarded as a golden age of children's literature.[1] The famous classics of that age are often praised because they subvert tradition, but many more books written for children reinforce and justify tradition than undercut it. Certain circumstances of British political and social life in the years prior to World War I explain a remarkable burst of historical novels that present the Middle Ages to a juvenile audience, as well as many versions of *Beowulf* for children and youth. These share common characteristics of racial definition, heroic behavior, chivalric idealism, and Christian piety. Reasons for the outpouring of Edwardian children's fiction and history that sought to influence and form an Anglo-Saxon character are complex and include nineteenth-century nationalism and racialism. Although an enthusiasm for the Crusades and Froissart yielded a significant number of chivalric stories, the Anglo-Saxon period is the more frequently chosen one. This richness can be explained in several ways.

Certainly Victorian evocation of the greatness of King Alfred, which culminated in the King Alfred Millenary of 1901, was a crucial inspiration to those who sought noble precedents. The choice of the first year of the new century to mark Alfred's death, although technically incorrect (for that king died in 899, not 901), reflected a wish to strengthen the analogue between present and past national achievements, and Victoria's death reinforced it.[2] A prolific and admired writer for children, the Reverend A. J. Church, composed a funeral sermon for the queen that,

besides deploying familiar maternal imagery, expressed national sentiments by tying Victoria to King Alfred, who is lauded for saving the
country from heathen invaders, for building a fleet that began the nation's
glory and defense, for adorning life with culture, and for making the
realm orderly with laws.[3] Thus Church evokes militarism, piety, tradition, and stability, while preaching in the words of the psalmist "A
thousand years are in Thy sight but as yesterday," and he encourages his
countrymen with the reminder that Alfred's son, like Victoria's successor,
was an Edward (14). In this moment of great transition at the start of a
new century, medievalism—a discourse through which the present, especially its anxieties and discontents, can be articulated through a repository of belief and images—served British national interests, and many
authors in the years before World War I continued to rely upon and
exploit the nation's heritage from the age of Alfred.

In addition, values specifically conducive to the period of empire
found confirmation in the Anglo-Saxon past. The Anglo-Saxon myth is a
complex one, but especially appealing to people of the Victorian and
Edwardian periods were military success in a time of need, the ideal of
free and equal citizens united through representative institutions (as
opposed to the oppressive Norman yoke), and the comfort and power of
a strengthening Christianity that enhanced unity and stability.[4] Interest-
ingly, the historical novel as a modern genre begins with Anglo-Saxonism.
Sir Walter Scott's *Ivanhoe* explores Enlightenment views of historicism,
invokes the importance of historical development and its relation to
nationalism, and confronts the post-Revolutionary era and the collapse
of Napoleon by resolving the conflict between conquerors and conquered
through "the middle way" that reconciles racial differences, showing
both the virtues of an aristocracy and the strength of lower classes. Scott
thus celebrates a new "Englishness."[5] G. K. Chesterton, a notable detrac-
tor of empire, advocated as its alternative an Edwardian "Englishness"
that stressed smallness and rural values, largely lost through industrial-
ization and the disappearance of the peasantry who were vital in early
medieval communities. The continuing popularity of Scott's *Ivanhoe*
demonstrates, in part, its usefulness as a gloss at a time when Europeans
were deeply interested in historical continuity and ideas of "racial"
survivals, theories that were both developed and applied in the nineteenth century. Another ardent proponent of medievalism, William Morris (1834–96), added socialist ideology and a tremendous enthusiasm for

northern identity to the medievalism of his time by both translating Icelandic sagas and writing his own imitative romances. Similarly, the operas of Richard Wagner (1813–83), their stories frequently retold for children, fostered the Teutonic race and enhanced representation of the Anglo-Saxon.[6] The Victorian self was prefigured in past cultures, and the Edwardians continued these projections, especially through children's literature.

Endless representations of fighting fill the pages of the juvenile novels of this period, inciting readers to a heroic ideal of manliness. Such novels were preceded by mid-century work like Sir Edward Bulwer-Lytton's *Harold: The Last of the Saxon Kings* (1848), which makes Harold a liberal patriot, and Charles Kingsley's *Hereward the Wake* (1866), which asserts the "berserker" spirit as needed for the regeneration of the English. The Crimean War inspired Kingsley's efforts, and at the end of the century the Boer War demanded similar complex responses. Nothing justified or evoked national enthusiasm for the army more vigorously than the holding of Mafeking in 1900, when "pluck and valour" inevitably triumphed in a "right cause," and the credit went to a small band of warriors who were victorious against heavy odds. Along with Lord Roberts, former commander of the Indian forces and hero of the war in South Africa, and Lord Kitchener, his chief of staff, the hero of the hour was Robert Baden-Powell, founder of the boy scout movement. Recognizing his nation's "great military proclivities," Edward Elgar composed the *Pomp and Circumstance Marches* (1901 and 1905), a large-scale treatment of the ordinary quick march. The 1905 composition includes "Land of Hope and Glory," but Elgar's *Enigma Variations* (1899) express much darkness, and that title suggests the tension that J. B. Priestly identifies as the salient characteristic of the Edwardian age.[7]

The designation *Great Britain* derives from Sir Charles Dilke's book *Greater Britain* (1867), an account of his travels, and this term for expanding empire fostered a strong sense of affinity among white English-speaking societies around the globe. A good example is a readable children's history, Eleanor Bulley's *Great Britain for Little Britons;* by 1887 there was a third edition, and a sixth was issued in 1904, with a dedication both to the specific children for whom it was written and "to all English-speaking children." An epigram on the title page asserts, "The youth of a nation are the trustees of posterity."[8]

The first literary history of *Children's Books in England* was written by F. J. Harvey Darton in 1932; its subtitle is *Five Centuries of Social Life*.[9] Darton anticipates the contemporary claims of those who read children's literature and justify its place in the canon of English studies with the argument that these books have much to say about cultural history and values. In the same year Paul Hazard in *Books, Children and Men* made a broader analysis, with special attention to national traits. Writing in France, he yet included other countries and observed, "England could be reconstructed entirely from its children's books."[10] Children's books are significant not only because they instruct and entertain children when they are read but also because their impact is long lasting. As the American author and illustrator Howard Pyle (1853–1911) observed: "In one's mature years one forgets the books that one reads, but the stories of childhood leave an indelible impression, and the author always has a niche in the temple of memory from which the image is never cast out to be thrown into the rubbish-heap of things that are outgrown and outlived."[11] Children's literature is the only one defined by its audience, but its definition is controlled by adults who write, select, buy, teach, and give to children the books that present views of history, character, and morals as adults wish these to be experienced. The temple of memory of which Pyle speaks was filled with countless vivid images and stories that defined the minds of the generation who lived an Edwardian childhood.

There are some national differences, but children's books in the United States were typically much the same as those in Britain, not least because of the values of the New England establishment and American enthusiasm for England, illustrated vividly by the expatriots Henry James and John Singer Sargent, quintessential Edwardian novelist and painter. Writers for children crossed the Atlantic easily in both directions, editions were often printed concurrently, and some authors appealed to Queen Victoria's creation of "a wider Anglekin the world over."[12] While stories of American Indians and the Far West were popular in England, heroic adventure and medieval chivalry found a large audience in the United States through both individual books and stories in encyclopedias.

Children's literature, then, is a potentially rich resource for defining one area of modern Anglo-Saxonism. After reviewing some essential contexts for the Edwardian moment, I use two examples to illustrate the relation between Anglo-Saxonism and juvenile historical novels: first, novels and histories centered on King Alfred, and second, the historical novels of Charles W. Whistler, perhaps the most singularly devoted writer of Anglo-Saxon stories for children. His careful research and ability to tell exciting stories were deployed in many books, each centered on a specific event in history before the Norman Conquest.

Defining the Anglo-Saxon and Educating the Children

John Sutherland's survey of Victorian fiction describes historical fiction as "the most numerous and least honoured of Victorian fictional genres."[13] This popularity was sustained and enlarged with increasingly nationalistic concerns at the beginning of the twentieth century. Autobiographies and accounts of Edwardian childhoods contain many references to Sir Walter Scott, widely acknowledged as the creator of the historical novel, and to other prolific novelists like H. Rider Haggard, Charles Kingsley, Edward Bulwer-Lytton, and G. A. Henty. It is worth noting that the line between adult and juvenile reader is not a clear one. Rider Haggard, for example, prefaces *King Solomon's Mines* (1885) with Allan Quartermain's dedication of "This faithful but unpretending record of a remarkable adventure . . . to all the big and little boys who read it." The reviewers of many juvenile novels sustain this congruence of audience, and over time there are shifts. Many juvenile novels about the Anglo-Saxon past may be described as "Edwardian invasion literature." This is the term used by Samuel Hynes to identify publications in Britain that reflected a heightened anxiety about invasion in the years from 1900 to the start of World War I. Publications were as numerous as for the preceding thirty years, when there had been two earlier occasions for anxiety, and distribution was wider, with a peak of publication in 1906–9 and a concentration upon Germany as the enemy.[14] Hynes judges "Edwardian invasion scare" as "primarily a Tory creation" (43), inspired by the militaristic group around Lord Roberts and Northcliffe (53).[15] The obvious correlation between adult and juvenile fiction is that the best invasion novel, Erskine Childers' *The Riddle of the Sands* (1903), is today regarded as juvenile fiction. Many historical novels written specifically for Edwardian children are a manifestation of the same invasion anxiety and a plea for conservative values. Adult invasion literature tended to be contemporary or futuristic; juvenile novels are set in the past, and this is reassuring—the invasions have been survived and indeed have contributed to the formation of the British character and nation or race. Published in different editions, these books were aimed at a middle-class audience and frequently given as school (and Sunday school) prizes. Their Tory sentiments are strong, but the effect is to reassure and inspire the young reader. The patriotic ideals are those of favorite nursery histories, H. E. Marshall's *Our Island Story* (1905) and *Our Empire Story* (1908).[16] Toy knights vied with regiments of empire. The same interests are clear in juvenile historical novels, and they evolved from a Victorian tradition of historical fiction.

The unchallenged favorite was Sir Walter Scott, frequently read aloud and also readily available in simplified retellings for children.[17] Several of Scott's historical novels are set in the Middle Ages; *Ivanhoe* (1819), of course, explores the survival of Saxon values after the Norman Conquest. Scott is the initiator of a complex enthusiasm for chivalric stories in Britain and the United States, especially in the Deep South before the Civil War. The name of the wrecked riverboat in Mark Twain's novel *Huckleberry Finn* is the *Walter Scott,* not surprisingly since for Twain, Scott's romances also foundered and southern emulation of their chivalric idealism was a principal cause of the war.

Unquestionably, Scott inspired a revival, Gothic and Arthurian, that was expressed not only in literature but also in art and architecture and indeed in life, with the formation of the English gentleman in the role of knight.[18] A precocious but not unique example is William Morris, who had read all of Scott's novels by the age of seven; Morris was given "a little suit of armour in which to ride through the Forest."[19] *The Education of Henry Adams* describes delight in reading Scott, and *Ivanhoe* was favored by generations in a southern family of writers, William Alexander and Walker Percy.[20] *Ivanhoe* was such an instant success that almost immediately there were theatrical productions, at least five in London in 1820.[21] Scott's medievalism stems from the work of late eighteenth-century English antiquarians like Thomas Warton, Richard Hurd, Joseph Ritson, and George Ellis; his formation of the Bannatyne Club in 1823 was part of the same interest. Very influential was Sharon Turner's *The History of the Anglo-Saxons* (1799), which Scott identifies in the preface to *Ivanhoe* as most helpful. Turner exemplified the Romantic view of history as organically unified: "the past is seen as a peculiarly national affair, as having a direct connection with the present fortunes of the nation, and as an organically intertwined and self-validating system of institutions and values."[22] Turner, incidentally, claimed that he was the first to note the significance of *Beowulf,* which he brought to the public's attention in 1805.

A significant characteristic of European Romanticism, including its English manifestation, was the recovery and recreation of the Middle

Ages. In the nineteenth century there were many intense attempts to exalt medieval ideals as a counterargument to the perceived decline in religious values and community. Enthusiasm for northern stories steadily increased, a sign of emerging European national interests, though the success of Wagner indicates also regional affinities. Nationalism is obvious in the title of M. I. Ebbutt's collection of retellings for children, *Hero Myths and Legends of the British Race* (1910),[23] of which the first is *Beowulf*. Also included are *Havelock, King Horn, Hereward the Wake, Roland*, and several Celtic items, as well as *Constantine* for Christian virtues and outlaws like *Robin Hood* and *William of Cloudslee* for insubordination and defiance. Ebbutt's introduction surveys those who have lived in Britain to form the "race"—from cavemen to Iberians to "the proud Aryan Celtic race" ("tall, blue-eyed, with fair or red hair," xxi), to Romans, to "Teutons, whether as Saxon, Angle, Frisian or Jute" ("tall and fair, grey-eyed and sinewy," xxii), who became the English, to be conquered by the Normans, after which "England has welcomed men of many nations—French, Flemings, Germans, Dutch" (xxvii). She then notes geographically "the admixture of races in our islands": descendants of Iberians are in Ireland, the Hebrides, central and south Wales, and Cornwall; blue-eyed Celts dwell in the Highlands and the greater part of Wales, Hereford, Shropshire, Worcestershire, and Cheshire; Danish traces show in Cumberland, the fen country, East Anglia, and the Isle of Man; "stolid Saxons" are south of the Thames from Sussex to Hampshire and Dorset; the Lowlands of Scotland contain Angles with Celts on the western fringe; Flemish blood shows in Pembroke and Norfolk (xxvii–xxviii). Ebbutt's details are precise and argue a distinctive British identity that is largely northern European.

Such physical characteristics are significant for the Edwardian ideal racial type. Rider Haggard's Allan Quartermain describes Sir Henry Curtis as big-chested and long-armed; with "yellow hair, big yellow beard, clear-cut features, and large grey eyes . . . he reminded me of an ancient Dane."[24] The analogue is emphasized in the great fight, when Curtis is "like his Bersekir forefathers" (183): "There he stood, the great Dane, for he was nothing else, his hands, his axe, and his armour, all red with blood, and none could live before his stroke" (182). In the African adventures Curtis is the traditional heroic male; he weds Nylepha and becomes king, and "their son and heir" is "a regular curly-haired, blue-eyed young Englishman in looks, and though he is destined, if he lives, to inherit the throne of Zu-Vendis, I hope I may be able to bring him up to become what an English gentleman should be, and generally is."[25] Not surprisingly, such romances and historical novels reinforce the identity celebrated in myths and legends of the north, and Anglo-Saxonism was a crucial element in the reading of the young and in the definition of British imperialism.

Advocacy of Anglo-Saxonism was part of a larger context of educating children. Katherine Dunlap Carter's *Educating by Story-Telling* is a compelling gloss on attitudes at the start of the twentieth century. The book, published in 1919, is based on work of the Demonstration Play School of the University of California, Berkeley, first used in the summer of 1914. Its thesis is that story is the natural form for revealing life and has two functions in education: as molder of ideals and illuminator of facts (14).[26] Carter defines periods of childhood interests, and the relevant phase is the "Heroic Period," for the age eight to twelve years. At this time adventure stories, with emphasis upon physical bravery, are what interest children and what they need. Boys and girls share this "ravenous appetite" (58), and national epics are the proper material. Carter favors Robin Hood, suggests Hiawatha, and names a few Greek heroes and Charles's peers. But Beowulf and other northern heroes like Sigurd, Frithiof, some figures from the *Mabinogion,* and a discreet selection of King Arthur stories receive much praise. "Boys and girls love the epical stories because they are true in spirit, but they also love those that are true in fact" (63), and the first person from history is Alfred, whose story of entry into the Danes' camp as a harper is also an example for "Teaching Music" (114). A chapter on "Story-telling and the Teaching of Ethics" defines the teacher's role as trying "to bring children to an understanding of what is generally accepted as right and wrong, and implant in them convictions strong enough to cause them to adhere to those standards" (158). Juvenile novels that present Anglo-Saxonism adhere to these objectives; in this they mirror adult values while they favor historical fiction.

The Role of Anglo-Saxonism in Nineteenth-Century Historical Novels

For Marxist critic Georg Lukács, *Ivanhoe* is a prime example of the classical form of the historical novel. It centers on the rise of the British nation, which comes with the struggles of Saxons and Normans, and Scott establishes a middle way, the archetypal British compromise; the hero is an average English gentleman, not the flamboyant Romantic

Byronic type. Wilfred of Ivanhoe is a Saxon; he serves the Norman King Richard I, who in fiction has an epic character. Together they go on crusade, but they return at a time of crisis to save Britain from the machinations of King John, and the changes affect everyone, notably the peasants, minor figures but Scott's most authentic characterizations.[27] Dedication to Anglo-Saxonism is explicit in the reconciliation scene between father and son. Ivanhoe's father Cedric forgives him; however, Cedric warns: "But let me see thee use the dress and costume of thy English ancestry: no short cloaks, no gay bonnets, no fantastic plumage in my decent household. He that would be the son of Cedric must show himself of English ancestry" (404). Moreover, Ivanhoe's marriage to the Lady Rowena is to be delayed by two years of mourning for her be-trothed Athelstane, "the last sprout of the sainted Confessor" (289). At this moment Scott resuscitates Athelstane, "a violent breach of probabil-ity," to which he "was compelled by the vehement entreaties of his friend and printer, who was inconsolable on the Saxon being conveyed to the tomb" (448, n. 28). Thus reconciliation replaces destruction. *Ivanhoe* also gave impetus to evolving legends of Robin Hood, the outlaw hero who leads his band by consent.[28] Scott, then, not only spawns a nine-teenth-century tradition of chivalry but also initiates a strong advocacy for Anglo-Saxonism.

Few were able to match Scott's artistry, but all major Victorian novel-ists, as well as many lesser ones, wrote historical fiction. A particularly successful novel was Bulwer-Lytton's *Harold: The Last of the Saxon Kings* (1848). Its hero, a type of the liberal patriot, poses the claims of the Saxon, thus asserting a Teutonic heritage for the British race. Lord Lytton's fiction seems tractlike to some readers, but his moral passion still burns, as when he says of the lack of support for Harold: "The main causes for defection were . . . to be found in selfish inertness, in stubborn conceit, in the long peace, and the enervate superstition which had relaxed the sinews of the old Saxon manhood; in that indifference to things ancient, which contempt for old names and races engendered; that timorous spirit of calculation, which the overregard for wealth had fostered."[29] Bulwer-Lytton's choice of moments of change and crisis, indicated by his titles (*Harold: The Last of the Saxon Kings, The Last Days of Pompeii, The Last of the Barons*), makes him a fine example of Lukács's argument, but should not obscure his advocacy of hardy virtues thought to be rooted in Anglo-Saxon identity. His novels come early in the process well described by the title of Clare A. Simmons's book

Reversing the Conquest: History and Myth in Nineteenth-Century British Literature (1990).

Even more aggressive than Lord Lytton's advocacy is Charles Kingsley's *Hereward the Wake: The Last of the English* (1866), a celebration of the man who refused to yield to the Norman yoke, one whose name recognized his alertness. Hereward is the final ferocious fighter, a youth outlawed for his excesses, a slayer of a polar bear, one who overcomes more civilized knights. His first major feat is slaying a giant, Ironhook, and he is explicitly identified as David against Goliath, a foreshadowing of his role as leader of a rebel army in the fens. Finally Hereward falls before William's superior forces, who are abetted by female wiles that provoke his self-indulgence. With Hereward Kingsley evokes the old berserker spirit, a primitive energy and simplicity much needed to save mid-nineteenth-century Britain:

> The vices of incivilization are far worse, and far more destructive of human life [than the vices of civilization]; and it is because they are so that rude tribes deteriorate physically less than polished nations. In the savage struggle for life none but the strongest, healthiest, cunningest have a chance of living, prospering, and propagating their race. In the civilized state, on the contrary, the weakliest and the silliest, protected by law, religion, and humanity, have their chance likewise, and transmit to their offspring their own weakliness and silliness. In these islands, for instance, at the time of the Norman Conquest, the average of man was doubtless superior, both in body and mind, to the average of man now, simply because the weaklings could not have lived at all; and the rich and delicate beauty, in which the women of the Eastern Counties still surpass all other races in these isles, was doubtless far more common in proportion to the numbers of population.[30]

Kingsley, who was Victoria's favorite preacher and tutor of Edward, Prince of Wales, here voices sentiments that are basic to what he aptly identified—and some contemporaries ridiculed—as "muscular Christianity," a chivalric ideal that exalted manliness found in physical health and strength, which were deemed crucial for pureness of heart. The ideal is well expressed in Hereward, the last of the Anglo-Saxons, whose virtues could be used as an example of Teutonic manhood that Victoria could identify in her Saxon Prince Albert. Subsequent emphasis on sport in English schools is a part of the heritage of such Anglo-Saxonism.[31]

Anglo-Saxon heroism is crucial in Douglas C. Stedman's *The Story of Hereward: The Champion of England* (1909), a more authentic historical novel than Kingsley's romance. Stedman made extensive use of chronicles, provides a pronunciation guide for Old English, and gives youthful readers a liberal model in Hereward: "Defender of the downtrodden serf, avenger of the robbed yeoman, the name they had given him, 'England's darling,' was ever on their tongue, a blessing for him ever in their hearts. He brought them freedom from fear."[32] Patriotic achievement supplants youthful excesses. The fatal second marriage to Alftruda is rationalized as a wish for a son, and the virtuous wife Torfrida, from the convent, explains to the "fool" for whom Hereward never really cared: "Love looks for no reward. It gives and asks naught. It hopes, but wins—on earth never. It burneth the soul black, but looketh for no balm to ease the self-given torture. But the sacrifice is so glorious that Love rejoiceth in its self-inflicted bane" (276). The reading of such historical novels was a familiar part of Edwardian childhood, and the books read inspired ideals and action. An amusing deployment of historical traditions is "Two Modern Anglo-Saxons" in Stedman's *Captains and Kings* [1915]. In Brussels before the battle of Waterloo, a brother and sister who have read Hereward's story attend the Duke of Richmond's ball "arrayed in the pretty barbaric garb of the Anglo-Saxons" (304). Inspired to emulate heroic action, the modern Hereward and Torfrida please the Duke of Wellington by volunteering to live the legend, to fight the French and to nurse; their father Doctor Forrest adds Moira to his staff and allows Thornhurst "to fight as became an Anglo-Saxon chief and an officer of the British army."[33] Not least among characteristics of stories of Anglo-Saxonism for children is the frequency with which girls play active roles and are praised. This is a significant alternative to the anxieties about the New Woman in much influential Edwardian adult fiction.

King Alfred

There were many tales of resistance against the Danes, of Viking voyages, of sagas. Most favored was the noble character of King Alfred, an analogue for Queen Victoria. At her Diamond Jubilee in 1897 Poet Laureate Alfred Austin recalled:

> . . . with grave utterance and majestic mien
> She with her eighteen summers filled the Throne

Where Alfred sate: a girl, withal a Queen,
Aloft, alone![34]

The previous Poet Laureate, Lord Tennyson, was, of course, also "Alfred,"
and Tennyson's King Arthur is associated with Prince Albert. William
Theed's monument at Windsor Chapel shows Albert as an Anglo-Saxon
chief and Victoria as a Saxon queen. The Hanoverians established a
strong link with Germany, and Victoria and her children added to this
significantly. The year 1901 was planned as a millenary of Alfred the
Great, but it proved to be the year of Victoria's death.

The Reverend Edward Gilliat in that year published *God Save King
Alfred,* arguing that the great king of Wessex was "a National hero and
Saint who is more worthy of our reverence than the mythical St. George—
even with his dragon thrown in! But who is to make Alfred a Saint for us?
Have we not lost the art? What would the Nonconformist conscience,
what would the militant Protestant say! Alas! the age of Reverence is past
and gone!" (v–vi). Having shown his Tory stance, Gilliat follows this
lament with consolation: the city of Winchester is doing homage to
Alfred and thus "will atone for her old neglect in allowing Saint Alfred's
ashes to be carted away from Hyde Abbey—for rubbish. Every Englishman, and every American too, regrets that untoward carelessness now"
(vi). The book's handsome red cloth cover, stamped in gold, carries the
image of Winchester's statue of the Anglo-Saxon king. Alfred is identified
as the one who "united Anglekin in England," and "Victoria united a
wider Anglekin the world over" (vi). Here is evidence of an English-
speaking audience for this juvenile novel. The American writer for children Eva March Tappan also wrote of "this blameless king." *In the Days
of Alfred the Great* (1905) fervently marks "the one thousandth anniversary of his life": "Little of the legendary, less of the miraculous, has
obscured the fame of the real Alfred. His deeds are his own,—great in
themselves, greater in that they are the manifestation of the thought of a
great mind. Even in 'that fierce light which beats upon a throne,' it is
hard to find a flaw in the character of this man who believed in God, this
king who never failed to do his best."[35]

An earlier juvenile novel, Eliza F. Pollard's *A Hero King: A Story of the
Days of Alfred the Great* [1898], anticipates the identification of Saxon
and empire.[36] She notes that the union of Baldwin and Alfred's third
daughter Elfreda, the stems of Charlemagne and Alfred, sends branches
"far and wide over many lands, but the noblest branch, soaring high
above all others, is our own royal house of England and our gracious

Queen Victoria" (405). The last observation is: "A thousand years have passed away, but still the laws of Alfred the Great govern our vast empire, and she, the lady of the land, chief of the Saxon race, upon whom all eyes gaze with love and reference, has ever walked in the footsteps of her great ancestor, making—'The bounds of freedom wider yet'" (426). Pollard was perhaps better known for *A Saxon Maid* (1901), which recounts the life of a child, Edith, placed for safety in a convent. There she resists the veil, until she is revealed as Princess Maud of Scotland and becomes queen of England, a role for which she was well prepared by living a simple life and learning "that lesson which all who strive after goodness must learn sooner or later, forgetfulness of self."[37] Her discovery of her true parentage effects a suitable transformation: "Beautiful she was by nature, but when this knowledge came to her, a great glory shone in her face, so that those who looked at her marvelled" (111–12). Thus the Norman Henry I unites with the Saxon. There was an abbreviated version [1912] of this inspiring story in "Blackie's Stories Old and New Series, A Juvenile Library" for children aged eight to ten years.

G. A. Henty, whose novels of adventure were the foundation of Blackie's success, characteristically compares early history with empire; he explains in the preface to *The Dragon and the Raven; or, the Days of King Alfred* how "dear lads, living in the present days of peace and tranquility" can imagine "the days of King Alfred, when the whole country was for years overrun by hordes of pagan barbarians, who slaughtered, plundered, and destroyed at will." They are to think of India at the time of the Mutiny with the English population as the natives and the mutiny triumphant:

> The wholesale massacres and outrages which would in such a case have been inflicted upon the conquered whites could be no worse than those suffered by the Saxons at the hands of the Danes. From this terrible state of subjection and suffering the Saxons were rescued by the prudence, the patience, and valor and wisdom of King Alfred. In all subsequent ages England has produced no single man who united in himself so many great qualities as did this first of great Englishmen. He was learned, wise, brave, prudent, and pious: devoted to his people, clement to his conquered enemies. He was as great in peace as in war.[38]

King Alfred is a favored historical figure, but Henty's hero is a young Saxon thane who fights in Alfred's battles, goes to sea to combat the

Danes, and escapes up the Seine so that he is at the long siege of Paris. The prolific Henty does not exalt Anglo-Saxonism in simple terms; in *Wulf the Saxon: A Story of the Norman Conquest* (1894), he chronicles events in the life of Harold's page and thane—including a negligent King Edward's hunting, Edith's giving up Harold for the good of England, and the battle at Stamford Bridge—that culminate in the battle of Hastings. Henty judges the Norman victory a good thing because

> that admixture of Saxon, Danish, and British races which had come to be known under the general name of English, was in most respects behind the rest of Europe . . . the island distracted by internal dissensions. . . . The enterprise that had distinguished their Saxon and Danish ancestors seems to have died out. There was a general indisposition to change. . . . The arrival, however, of the impetuous Norman race, securing as it did a close connection with the Continent, quickened the intellect of the people, raised their intelligence, was of inestimable benefit to the English, and played a most important part in raising England among the nations. Moreover, it has helped to produce the race that has peopled Northern America, Australia, and the South of Africa, holds possession of India, and stands forth as the greatest civilizer in the world. The Conquest of England by the Normans was achieved without even a shadow of right or justice. It was at the time an unmixed curse to England; but now we can recognize the enormous benefits that accrued when in his turn the Englishman conquered the Norman, and the foreign invaders became an integral portion of the people they had overcome.[39]

Such Anglo-Saxonism echoes the resolution of *Ivanhoe* and the dismay of Bulwer-Lytton and Kingsley. It also shows a strong sense of the British "race" that holds sway in the modern world.

Yet another example of such historical fiction for juveniles is the work of Paul Creswick, author of *In Ælfred's Days: A Story of Saga the Dane* (1900) and *Under the Black Raven: or Saga, the King from out of the Sea* (1901).[40] Alfred is the historical personage and the Danish hero represents those whom he had to contain. The first book tells of the Danish invasion, and the second continues the story of his "despairs, defeats, and ultimate victory" with much vigorous action and physical violence as well as the blushes of "the boy-maid Isolde" to enhance "the romantic histories." Some such combination was typical of Edwardian historical novels, but the emphasis is on daring deeds, technical information about weapons and sailing, the spread of Christianity, and high sentiment.

The common element in the representation of Alfred in historical novels and in stories from history is the king's character: his heroism, wisdom, and faith. H. E. Marshall cites his names ("Alfred the Great, Alfred the Truthteller, England's Darling") in *Our Island Story* (76). She begins with the story of Alfred's learning to read and winning the book from his mother, continues with the burning of the cakes, which is probably the event in his legend that is most frequently told, and then goes on to his victory over the Danes, telling how he went into the Danish camp as a harper, fought bravely, built many ships, and made peace, encouraging learning, translating Latin into Old English, and strengthening Christianity. Other Edwardian histories for children present the same stories.[41] The intention is to foster behavior rooted in the past but still present in ideals of Anglo-Saxonism: love of reading, competition, courtesy, honesty, physical prowess, skill in music and story, a willingness to fight but always a desire to establish peace, and the missionary ideal of bringing Christianity to the heathen. Alfred was for many reasons an archetype, but many less famous heroes also thrilled and inspired.

Charles W. Whistler's Novels of Anglo-Saxonism

The most remarkable writer of Anglo-Saxon historical novels for juveniles is Charles W. Whistler (1856–1913), son of a clergyman, who was first a surgeon and then in midlife took holy orders. He was educated at the Merchant Taylors' School, St. Thomas Hospital, and Emmanuel College, Cambridge. In the last twenty years of his life Whistler wrote many historical novels for children, each one precisely dated and typically built around a major event, mostly in the Anglo-Saxon period. This is his special interest, expressed also in membership in the Somerset Archaeological Society and Viking Club. His objective as a writer for children is to provide knowledge of early Britain, to create characters who manifest archetypal English qualities, and to entertain and inspire through stories of youthful heroes. Often the location is East Anglia, where the series of Danish and Viking invasions provide much of the action. Whistler describes a world in which Dane, Icelander, Norwegian, and Viking are interrelated with men of Mercia, Anglia, Wessex, and fiercer tribes on the borders. Into each novel he introduces a breadth of political and cultural history as well as romantic descriptions of nature, richly detailed accounts of costume and armor, and sea and battle lore. Plots are usually fast-paced, and there is often a mystery in these exciting stories of young men who develop warrior skills and companionship, loyalty to thane and king, chivalric virtues, and not only a simple dedication to Christianity but also awareness of and respect for older heathen customs and experience. Usually narration is in the first person, often by a foster brother of the legendary hero. The world of a Whistler novel is filled with heroic songs and tales, frequent performances, and allusions to medieval literature—sagas, *Beowulf*, Arthurian legend. His sources are the *Anglo-Saxon Chronicle*, sagas, early epics, and romances. The latter are especially significant in heightening roles for female characters. Powerful queen; thane's competent wife; young woman of courage, independence, and energy; wise woman with second sight—these female figures are almost as familiar as youthful warriors and threatened kings.

Whistler retold the two earliest English romances about Anglo-Saxon Britain: *Havelock the Dane* (1900) and *A Prince Errant: The Story of Prince Horn and Princess Rymenhild,* as told by Athulf, Horn's foster brother [1908]. These medieval romances provided a model that most deeply influenced Whistler, even though much of his source material came from chronicles and sagas. Historical periods are often indicated in his titles, which show his dedication to Anglo-Saxonism: *A Thane of Wessex: Being the Story of the Great Viking Raid of 845* (1896); *Wulfric the Weapon-Thane: The Story of the Danish Conquest of East Anglia* (1897: hagiography of King Eadmund); *King Olaf's Kinsman: A Story of the Last Saxon Struggle against the Danes in the Days of Ironside and Canute* (1898); *King Alfred's Viking: A Story of the First English Fleet* (1899); *A Prince of Cornwall: A Story of Glastonbury and the West in the Days of Ina of Wessex* (1904); *Dragon Osmund: A Story of Athelstan and Brunanburh* (1915); *A King's Comrade: A Story of Old Hereford* ([1905]: centers on Offa); *A Son of Odin: A Romance of Old Norway* ([1915]: set in 995, features Olaf Tryggvasson); *A Sea-Queen's Sailing* ([1906]: set in 935, with Hakon).[42]

Whistler's skill in evoking the Anglo-Saxon period appears in his use and explanation of *Beowulf* in *A Thane of Wessex*. When the outlawed Heregar approaches a fire on the fens, the collier of the kiln flees. In the morning Heregar wakes to a small boy's saying, "Ho, Grendel!" A bit later a priest, summoned to exorcise the devil Grendel, explains: "They sing the song of Beowulf and love it, heathen though it be, better than aught else, and will till one rises up who will turn Holy Writ into their mother tongue, as Caedmon did for Northumbria. Howbeit, doubtless those who were fiends in the days of the false gods are fiends yet, and if Grendel then, so Grendel now, though he have many other names" (54). The priest deploys this mini–literary history of Anglo-Saxon poetry to speak against vengeance. Whistler later develops it when Heregar is at a monastery, where he hears the stories of the lay brethren, read "in some secrecy." When Guthlac reads, "such power has verse like this in the mouth of a good reader, [that] they started up, one and all" (184). A subprior chides such heathen "pagan vanities" and imposes a penance of reading David and Goliath, Ahab at Ramoth, and Joshua at Jericho. These choices show a distinct sympathy with warrior interests, and Heregar records the subprior's observation that "maybe it was laudable to search even pagan books for the manners of fiends, seeing that forewarned is forearmed." Heregar provides the further information that this religious man "was minded to make the old rhyme more Christian-like, if he could, writing parts of it afresh. And this he has done since, so that any man may read it; but it is not so good as the old one" (186). A helpful footnote explains that "the 'Saga of Beowulf' as we have it is the work of a Christian editor of King Alfred's time."[43] If this judgment appears unexpected from an Anglican clergyman writing for children, reassurance comes later when Wislac, Heregar's companion, observes, "Howbeit, I always did hold that there was none so much difference between a fighting-saint and one of ourselves" (188).[44] Thus Whistler's representation of Anglo-Saxon monastic life is not as a monolithic institution of the Late Middle Ages but an ambience of lay and religious, where pagan and Christian elements achieve a synthesis. This interpretation is recognizable in some of today's medieval scholarship.

Dragon Osmund: A Story of Athelstan and of Brunanburh [1915] is perhaps Whistler's best historical novel for children. As the subtitle indicates, the center is the great Anglo-Saxon victory of 937, celebrated in a poem that is the finest elaboration in the *Anglo-Saxon Chronicle*. In the novel this song is first sung at the victory feast, and historical persons and details are enriched with the successes of fictional heroes. Brunanburh was long recognized as a high point of Anglo-Saxon achievement; it was an important victory, and the poem that commemorates it stands out by contrast to the elegiac qualities of much Old English poetry. Its legendary significance was subsequently expanded when the Norman chronicler Peter Langtoft tied the victory to the popular hero Guy of Warwick, whose defeat of a Danish giant survived as "historical fact" until the eighteenth century.[45] Brunanburh is the climax of Whistler's book: the summoning of warriors to Stamford by the broken war-arrow, delays for negotiation about ransom with a hope that the Danes will not fight or at least that Athelstan's forces will have time to gather for a defense, an initial Danish sally stopped by a Viking force of tough and eager warriors allied with Athelstan, and finally the furious battle itself—including the use of a wedge of men to drive through the Danes, battle cries, and blows. The great victory banquet that follows is an occasion of celebration and grief. All are vividly described, and in the thick of the battle are Osmund and his friends, for the resolution of Osmund's personal dilemma is postponed in the face of public need.

There is a well-articulated interlacing of events; at the battle of Brunanburh Osmund is reunited with King Athelstan after an exile of three years, and the circumstances of his disappearance are soon to be revealed. Whistler uses several major elements in the chronicle account of Athelstan. The king's reign was darkened by an accusation that he was responsible for the drowning of his brother Edwin, who was seen as a threat to the throne. Whistler exonerates Athelstan by identifying the king's cupbearer, here called Orgar, as the culprit. Exposure of this traitor comes later at a London banquet, where the heathen Bragi-beaker (original of the Twelfth Night beaker at Yule celebrations) is presented and the betrothal of Osmund and Elfgiva is to be celebrated. When Orgar enters as cupbearer, festivity becomes an occasion of British justice. Athelstan, then, not only has a military triumph over the Danes but also gains the hearts of his people. The scene is highly dramatic, different warriors rising to accuse Orgar and to exonerate both the king and Osmund, who had accompanied Edwin on the fatal voyage and brought him to shore although he could not save the life of his foster brother. Thus the battle feast of Brunanburh is the occasion for final resolutions.

The fictional theme of the novel is the animosity between Osmund and Orgar, who constantly challenges and tries to kill the hero to prevent exposure of his treason. Orgar is proud, an aggressive villain who falsely claims property, makes night raids, takes a young woman hostage, hires murderers, and so on. He is the man of trust and responsibility who betrays, the dark side of loyalty. Osmund, moved by a Christian belief in forgiveness and respect for honor in Orgar's past, allows him to fight the battle of Brunanburh, a chance for death as a warrior rather than hanging as a murderer. Orgar's one noble action is at a crucial point in the fighting when the evil plotter helps Osmund. He subsequently flees, later tries to defame Osmund, and even accuses the king himself of killing Edwin. Osmund's integrity makes him acknowledge Orgar's assistance on the field of battle, while others make the case against the man who has tried to destroy him. Such nobility is amply rewarded by the king's favor, high office, and an appealing marriage.

Whistler is interested in the sea, and *Dragon Osmund* contains many fine passages about the rigors of sailing, the danger of a small boat, the terror of being cast overboard and struggling ashore, the practice of salvage with its correlative rivalry for gain. The hero's name comes from an exhilarating episode that provides a fine image. In the fury of a storm off the Wash, Osmund goes into the sea, as the decorative head breaks off from the Viking ship on which he is sailing. He rides the dragon into the shore and quickly is known as Dragon Osmund. Later the huge wooden device is used as a defense against attackers in a raid. Among the salvage is a chest that contains fine mail and a sword, Dragon-Fang, with a runic inscription that identifies it as a weapon of Osmund's family. This gift of Odin is reclaimed in the midst of the battle of Brunanburh when the god appears as an old warrior whose sword breaks Dragon-Fang. A mingling of pagan and Christian recalls the juxtaposition that occurs in *Beowulf,* which Whistler so eloquently evokes in *A Thane of Wessex.* Monasteries are burned and rebuilt, prayers offered, good priests serve; however, there are several dreams and visions, and second sight is respected.

The latter is the special gift of Lady Orvenna, whose role is counselor, and she is a woman greatly respected by Osmund, her son Aska who is his companion, and King Athelstan himself. A distinction of *Dragon Osmund* is its strong roles for women. The Lady Elfgiva is a good match for Osmund: she helps the exhausted hero ashore after his dragon ride in rough seas, and she escapes from Orgar by loosing the saddle girths so that he falls while she rides away bareback and spears a man who tries to stop her. This escape sequence is wonderful daring-do, especially thrilling for girl readers, who would empathize further when foster brother Aska teases her but says that the deed will be remembered in song. That she is niece of Thorfin, the great Viking chief, seems fitting. In another episode Elfgiva, who rows ably on the fens, follows a hawk and thus rescues Athelstan with practical expedients when his horse is stuck in the bog. Her reward is the king's gray falcon. Nevertheless, Elfgiva preserves a gentle femininity; she blushes, she encourages men before battle, giving Osmund her brooch to wear, and her vulnerability as a woman is clear.

Elfgiva thus attractively combines qualities of the powerful female warrior of Teutonic myth with the gentle and loving lady of chivalric romance, a model reflected in Edwardian ideals for women.

Osmund's appeal is continued in a sequel, *A Son of Odin: A Romance
of Old Norway* [1914], when an old warrior from Brunanburh recognizes Osmund's grandson, Leofric. The date is 995, when Olaf Tryggvasson
succeeded in Norway and the struggle between the old and the new faiths
began, but a Saxon atheling could claim descent from the old god Woden,
regarded as a deified hero, without jeopardizing Christian belief. Again
Whistler puts complex historical circumstances into a form readily accessible. Edwardian children reading these books would learn a great deal
about history, archeology, and the spread of Christian religion amid
lingering pagan survivals; they would also have models for behavior and
reasons to rejoice in their Anglo-Saxon heritage. Whistler is only one of a
dozen novelists who conditioned Edwardian youth to become Anglo-
Saxon heroes; there were all too soon many battles for them to fight as
"Happy Warriors."[46]

Conclusion

A notable part of nationalism in Britain (and the United States) in the
period before World War I is the enthusiasm for the Teutonic, of which
Anglo-Saxonism is a substantial part. Public events, as well as fiction,
celebrated the past. Historical pageants were popular in the early years of
the century—at Winchester, Bury St. Edmund's, Oxford, Colchester,
Warwick—and their opening episodes are Anglo-Saxon.[47] In the nineteenth century history was esteemed and cultivated, as the Victorian way
of hanging paintings, first prescribed by Sir Joshua Reynolds, shows. The
image is of hierarchy: historical and religious subjects have pride of place,
followed by landscapes, genre paintings, and still lifes, then life studies
and copies of Old Masters at the bottom. This Edwardian privileging of
history is an agreeable alternative to the dictum of Henry Ford that
"history is bunk."

The neglect of historical fiction in recent years is evident in the paucity
of analyses of it. Lukács's study holds a singular place, but Irving Howe's
1963 preface to the American edition of *The Historical Novel* noted that
"the work—indeed the very name—of Georg Lukács is barely known in
the United States." Twenty years later, Frederick Jameson's introduction
to a new edition of this study identified it as "perhaps the single monu-

mental realization of the varied program and promises of a Marxist and a dialectical literary criticism" (1). He adds that Lukács succeeds in "articulating the aesthetic text and its historical or 'social' context" by demonstrating "the coordination between an emergent new *form*, the historical novel, and an emergent new type of *consciousness*, a new sense of history and a new experience of historicity." Between these two editions Avram Fleishman wrote, in 1971, the first book-length study of *The English Historical Novel*, limiting himself to adult fiction but considering the period from Walter Scott to Virginia Woolf. I hope that I have indicated the possibilities and significance of juvenile historical fiction, at least for the study of Anglo-Saxonism among Victorians and Edwardians.[48] Reading such books shows a great deal about changes in appeal and values—and reminds us of a time when stirring stories and virtuous behavior were admired and encouraged so that hundreds of historical novels were deemed a good read, especially to form the character of the young.

This intention is well epitomized by a comment that introduces practical suggestions for reading *Stories of Legendary Heroes*, volume four in Eva March Tappan's ten-volume collection *The Children's Hour*: "Courage, generosity, politeness, consideration of the weak, and self-respect before the strong, a high sense of honor and a steadfast devotion to duty,—in a word, all that goes to make up true manliness, is found in these old tales without a hint of moralizing, but as a series of beautiful and noble pictures to be admired and remembered forever."[49] The first hero named is Beowulf; others included are Havelok and Siegfried. The "Suggestions for Further Reading" are all other children's versions of stories from medieval European literature. Of six recommended historical novels, three present versions of Anglo-Saxonism: Kingsley's *Hereward the Wake*, Bulwer-Lytton's *Harold: The Last of the Saxon Kings,* and Scott's *Ivanhoe*.

The effect of this large body of juvenile literature featuring Anglo-Saxon themes is difficult to assess. World War I began with the high sentiments evoked by legendary heroes and reiterated in historical novels that fostered Anglo-Saxonism, notably a definition of manliness as a warrior's strengths. In *The Great War and Modern Memory* Paul Fussell early gives a table of equivalents for an "essentially feudal language" and makes an eloquent case for "a literary war" that is now hard to imagine.[50] Fussell analyzes the significance of British literature at the Edwardian moment; he shows how romance quest and vocabulary were a means to describe World War I, to remember and mythologize the events that changed the perception of heroism and of the world. A concentration upon the books that children read shows repeatedly how crucial these early experiences were in forming their character as adults and confirms that a child's "temple of memory" remains throughout life.

Autobiographies that describe Edwardian childhoods are replete with references to reading that urged the heroic military ideal. The tie between literature and life is obvious in the dashing heroics of T. E. Lawrence, in many ways a reliving of boys' adventure stories. Lowell Thomas acknowledged this connection to juvenile literature in his book *With Lawrence in Arabia;* the title deploys the characteristic usage of G. A. Henty, the progenitor of historical novels that celebrated the British Empire and the Middle Ages, which seem remarkably similar in ideals and adventures for young heroes with pluck. One final example will illustrate the complexity of understanding the relation of literature to life and the impact of mature comprehension and historical change on minds influenced by their childhood reading. Siegfried Sassoon's writings are highly praised for his delineation of the brutality and futility of war; nevertheless, in his autobiography, *The Old Century and Seven More Years* (1938), he describes with some irony how as a child he "took . . . interest in the Danes, who . . . had done a lot of damage, of course, but Alfred . . . had converted them into being almost the same as the English, so after all they were all right." At that time he had no doubt that "God . . . wanted little boys like myself to grow up into splendid soldiers who won the Victoria Cross."[51] In *The Complete Memoirs of George Sherston* (1937), Sassoon gives a full account of the experience of World War I. He reiterates an initially exciting wish to be "heroic" and a subsequent recognition that feeling heroic was the only way that he could carry on after the experience of both the trenches and civilians in England. The values of a modern Anglo-Saxon soldier echo those of an earlier age; but Sassoon's vision is binary, varying "between happy warrior and bitter pacifist" (Fussell, pp. 90, 98).

J. B. Priestly has well argued the ambiguity and poignancy of nationalism, which he calls "honest regionalism tainted and manipulated by ambitious politicians."[52] Even after stripping away the illusions of which Sassoon speaks, Priestly can still see "something solid" in the idealism of Edwardian England, "that gleam of real gold in the wreck." He preserves that vision, again with some irony, while still sounding an elegiac note: "Had there been no Great War, we might have saved ourselves and the world" (289). One conclusion that follows from my survey of Edwardian juvenile literature is that historical novels that taught Anglo-Saxonism should be recognized as one key factor in the emergence of attitudes that produced, among many glorious achievements, a war of unparalleled proportions.

Notes

1. Humphrey Carpenter's *Secret Gardens: A Study of the Golden Age of Children's Literature* (London: George Allen & Unwin, 1985) is notable and characteristic in being limited to "classics "or "favorites" without taking into account many other books that were both popular and influential.

2. See Allen J. Frantzen, *King Alfred* (Boston: Twayne, 1986), pp. 2–3, 115. For a full account, see C. Lloyd Engström, *The Millenary of Alfred the Great, Warrior and Saint, Scholar and King* (London: Longmans, 1901).

3. Rev. Alfred J. Church, *A Mother in Israel* (London: Seeley & Co., 1901), p. 9. Church preached in St. Peter's Church, Ightham on Sunday, January 27, 1901, describing the grief of the "voices of civilized mankind" and "the almost inarticulate cry of humbler races, dim multitudes who, for all their ignorance, knew that this splendid Queen was yet the Great White Mother who loved and cared for her meanest and weakest children."

4. Useful current theoretical discussions are Paul Rich, "The Quest for Englishness," in *Victorian Values: Personalities and Perspectives in Nineteenth-Century Society,* ed. Gordon Marsden (London and New York: Longman, 1990), pp. 211–25, and Chris Waters, "Marxism, Medievalism, and Popular Culture," in *History and Community: Essays in Victorian Medievalism,* ed. Florence S. Boos (New York: Garland, 1992), pp. 137–68.

5. This analysis summarizes Georg Lukács, *The Historical Novel,* trans. Hannah and Stanley Mitchell (1938; rpt. with new introduction, Lincoln and London: University of Nebraska Press, 1962).

6. A notable case of the impact of a child's reading is C. S. Lewis's encounter with "Northernness" upon seeing *Siegfried and the Twilight of the Gods,* illustrated by Arthur Rackham. See *Surprised by Joy: The Shape of My Early Life* (New York: Harcourt, Brace & World, 1955), pp. 72–77, 165–66.

7. J. B. Priestly, *The Edwardians* (New York and Evanston: Harper & Row, 1970), p. 91.

8. Eleanor Bulley, *Great Briton for Little Britons* (London: Wells, Gardner, Darton & Co., 1904).

9. Revised third edition rewritten by Brian Alderson (Cambridge: Cambridge University Press, 1982). Darton's family were distinguished publishers of children's books, beginning about 1785 and continuing for 150 years, until 1928; the firm printed most of F. J. Harvey Darton's books.

10. Paul Hazard, *Books, Children and Men,* trans. Marguerite Mitchell (Boston: Horn Book, 1944), p. 128.

11. Quoted by historian Henry Steele Commager in his introduction to Cornelia Meigs, Anne Eaton, Elizabeth Nesbitt, and Ruth Hill Viguers, *A Critical History of Children's Literature* (New York: Macmillan, 1953), p. xv.

12. Rev. E. Gilliat, *God Save King Alfred* (London and New York: Macmillan, 1901), p. vi.

13. John Sutherland, *The Longman Companion to Victorian Fiction* (Harlow, Essex: Longman Group UK, 1988), p. 297.

14. Samuel Hynes, *The Edwardian Turn of Mind* (Princeton: Princeton University Press, 1968), pp. 34–35.

15. R. J. Q. Adams, "Field-Marshal Earl Roberts: Army and Empire," in *Edwardian Conservatism: Five Studies in Adaptation,* ed. J. A. Thompson and Arthur Mejia (London, New York, Sydney: Croom Helm, 1988), pp. 58–69, gives a more positive view of the experienced heroic commander's advocacy of Britain's need for military preparedness, including conscription.

16. At least one Edwardian admits that "the only history I can now remember" was the simplistic accounts in H. E. Marshall, *Our Island Story: A Child's History of England* (London: T. C. and E. C. Jack, 1905), illustrated by A. S. Forrest; see Joanna Smith, *Edwardian Children* (London: Hutchinson, 1983). The pink (British Empire) covered much of the map.

17. A few representative examples are E. P. Prentys, *Ivanhoe* (London: Harrap, 1913), Alice F. Jackson, *Ivanhoe Retold for Children* (London and Edinburgh: T. C. and E. C. Jack, n.d.), *The Story of Ivanhoe for Children* (London: A. and C. Black, 1899; facsimile, London: Lamboll House, 1986), Sir Walter Scott, *Ivanhoe: A Romance,* Windermere Series (Chicago and New York: Rand McNally & Co., 1918). S. R. Crockett, *Red Cap Adventures* (London: A. and C. Black, 1908) includes five "Tales Told from 'Ivanhoe.'"

18. Mark Girouard, *The Return to Camelot: Chivalry and the English Gentleman* (New Haven and London: Yale University Press, 1981), richly documents the impact of the ideals not only in literature and art but also in popular culture and education and in politics. Debra N. Mancoff's review in *History and Community: Essays in Victorian Medievalism* (New York: Garland Publishing, 1992), pp. 209–20, raises some counterarguments. See also her *The Arthurian Revival in Victorian Art* (New York: Garland Publishing, 1990).

19. George Wyndham was inspired to similar dress by his mother's reading from Malory's *Morte d'Arthur* and dreamed of "doing knightly deeds if they came his way." See J. A. Thompson, "George Wyndham: Toryism and Imperialism," in *Edwardian Conservatism,* ed. Thompson and Mejia, p. 109.

20. William Alexander Percy, *Lanterns on the Levee* (1941; rpt. with new introduction, Baton Rouge and London: Louisiana State University Press, 1973), recalls as part of his American experience of an Edwardian childhood that his senator father judged, like Moses, what fiction he wanted read; *Ivanhoe* was to replace Aunt Nana's romantic gem, and "no other novel-reading was to poison my mind until I had finished Scott, Bulwer-Lytton, Dickens, and a little Thackeray"

(56). William Percy later realized that his hardworking father would have preferred a life of golf, hunting, or "merely to lie on the deck of a sunny steamer with
a hundred detective novels, *Ivanhoe*, and *The Light of Asia*" (143). Novelist
Walker Percy recounts his own analysis of his uncle by using the analogue of
Richard and Saladin (xii).

21. In 1888 Edward Salmon published *Juvenile Literature As It Is* (London:
Henry J. Drane), which included a poll of children's preferences in reading. The
results of a poll of 790 boys placed Scott third (128 nominations), after Dickens
(223) and W. H. G. Kingston (179). Among favorite books, from a longer list,
Ivanhoe was fourth. Cited in Humphrey Carpenter and Mari Prichard, *The
Oxford Companion to Children's Literature* (Oxford and New York: Oxford
University Press, 1984), p. 285.

22. Avram Fleishman, *The English Historical Novel* (Baltimore: Johns Hopkins
University Press, 1971), p. 19. See also Clare A. Simmons, *Reversing the Con-
quest: History and Myth in Nineteenth-Century British Literature* (New Brunswick,
N.J.: Rutgers University Press, 1990), pp. 55–60.

23. M. I. Ebbutt, *Hero Myths and Legends of the British Race* (London:
Harrap, 1912); the preface is dated 1910.

24. H. Rider Haggard, *King Solomon's Mines* (1885; quotation from Puffin
Books edition, New York: Viking Penguin, 1958), pp. 13–14.

25. H. Rider Haggard, *Allan Quartermain* (1887; rpt. London: Hodder and
Stoughton, 1919), p. 319. This information is in a letter to George Curtis that
accompanies the manuscript sent by Sir Henry Curtis after Quartermain's death.
The novel contains a dedication: "I inscribe this book of adventure to my son
Arthur John Rider Haggard in the hope that in the days to come he, and many
other boys whom I shall never know, may in the acts and thoughts of Allan
Quartermain and his companions, as herein recorded, find something to help him
and them to reach to what, with Sir Henry Curtis, I hold to be the highest rank
whereto we can attain—the state and dignity of English gentlemen." Haggard
never spoke of his small son's death except to his friend Rudyard Kipling, whose
son was killed in World War I. Both men were part of empire, writers of fiction
that delighted and inspired many young people.

26. Katherine Dunlap Carter, *Educating by Story Telling* (London: Harrap,
1919), from the editor's introduction by Clark W. Hetherington.

27. Lukács, *Historical Novel*, pp. 19–63. Quotations are from Sir Walter
Scott, *Ivanhoe: A Romance* (New York: Bantam Classic, 1988).

28. Simmons, *Reversing the Conquest*, pp. 76–87. R. B. Dobson and J. Taylor,
Rymes of Robyn Hood (London: Heinemann, 1976), pp. 58–61, briefly mention
juvenile accounts. Enthusiasm in the United States was much fueled by Howard
Pyle's *The Merry Adventures of Robin Hood* (New York: Charles Scribner's Sons,
1883; facsimile, New York: Dover Publications, 1968), which is a coherent
narrative based on the ballads. Among Edwardian versions many are notable:
Henry Gilbert, *Robin Hood and the Men of the Greenwood*, illustrated by H. M.

Brock and Walter Crane (London, Edinburgh, New York, Toronto, Paris: Thomas Nelson and Sons, 1912); a simplified version appears as part of "In Days of Old Series" with only Crane illustrations (London: T. C. and E. C. Jack; New York: Frederick A. Stokes, [1915]); Jack also published H. E. Marshall's *Stories of Robin Hood,* illustrated by A. S. Forrest for the "Told to the Children" nursery series (London: T. C. and E. C. Jack and New York: E. P. Dutton, 1905); J. Walker McSpadden and Charles Wilson, *Robin Hood and His Merry Outlaws: Retold from the Old Ballads,* illustrated by N. C. Wyeth (London: Associated Newspapers, 1917); F. C. Tilney, *Robin Hood and His Merry Outlaws,* illustrated by Ione Railton (London: J. M. Dent; New York: E. P. Dutton, 1913); Dorothy King, *Greenwood Tales: Stories of Robin Hood and His Merry Men* is part of the "Stories Old and New" series (London and Glasgow: Blackie, [1920]). The Robin Hood stories are also in many collections of medieval narratives for children; for example, Andrew Lang's *The Book of Romance* (London, New York, Bombay: Longmans, Green, and Co., 1902), Ebbutt's *Hero-Myths and Legends of the British Race* (see note 22), Lewis Marsh, *Tales of the Homeland* (London: Henry Frowde, Hodder & Stoughton, [1910]), and American James Baldwin's *Fifty Famous Stories Retold,* 13th ed. (Shanghai: Commercial Press, 1917). (Throughout this essay I use square brackets to indicate the actual date of publications for which no date of publication appears on the title page.)

29. Sir Edward Bulwer-Lytton, *Harold: The Last of the Saxon Kings* (1848; London: Routledge's Railway Library, n.d.), p. 326.

30. Charles Kingsley, *Hereward the Wake: "Last of the English,"* quoted from the New Century Library edition (London, Edinburgh, Dublin, New York: Thomas Nelson, 1908), p. 4.

31. See Girouard, *The Return to Camelot,* pp. 129–44 and 232–48, on the moral value of games.

32. Douglas C. Stedman, *The Story of Hereward: The Champion of England,* quoted from the New Century Library edition (London, Edinburgh, Dublin, New York: Thomas Nelson, 1909), p. 246.

33. Douglas C. Stedman, *Captains and Kings: A Second Book of Stories from History* (London, Dublin, New York, Paris, Leipzig: Thomas Nelson and Sons, [1915]), p. 309.

34. Cited by Simmons, *Reversing the Conquest,* p. 175.

35. Eva March Tappan, *In the Days of Alfred the Great* (London: Hutchinson & Co., 1905), preface.

36. Eliza F. Pollard, *A Hero King: A Story of the Days of Alfred the Great* (London: S. W. Partridge & Co., n.d. [1898]).

37. Eliza F. Pollard, *A Saxon Maid* (London, Glasgow, Dublin: Blackie, n.d. [1901]).

38. G. A. Henty, *The Dragon and the Raven; or, the Days of King Alfred* (New York: A. L. Burt, n.d.), p. 3.

39. G. A. Henty, *Wulf the Saxon: A Story of the Norman Conquest* ([1894]; London, Glasgow, Bombay: Blackie, n.d.), preface.

40. Paul Creswick, *In Ælfred's Days: A Story of Saga the Dane* (London: Ernest Lister, 1900) and *Under the Black Raven: or Saga, the King from Out of the Sea* (New York: E. P. Dutton, 1901).

41. E. Nesbit and Doris Ashley, *Children's Stories from English History* (London: Raphael Tuck and Sons, [1914]), pp. 9–15, includes all the same stories. Agnes Sadlier, *Heroes of History in Words of One Syllable* (London: George Routledge and Sons, 1891), pp. 70–75, is more expository and factual, but refers to the same stories. Elizabeth O'Neill, *A Nursery History of England* (London: T. C. and E. C. Jack, [1912]), pp. 30–35, has four paragraphs and four colored illustrations for reading, Danish defeat, cakes, and conversion to Christianity. Hazel Phillips Hanshew, *My Book of Best Stories from History* (New York: Funk and Wagnalls, 1917), which stresses storytelling and uses examples from many lands, includes only the cakes (pp. 45–50). Hamilton Wright Mabie, *Heroes Every Child Should Know* (New York: Doubleday, Page & Co., 1906) is more analytical about the relation of history and legend. The Edwardian stories from history are, of course, a continuation of what was established in such Victorian books as *Picture Lives of Great Heroes* (London, Edinburgh, New York: Thomas Nelson and Son, [1884–85]), a fine volume that includes the stories of Alfred the Great, Robert the Bruce, Edward the Black Prince, and Columbus.

42. Whistler's publisher is either Blackie and Son or Thomas Nelson and Sons. Quotations are from *A Thane of Wessex* (London, Glasgow, Bombay: Blackie and Son Limited, 1896). The Boston Public Library, which includes all of his Anglo-Saxon historical novels, gives evidence of Whistler's reputation and influence in the United States.

43. There are several good Edwardian children's versions of *Beowulf*. Two attractively illustrated little books for very young children are H. E. Marshall, *Stories of Beowulf*, in the "Stories Told to the Children" series (London: T. C. and E. C. Jack, 1908), and Thomas Cartwright, *Brave Beowulf*, in a six-volume Every Child's Library (London: Heinemann, 1908) that also includes two versions— *Volsung Saga* and *Lay of the Nibelungs*—of the story of Sigurd the Dragon Slayer. Ernest J. B. Kirtlan, *The Story of Beowulf* (London: Charles H. Kelly, 1913) is a fuller translation suitable for juveniles, as is Zenaïde A. Ragozin, *Siegfried and Beowulf: Tales of the Heroic Ages* (New York and London: G. P. Putnam's Sons, 1899). The epic of the Anglo-Saxon race is in most of the important collections: H. A. Guerber, *Legends of the Middle Ages* (London: Harrap, 1896), and *The Book of the Epic: The World's Great Epics Told in Story* (London: Harrap, 1919), A. J. Church, *Heroes of Chivalry and Romance* (London: Seeley and Co., 1898), Hamilton Wright Mabie, *Legends Every Child Should Know* (New York: The Parents' Institute, Doubleday, Page & Co., 1906), E. M. Wilmot Buxton,

Britain Long Ago (London: Harrap, 1906), Eva March Tappan, *Old World Hero Stories* (Boston, New York, Chicago: Houghton Mifflin, 1911) and *Heroes of the Middle Ages* (London: Harrap, 1911), Joyce Pollard, *Stories from Old English Romance* (New York: Stokes, 1912).

44. William Canton, author of the popular *A Child's Book of Saints* (1898), issued in Everyman's Library (London: J. M. Dent; New York: E. P. Dutton, 1906), also wrote *A Child's Book of Warriors* (London: J. M. Dent and E. P. Dutton, [1912]), which includes several Anglo-Saxon saints.

45. See my *Legend of Guy of Warwick* (New York: Garland, 1996), pp. 65–68, 305–6.

46. The phrase is Wordsworth's; it is also the title of George Watts's famous painting, a version of which hangs in Eton chapel; copies were in many nurseries. Henry Newbolt's *The Book of the Happy Warrior* (London, New York, Bombay, Calcutta, Madras: Longmans, Green, and Co., 1917) combines retellings of heroic medieval stories with analysis of the public school spirit and patriotic urgings after years of fighting in World War I.

47. Just as the many vivid illustrations of Anglo-Saxon men, women, and children add much to the impact and interest of Edwardian children's books, so the postcards of the pageants, souvenir programs, and photographs of performers show redoubtable figures distinguished by contemporary conceptions of Anglo-Saxon times. The first episode for the Winchester Pageant of 1908, for example, is the Danes Camp, while the second episode of the Bury St. Edmund's Pageant of 1907 is the Martyrdom of King Edmund. Some photographs of the performers and properties used for the Anglo-Saxon hero of the Warwick Pageant of 1906 are among the illustrations of my *Legend of Guy of Warwick,* figs. 68, 69. Typically costumes show an influence of Pre-Raphaelite painting.

48. Another significant type of juvenile historical fiction was that published by religious printing houses. A few authors and titles indicate something of the range of this historical fiction about Anglo-Saxonism: Gertrude Hollis, *A Scholar of Lindisfarne: A Tale of the Time of S. Aidan* (London: Society for Promoting Christian Knowledge; New York: E. & J. B. Young, 1902); J. F. Hodgetts, *Harold, the Boy-Earl: A Story of Old England* (London: Religious Tract Society, [1888]). There is not space here to consider the many novels about Vikings, such as Ottilie A. Liliencrantz, *The Thrall of Leif the Lucky: A Story of Viking Days* (Chicago: A. C. McClurg & Co., 1902), and Captain Charles Young, *Harald: First of the Vikings* (London: Harrap, 1911). Such books were part of the development of Anglo-Saxon ideals for youth.

49. *A Guide to Good Reading with Practical Directions for the Use of "The Children's Hour" in the Home* (Boston: Houghton Mifflin, 1912), p. 26. The words are those of Walter Taylor Field. Eva March Tappan, *The Children's Hour* (Boston: Houghton, Mifflin and Co., 1907), is one of several American collections of stories—renderings of traditional literature—for children and juveniles.

50. Paul Fussell, *The Great War and Modern Memory* (London, Oxford, New York: Oxford University Press, 1975), pp. 21–22, 158.

51. Siegfried Sassoon, *The Old Century and Seven More Years* (London: Faber & Faber, 1938), pp. 49–51.

52. Priestly, *The Edwardians,* p. 254.

9. Appropriations
A Concept of Culture

John D. Niles

> Somewhere among us a stone is taking notes.
> —Charles Simic

A STONE AMONG US is taking notes? What good reading that will be! To date, not many people concerned with either the general study of the Middle Ages or the specific phenomenon of Anglo-Saxonism have taken a stone's-eye-view of their subject.[1] When most people think of the Middle Ages, they are likely to envision a grand sequence of kings and conquests, heroes and adventures, all unfolding providentially in the direction of a higher plane of being that culminates not far from their own time and place. History abhors a clod. There are advantages, however, to the move toward grassroots social history that is a feature of the historical writing of recent years.[2] In addition, as soon as one begins to regard the past as one aspect of a history of mentalities rather than as a sequence of noteworthy events,[3] one is led to a view of cultural processes as many-layered and potentially fissured rather than as progressing steadily according to some smoothly flowing teleological design. I will therefore ask for patience as I direct attention to an imagined case history, one that introduces a few suggestions concerning the dynamics of Anglo-Saxonism and of cultural change in general.

Suppose that a stone had been patiently taking notes in a single place over the past two thousand years. For us that may seem rather a while, but for a stone it might be no more than a few blinks of an eye, as it were. What place? Many might do for our purposes, but let me arbitrarily single out the valley of the river Taff, or Cwm Taff, to use the vale's more ancient name.

Today, as the Taff flows toward the Bristol Channel through the modern city of Cardiff, spilling down a channel that glaciers once scoured out from ancient highlands, it runs through the grounds of Cardiff Castle, passing just west of the castle gate. Let us imagine that our stone is now part of that castle, having been quarried from a point higher up the valley. Where in the castle is it? For the sake of its sense of self-importance, let us set it high in the castle wall. The stone is blessed, as stony blessings go. From its niche beneath the clock tower it now has a fine view toward the Norman keep and the castle's inner grounds.

The fortunes of this stone have not always been so blessed, however, for Cardiff has known the ups and downs of time. The castle's present walls and towers are largely the result of a major reconstruction undertaken by John Patrick Crichton-Stuart, third Marquess of Bute (1847–1900), who hired the architect John Burges to restore the estate in medieval style. Burges set about the task with dedication and wit. Working in collaboration with Lord Bute, whose interest in this project ran as deep as his purse (and whose purse ran as deep as the coalfields of South Wales), Burges constructed a set of rooms and towers, the interiors of which he decorated in magnificent arts-and-crafts style. The result was one of the epiphanies of nineteenth-century medievalism. To complete the effect, Lord Bute restored the Norman keep, drained its moat, and cleared and replanted the grounds.[4]

These, however, were not the first modern improvements on the site. To turn his grand scheme into a reality, Lord Bute not only had to rebuild the castle walls, which were discovered to have been built on top of Roman fortifications. In addition—and this was his major challenge—he had to integrate into his design the substantial country house into which the former castle had been converted. This house was the result of a sequence of building projects undertaken from the fifteenth to the eighteenth centuries. As Lord Bute, who knew what he liked, put it in a letter to his fiancée in 1872, the place had been "the victim of every barbarian since the Renaissance."[5]

In short, our stone has witnessed momentous changes. As a prelude to a larger argument, let me introduce the notes that our stone might have jotted down from time to time over the years.

Exhibit A: The Diary of a Stone

75 A.D. *Myn brain i!*[6] Quarried today. Stacked by the Taff like a load of fish. Big works in progress.

254 Hoisted to 20th tier of vallum and polished off—rather a nice job, I must say.

434 Legionnaires breaking camp, heading east. Things looking anxious.

786 *Dammo*! Took a fall. Heaps of rubbish above me.

1092 Big motte under construction; *beaucoup de monde ici*.

1184 A Welsh attack, I'm told. Some damage in my sector.

1645 Commotion overhead: King Charles to visit this week.

1778 Rain for a fortnight. Noise from construction above.

1867 Found at last, I've been found at last! They've set me out and refaced me. The new Lord has no end of schemes, they say.

1872 I've been given a place of honor in the clock tower![7] Mother, come see me now!

1875 The Marquess and Master John were up smoking today.[8] Peacocks, parrots, and incense.

1947 Castle under new management. No more pipe dreams, I fear.
. . .

Since a stone writes slowly I will leave off here, asking you to imagine that the diary yields as yet no further information as to how the stone enjoys being part of what is now a large civic museum with gardens.

This is well and fine, you may say. Playing with point of view can do no harm. But where does a history of this kind lead?

What the stone's story leads to is a different concept of cultural processes than most people who have concerned themselves with that subject have assumed.[9] While I cannot claim to have read all the authorities on a subject that, leaving biology aside, encompasses virtually everything that makes us human, still I have the impression that scholars have sometimes underestimated the power of individuals or groups to produce culture by selecting, organizing, and recasting its existing elements. Sociologists, for example, often rest content with analyzing synchronic patterns of culture without necessarily considering the ways in which these patterns have come into being over successive eras, sometimes via loops back into the past. While some anthropologists take a chronologically deep view of their subject, they tend to orient their discussion of cultural change around two key terms, *acculturation* and *assimilation,* that can account only partially for long-term impersonal processes. The first of these encourages a view of culture as something already formed, ready to be passed on from one group to another when people come into direct contact with one another. The second directs attention to the largely unselfconscious merging of races, institutions, and traditions. Neither concept foregrounds human agency. Neither leaves much room for discontinuities and reinventions, the jerks and starts of cultural evolution. These matters might be thought to fall under the purview of historians and literary scholars, who routinely address questions of tradition and individual talent; but not many scholars in these fields approach culture systematically, focusing on large anonymous processes as well as on singular events and achievements. Fewer still devote much attention to cultural ruptures and unconformities, as opposed to the achievements of a single era.

From the perspective advocated here, culture is chiefly produced through a complex series of purposeful appropriations either of the past or of someone's present property (whether material, linguistic, or intellectual in nature).[10] Whether these appropriations are the work of individuals acting in relative isolation or of groups acting in consort, the results of this activity tend to be expressive of an underlying ideology that is characteristic of a given time and place as well as of specific class interests, ethnic allegiances, and so on.

To *appropriate* something, literally, is to make it one's own property (from Latin *ad,* "to," plus *proprius,* "one's own"). While the word can be used in a neutral tone (as I am using it here), it more often bears a negative connotation. There is a mercenary motive lurking beneath its surface, an opportunistic vigilance, as is evident from the medieval use of the term *appropriation* to denote the transfer to a monastic house of the full receipts of a parish church.[11] The makers of Webster's dictionary make the forked character of the word explicit in their succinct definition: "*Appropriate,* v.t.: 1. to take for one's own or exclusive use; hence, 2. to steal."[12]

Stealing is a hard word, one that more often reflects the point of view of the taken-from than that of the taker. Still it denotes a practice that sometimes has its uses, in the cultural sphere at least. As T. S. Eliot remarked in his appreciation of playwright Philip Massinger, "Immature artists imitate; mature poets steal."[13]

The Anglo-Saxon period abounds with examples of what might be called "creative appropriation," as anyone who has studied that era will know. To take an example from the religious sphere: the history of the acceptance of Christianity by the people of Britain during the sixth and seventh centuries A.D. is often recounted as a tale of conquest. The heroes of Bede's *Ecclesiastical History* are the missionaries who came from Rome to save the pagan Saxons from their misguided ways. Bede was the first person to tell of these events as a heroic narrative played out against a providential view of history, and for some 1,250 years other historians have followed suit. But this is not the only way to tell the tale. One could also tell it from the point of view of Protestant reformers of the time of Queen Elizabeth I, for example. For Matthew Parker and John Foxe, if Bede was not a liar then he was at least mistaken, for the foundation of Christianity in England went back to Joseph of Arimathea. Pope Gregory the Great's missionaries had found Christians on the island and had corrupted them.[14] The same story could also be told from the perspective of members of a native British aristocracy who in late Roman times worshipped (let us say) their choice of Mithra, Isis, Jupiter, Christ, or sticks and stones; who then, during the troubled years of the sixth century, worshipped their choice of Christ, Woden, or sticks and stones; and who during the seventh century decided to restrict their worship to Christ.

Decided: the word is meant to denote a degree of agency on their part, a consciousness of actions to be taken after consideration of self-interest. It is precisely this agency that is effaced both by Bede's Roman neocolonial perspective and by the Protestant insistence on access to Christ unmediated by Rome. From a grassroots perspective, the conversion of the English was an act of appropriation of Christianity *by* the English, who were apparently able to preserve many of their time-honored customs (Eastertide, Yuletide, and Lammas celebrations, visits to holy wells, and autumn sacrifices of oxen, for example) while dedicating these activities to Christ or the saints. The shift from pagan rites to Christian rites was a pragmatic one that was influenced, surely, not only by theological concerns but also by the high prestige value of the new faith as was evidenced by books, icons, vestments, impressive masonry, overseas connections, and the like.[15]

By speaking of appropriations, by no means do I wish to negate originality as a major factor in the evolution of culture.[16] I wish only to refine somewhat what we mean by that term. Creative people will continue to shape the stuff of life into original patterns in defiance of any theory that would rule otherwise. If there is merit in the concept of appropriation that I am recommending, it is that through such a concept, even what appear to be new inventions can be seen to be new configurations of preexisting elements. One does not build a castle by inventing stones. One finds stones, and often good stones are to be had close to hand, whether dressed or as yet rough-hewn. People appropriate from what is available, taking what they want to make use of or what they are prepared to accept at a given moment. Whatever elements of past cultures they adopt, they transform, in accord with period-specific desires and circumstances.

No Things but in Ideas

If a historically informed concept of culture is to be found useful, it will have to elicit a widely shared recognition that it is capable of integrating beggars and kings, agriculture and industry, wrestling and soap powder[17] into a single field of vision with contours that are steady and capacious, so that what otherwise might appear as flux is revealed as meaningful connection. I have used Lord Bute's restoration of Cardiff Castle and Bede's story of the conversion of the English as two points of departure. Other examples could serve equally well: the change from Roman basilica to early Christian church, or from Roman villa to Benedictine monastery, or from medieval priory to Tudor country house, to cite three possibilities.[18] Or one could look at roads rather than buildings or estates. It is easy for motorists in the United Kingdom who drive the B6318 between Newcastle and Carlisle to overlook General Wade's eighteenth-century road, which lies either close beside or right beneath the modern road, hard by the Roman road that follows very much the same geographical contours, sometimes physically incorporated into the newer surfaces. And what is true of castles, churches, country houses, and roads is true of the physical landscape as well, with its ancient field boundaries that aerial photography has been able to reveal.[19]

"Our countryside is a palimpsest," Nora K. Chadwick remarked forty years ago.[20] Almost anywhere one looks in the British Isles, if one looks with care, one can perceive the traces of one or another act of appropriation whereby one civilization has superimposed itself upon others, drawing on preceding ones to further its own ends.

What is true of the lay of the land is equally true of verbal arts and social behavior, although here the traces of earlier forms are more challenging to discern. Moreover, what is true of the British Isles is by no means unique to those islands but can be perceived in almost any land that bears the marks of a long history of human habitation.

Could a full history of Anglo-Saxonism be written, it would read as the story of a series of appropriations of greater or lesser magnitude. In such a narrative, what would be of most significance would not be Anglo-Saxon England "as it was," whatever that lost object of desire may have been. Instead, it would be the *idea* of Anglo-Saxon England, as that idea has been formed, transformed, consigned to oblivion, or reconceived anew during every successive era since the time of the Anglo-Saxons themselves. Like the idea of Greece, which has been reconstituted again and again to serve various ideological interests,[21] the idea of early England has survived triumphantly because, like any symbolic construction, it has been able to convey forcefully a wide range of social meanings.

When we think of Anglo-Saxon England, as when we deploy practically any historical concept, we tend to picture something *out there,* in the past, that assiduous historical research can discover. We may flesh out that mental image by visualizing a particular land mass (Lowland Britain), by constructing a chronology of memorable dates (449, 597, 793, 899, 991, and 1066, for example), by naming a common language (English) as well as certain social institutions valued by most speakers of English (e.g., representative government, trial by jury, and the Christian Church), by invoking certain well-known personages and events (e.g., Hengist and Horsa, the Venerable Bede, St. Cuthbert, and King Alfred), and by calling to mind certain racial stereotypes or character traits (e.g., a race of fair-haired, fair-skinned people renowned for their bold manliness). At least these are some of the mental associations that authorities have invited us to adopt in the past, and we may be forgiven if we have come to take them for granted. But there is another way of considering the phrase *Anglo-Saxon England,* and that is as a creation of language. As such, the phrase is literally a figure of speech, one that has lent the concept that it denotes the semblance of solidity thanks to centuries of reiterated use.

It is this rhetorical trope to which I would like to call attention, for recognizing it as a trope leads to the discovery that as far as present-day people are concerned, Anglo-Saxon England is *nothing other than what it has been perceived to be* by historically grounded human beings, from the time of the Anglo-Saxons to the present moment. It is an idea, not a thing. It happens to be an important, dynamic, and sometimes contentious idea, for it served as an organizing principle of a kingdom for a number of generations before the Norman Conquest, just as in recent centuries it has served a foundational purpose for English-speaking peoples on five continents.

"Anglo-Saxon England is an idea, not a thing." A simple statement to make, but what a ruckus it can cause if spoken in the wrong company! It is hard to imagine the vehemence with which some professional Anglo-Saxonists resist this suggestion, not to mention some other people, most of them no part of the academic world, who take their Anglo-Saxon racial origins seriously. Such people do not like to think of Anglo-Saxon England as an idea—especially not as *their* idea. They continue to think of it as something to which their life or scholarly work is connected by almost tangible lines. To confirm the tensile strength of such lines they appeal to genealogies, genetics, archeology, the statements of reliable authorities, and any other evidence that comes to hand, unaware that the effect of all such efforts is only to tighten the web of mental inferences in which they and their personal orientations are suspended.

By calling Anglo-Saxon England an idea, then, I do not mean to deny its power. Quite the reverse. The power of ideas—their reality, in a sense that medieval philosophy understood—should never be underestimated. If Anglo-Saxon England is not out there but rather *in here*, as a feature of consciousness, then the process by which an idea of such magnitude came into being is worth knowing about. Here is where the tool that I have been honing has some use, for it is by a series of appropriations, beginning with the Anglo-Saxons themselves, that the idea of Anglo-Saxon England came into being and gained its later appeal.

The full story of that process would make for a long winter's tale. The essays included in the present volume tell fragments of the story, often in rich detail. Still, these are only episodes. No contributor to this volume takes an overview of the subject, nor is there any other book on hand that attempts to do so, although Allen Frantzen in *Desire for Origins* takes steps in that direction.[22] What still asks to be written is a narrative that will set forth the whole story: a book with a grand title like *The Invention of Anglo-Saxon England*.

Imagine such a book. It might include such chapters as the following.

Exhibit B: Prospectus for a Never-to-Be-Written Book

(1) "Anglo-Saxon Self-Fashioning." How a large number of the post-Roman inhabitants of the Isle of Britain began to think of themselves as a single people. How they fashioned their identity through selective appropriations from other cultures (Frankish, Scandinavian, Roman/Italian, Irish, Welsh, and others). How, using the resources of an advanced textual culture in both Latin and the vernacular, the West-Saxon kings established their hegemony over *Englalond* through selective appropriations from Northumbria, Mercia, and other regions.

(2) "The Norman Hiatus." How, with the passing of time, many inhabitants of Britain became complicitous with the project of effacing Anglo-Saxon England as a separate ethnic, cultural, or geopolitical entity, and how they came to cultivate an alternative idea of the British Isles as constituting one of the homelands of a far-flung Norman empire. How, with the fading of Norman power and the assimilation of the French-speaking aristocracy into the larger English stock, this second idea lost its cogency and the search for national origins resumed.

(3) "Renaissance Inventions of a National Past." How the idea of Anglo-Saxon England reemerged during Tudor and Stuart times, chiefly as a means of supporting accelerated national ambitions. How the idea was used to establish the validity of specific institutions in both Church and state, including the Church of England and a system of parliamentary rule based on suffrage for white male property owners. How Old English texts were first published and translated, with what aims and biases.

(4) "Anglo-Saxonism in the Empire and the United States." How the idea of Anglo-Saxon England continued to be cultivated in recent centuries as a means of promoting nationalism, imperialism, racialism, agrarianism, and democratic political institutions.[23] How the movement of English-speakers to various parts of the globe was represented in terms that replicated the Anglo-Saxons' own migration myth, thus anchoring colonial and postcolonial political configurations in a mythlike narrative of national origins.

(5) "Anglo-Saxonism in the Academy." How the modern canon of texts, people, and events relating to the Anglo-Saxon period was developed and confirmed, to reinforce what ideological ends. How the rise of scientific philology, with its emphasis on the Germanic origins of the English language, went hand in hand with political pan-Germanism, with what scholarly tensions and resistance. How Anglo-Saxon studies came to gain and then lose a central place in modern departments of English.

Well and fine, you may say again! A prospectus will do little harm as long as the book will not be written. For what author will be conversant with all the disciplines that would have to be mastered for its completion? In addition, what Anglo-Saxonist will undertake a book on a topic that is so volatile? Every year sees new turns in scholarly thought—new appropriative twists, one might say—concerning not only Anglo-Saxon England but also every one of the historical periods in which the idea of Anglo-Saxon England is embedded.

During the past twenty years or so, for example, we have seen the reputation of Æthelred the Unready rise rather substantially, in a move that undermines the myth of decadence that for many years had clouded the understanding of Anglo-Saxon England during the three generations or so preceding the Conquest.[24] The Conquest can now be seen as a trauma that could not well have been predicted, rather than as the fated outcome of some defect in the English themselves. In a parallel development, one that may have some relation to postwar Europe's movement toward economic unity, we have come to see the Vikings as vigorous contributors to a hybrid Anglo-Scandinavian civilization, not just as wreckers and pillagers.[25] Partly in consequence of this shift, we have learned to be skeptical of confident assertions of a pre-Viking date for *Beowulf*, with the heritage of pan-Germanic ideology and the jitteriness concerning Vikings that that early date implies.[26] Shaking off a thousand years of entrenched thinking, we have come to question the historical basis of the migration myth that the English have often told of themselves. Appreciative of the possible continuity of the present inhabitants of Britain with the peoples of prehistoric times, some scholars now are asking if the origins of Anglo-Saxon England owe more to the Germanization of a resident Romano-British population than to invasion from across the North Sea.[27] Perhaps most significantly of all: through research into the historical roots of current scholarship, we have begun to conceive of Anglo-Saxon England as a process, not just a thing, and we have

begun to see ourselves as part of the process we are studying, whether as
the recipients or the victims of prior scholarly investments.

Who can say what new appropriative impulses will transform Anglo-
Saxon studies in coming years? Who knows what the future of the past
will be? One guess is as good as another as long as it is aligned with the
prevailing wind. To help determine the direction of that wind, let me call
attention to the current afterlife of two figures. These are, first, the
leading saint of Anglo-Saxon England, St. Cuthbert, whom Bede and
other early biographers shaped into a durable icon of English spiritual
identity; and, second, a leader in both peace and war, the beloved King
Alfred the Great.

Exhibit C: The Lindisfarne Brooch

Not long ago, a visitor to the United Kingdom paused in a gift shop
to admire a fine handcrafted silver brooch, one in a series of silver
articles advertised under the name "Our Celtic Heritage." The
brooch featured designs adapted from an illuminated page of the
Lindisfarne Gospels. An accompanying printed card explained that
St. Cuthbert of Lindisfarne is particularly to be revered as the first
person to establish a refuge for eider ducks. The same card assured
prospective customers that the Christian symbols that feature promi-
nently in Hiberno-Saxon illuminated gospels are of pre-Christian
origin.

St. Cuthbert as environmentalist saint? Why not! Stranger appropriations have been known. From St. Francis's birds to St. Cuthbert's eider
ducks is an easy progression, it seems, and one that naturally suits the
current era.

Christian symbols that are of pagan origin? Again, why not? Some
Christian symbols do predate the Christian era; this is a claim that
archeology can confirm. But regardless of its truth value, the making of
such a claim in the context of marketing a line of jewelry is a small event
worth noticing. Through the act of calling attention to putative acts of
appropriation by early Christians, the jeweler is engaging in a second act
of cultural appropriation, one that points in a direction exactly contrary
to the first. If this new direction has commercial appeal, that fact should
come as no surprise given the present-day decline of the Church and
commodification of the Celt.

But there is more going on here than marketing. Christian symbols
that are really of pagan origin—ones that are part of "our Celtic heri-

tage," as it is called without further ado—lend weight to a pagan, pan-Celtic originary myth that has a potent appeal in some present circles. It is no coincidence that if one visits West Kennett long barrow in Wiltshire, not far from where these brooches are being sold, one is likely to find there the remains of freshly cut flowers, together with candlewax drippings beneath some smoke-stained sarcens. West Kennet, dating from c. 3000–2500 B.C., is one of the most impressive megalithic chambered tombs of Europe. No one is making money from the flowers left there. Undisturbed and almost unnoticed, they bear witness to the moonlit rites that are practiced by present-day pagans at such sites in honor of the goddess who once dwelled there, as her acolytes like to believe.[28]

The silver brooch exhibit, however, leads us tangentially away from Anglo-Saxon studies in the direction of Celtic Britain, nature conservancy, and goddess worship, three stars that form an ascendant constellation just as the star of Anglo-Saxon England seems to be entering partial eclipse. Let us then return to the emotional core of Anglo-Saxon studies through reference to King Alfred.

Exhibit D: "The Tomb of Alfred."

This exhibit consists of a blank page, a landscape with no objects, and an ear cocked to the wind.

I must apologize if the display is enigmatic. Despite King Alfred's fame as "the only king in our history who has been honoured with the epithet of Great,"[29] there exists no tomb to honor him. Apart from statues unveiled at Wantage in 1877 and Winchester in 1901, when Alfred's star reached its zenith,[30] there is no appropriate site where one can pay one's respects to a king who has variously been styled "England's darling," "lord of the harp and of the liberating spear," and "in effect the founder of the English monarchy."[31]

The absence of a tomb of Alfred will seem strange unless one examines his reputation within the context of the reception history of Anglo-Saxon England.

After his death on October 26, 899, Alfred was buried in the Old Minster, Winchester. Shortly after the foundation of the New Minster in Winchester, Edward the Elder had his father's bones translated to that impressive site in the heart of his expanding kingdom. There, as that kingdom established and confirmed its supremacy in the Isle of Britain, the bones remained for close to two hundred years. Not long after the Norman Conquest, they were removed to nearby Hyde Abbey to make

way for another major rebuilding project in Winchester that was designed to promote Norman prestige and authority. Nothing further is
known about Alfred's remains until the Reformation. Hyde Abbey was
then broken up, together with much else that pertained to an age that
was discovered to have outlived its usefulness. There the trail of evidence
gives out. The last words on the subject are those of Pollard Wriothesley,
an agent of King Henry VIII and Thomas Cromwell and a future chancellor of England. As Wriothesley wrote in 1538, reporting on his seizure of
Hyde Abbey's lands and silver altarpiece, "We intend both at Hyde and
at St. Mary's to sweep away all the rotten bones that be called relics,
which we may not omit lest it should be thought that we came more for
the treasure than for avoiding the abominations of idolatry."[32]

   In any event, it was natural for Alfred's remains to disappear, for by
this time, thanks to the creative historiography of Geoffrey of Monmouth,
a new non-Saxon origin had been established for the people and crown of
Britain.[33] The figure of Alfred had been lost somewhere in the wastes that
were said to have extended between the fabulous days of King Arthur
and the sturdy reigns of William the Conquerer and the Angevin kings.
The absence of a prominent tomb for Alfred confirmed, for those who
gave any thought to it, the nullity of his people and his reign. There was
no one to reproach for this act of effacement. After all, where there is no
corpse there is no crime.

   It took the efforts of scholars living some time after the stripping of the
altars to recover and refashion the idea of King Alfred. Additional
centuries passed before that idea, increasingly invested with racial and
national dignity, was given a place of honor in the histories of Britain. By
the time of Queen Victoria, Alfred had become a paragon of the German
race, of which the English were believed to be one offshoot. In him could
be seen the type of the English gentleman: warlike yet pious, undaunted
in danger, yet deeply philosophical when the course of events permitted
him to cultivate the life of the mind. Stones were on the move again! New
monuments were commissioned; sculptors, artists, poets, and playwrights
vied with one another in the service of Alfred and national pride. But the
full story of the apotheosis of that monarch is a tale for another time.

✠

Four exhibits are now on the table. Each one is a special case. What links
them, besides their common connection with Anglo-Saxonism? What are
the laws by which the process of appropriation operates?

At the risk of oversimplification, let me distinguish one by one five leading principles of appropriation, with the understanding that none of them governs any conduct whatsoever. Like Danish folklorist Axel Olrik's famous "laws of folk narrative"[34] or any other laws that have been thought to operate in the cultural sphere, these principles are wholly descriptive in character, not proscriptive.

1. *The Law of High Prestige.* People regularly appropriate from a culture that they view as superior or of higher prestige, at least in the specific area of appropriation. Thus Anglo-Saxon England borrowed importantly from Gaul and Italy but concealed its debts to the Welsh and the Picts. Koreans readily appropriate a western style of dress that is summed up by Guess jeans and Reebok tennis shoes, but Americans do not normally appropriate traditional Korean dress. They do appropriate Korean martial arts, however, together with uniforms dedicated to that purpose.

2. *The Law of Dead Meat.* Appropriation proceeds without substantial impediment when the source culture is dead, or nearly so. My figure of speech here is drawn from the culinary sphere. It is easier to carve beef when it is on a plate than when it is on the side of a living bull. Scotland and the tartan provide an example of the "dead meat" principle. Only after the Highlands were pacified and the clan system was crushed, several generations after the disaster at Culloden (1746), did there arise a vogue for plaids and sporrans. From that period to the present, a taste for tartan has remained in Edinburgh and other parts of the Lowlands, as well as among people of Scots ancestry living abroad.[35] But most Highlanders today have little use for such relics. Resistance to appropriation is one of the last resorts of the powerless, when few other means of asserting oneself remain.

3. *The Law of Adaptation.* Appropriation works selectively, and once something is appropriated it is never the same as it was before. People accept what they need, or what they think they need, at a given stage of development; and whatever they accept, they remake in their own image. The Saxons fashioned shield-walls in imitation of the Roman phalanx, but using round shields and omitting the refinements of the *testudo.* Henry VIII made cannonballs out of the lead that had been used to cover priory roofs.

4. *The Law of Vested Interest.* Appropriation is never disinterested, although it routinely claims to be so. It can be an efficient

means of expressing ideology or status, and sometimes it can challenge the status quo. In Germany of the Third Reich, for example, the Nazis' appropriation of the Grimms' collection of fairy tales into a kind of national Bible represented a repudiation of internationalism, a celebration of rural values, and a claim regarding the antiquity and value of native German traditions, hence the status of the German *Volk*.[36] Precisely because acts of appropriation are expressive of ideology and prestige, their constructed nature often remains invisible. They are taken to have a high truth value, for almost every appropriation denies its own factitiousness.

5. *The Law of Rivalry*. People vie with one another as to what to appropriate, group against group, generation against generation. Prestige is a subjective and hence a contentious thing. As civilizations rise and fall they provide ever new opportunities for cultural raiding. For some Englishmen, the Roman Empire is "nearer to us spiritually than our own country in the Middle Ages,"[37] but the nation did not agree when it chose to rebuild the Houses of Parliament in Perpendicular style rather than with a classical facade. The claim that there exists any "original" cultural site, the source of later appropriations but the beneficiary of none, is either deceit or an illusion.

These, then, are five "laws" that describe the customary dynamics of appropriation. There is nothing sacred about them, and no one should be shot for breaking them. Their adequacy as a means of describing any specific phenomena should always be tested, in the spirit that Raymond Williams recommends for all intellectual dealings: one that maintains an "alert, open and usually troubled recognition of specificity and complexity," a recognition that is "always, in a thousand instances, putting working generalizations and hypotheses under strain."[38]

Standing on Solid Mental Ground

Two large questions still need posing. First, what are the chief aims or ends of appropriation? And second, what are the chief means by which it operates?

Mindful of Williams's words, and fearful also of Blake's remark that "to Generalize is to be an Idiot,"[39] I would answer the first question as follows: *The chief unstated aim of appropriation is to shape the ground on which the historical present rests.*

This claim is worth contemplating. What is the historical present, and what is the ground on which it rests? Here I would enlist the aid of R. G. Collingwood, whose words on the subject are both precise and important although half a century old. In his study *The Idea of History,* published posthumously in 1946, Collingwood makes a remark that has some relevance to the concept of Anglo-Saxonism: "Since the historical present includes in itself its own past, the real ground on which the whole rests, namely the past out of which it has grown, is not outside it but is included within it."[40]

To paraphrase Collingwood, the historical present is nothing other than our present consciousness, insofar as we are aware that we are beings whose identity has evolved over time. The ground on which this consciousness rests is of course the past. This is not a past that is *out there* in some sense, however. It is a past that now exists only within us as part of our present awareness.

The chief aim of the present essay is to add to Collingwood's point an additional claim concerning how the historical present is chiefly formed: namely, through endlessly varied acts of appropriation, the effects of which are to confirm a group's sense of identity and status, to reinforce its loyalties, values, and beliefs, and to liberate its capacity for powerful action.

To prepare for the second question, the question of means, I have already introduced examples so various as to suggest that the means by which acts of appropriation take place are practically limitless. Still, it may be useful to call attention to a few means of appropriation that have not yet been mentioned.

Through the power of names, according to the Book of Genesis, Adam established mastery over the beasts. Never since then have names ceased to be acts that assert power over the things named and thus exert influence over a world of larger relations. The land that Geoffrey of Monmouth celebrates in his twelfth-century *History of the Kings of Britain* no longer bears the false name *Englalond.* It has cast off the identity that Anglo-Saxon intruders imposed upon it and has become that more glorious and ancient thing *Britannia,* the land of the Britons, the descendants of the Trojan refugee Brutus. Through names, the aura of King Arthur (so strikingly invoked in the Galfridian calumny of the Anglo-Saxon past) is appropriated still at the present time, to judge from Mobil Oil North Sea oil rigs christened Avalon, Camelot, Excaliber, and Guinevere. By such means the drilling of offshore oil is given a patriotic mystique, as if twentieth-century technological adventures were fulfilling

long-deferred dreams and portents. Here as in other instances I have
noted, the assertion of power through names takes on a propagandistic
aspect as it serves material interests.

Through genealogy—"an ideological backbone of the social framework," in the words of Jan Vansina[41]—the past is made to yield a linear
pattern that culminates providentially in the historical present. If a noble
point of origin is not at hand, it can always be discerned. Henry Tudor's
claim of descent from Cadwallader—the last British king before the
Saxon hegemony, according to Geoffrey of Monmouth—was one weapon
in the genealogical wars of the fifteenth and sixteenth centuries, for it
legitimized Tudor claims to the united throne of England and Wales.[42]
The step-by-step extension of the West-Saxon royal line back in time
from Æthelwulf to Adam, as can be traced in the grandiose genealogies
attributed to West-Saxon monarchs from the late ninth century on,
provides another example of genealogical creativity.[43] With each extension of this pseudogenealogy, the prestige of the West-Saxon kings was
enhanced. Their authority as rulers of *Englalond,* not just of Wessex, was
made manifest, and the ground on which the historical present rested was
tilted first northeast to Scandinavia (via Scyld, Geat, and other legendary
northern kings) and then southeast, in the direction of the Holy Land.

Through translation, in the root sense of the word (from Latin *transferre,*
"to carry across"), a saint's bones are transported from one resting place
to another. The aura of the holy thus accrues to the new place. St.
Oswald's head and right arm are translated from Northumbria to
Gloucester; then again, somewhat later, they are brought from Gloucester
to the Old Minster at Winchester. It is an itinerary that mirrors step by
step a shift in political power from Northumbria to Wessex. Also through
translation, in the usual current sense of that word (once metaphorical,
now literal), a statement or book made in one language is rendered into a
different language. The power that is associated with that verbal artifact
is thereby made available at the new site. Sometimes the work of verbal
translation parallels the traffic in body parts. Bede writes a Latin life of
St. Oswald as part of his *Ecclesiastical History* (Book 3, chaps. 1–13),
and in time, once Oswald's relics have found a more southerly resting
place, Ælfric translates Bede's life of Oswald into his own English, not
word for word but freely expanding upon Bede's Latin in a limpid prose
that mimics the rhythms of verse. The story is thereby nationalized—that
is, made accessible to the English people as a whole.[44] Translation can
easily merge into adaptation, as it does here, or into imitation, as when

Asser, looking to write an official biography of King Alfred, does so with the model of Einhard's *Life of Charlemagne* in hand, thereby endowing that king of Wessex with an antique, quasi-imperial aura.

Through iconography and the display of visual images more generally, the course of history is confirmed, beliefs and values are reinforced, and status and allegiances are made clear. The place of the British Empire as successor to Rome finds expression in the figure of a seated, sceptered Britannia that was depicted on the old British penny, a replica of the personified figure of a triumphant Roma that the Emperor Nero depicted on the reverse of a coin issued after the city of Rome was rebuilt following the great fire of 64 A.D. Imperial ambitions were here given currency in an image that could be held in the palm of the hand. Tombs, statues, paintings, and monuments of all description lend solid physical form—and hence a high truth value—to whatever figures and events a given people cares to consider originary. The elaborate tomb of Geoffrey Chaucer that was erected in Westminster Abbey in 1556 announces a strong point of origin for an English national literature, much as Lord Bute's luxurious Chaucer Room, located near the summit of one of the towers of Cardiff Castle, pays homage to one of the high gods of Victorian medievalism. Wherever we look, it seems, our eyes meet the gaze of the dead who have been found memorable, and these managed splendors ensure that key elements of a people's past retain their foundational authority.

By extension, through historical dramas that function as a kind of animated iconography, audiences watch while designated people enact key moments from the past and keep those moments before us in visually impressive forms. The power of historical drama to encode ideology is enhanced when it is acted out in sites that themselves recreate an historical period, hence the importance of the major current project to restore the Globe Theater on the south bank of the Thames.[45] "Living history" exhibits illustrate the same principle. At the popular interactive historical site at Plymouth Plantation, Massachusetts, tourists are invited to imagine themselves holding conversations with the inhabitants of an English colonial settlement at a crucial originary moment for the United States. Those who visit such sites can come away impressed by their personal participation in the past, so to speak. "Seeing is believing," the saying goes. Since participatory dramas allow room not only for seeing but also for tasting, smelling, hearing, and touching, their power to promote ideology is enhanced.

This is a mere sampling of the myriad ways in which appropriations take place. The principle underlying each example is the same: people appropriate what they will, from wherever they can get it, as part of an effort—whether conscious or unconscious, implicit or explicit, successful or unsuccessful—to shape the ground on which the historical present lies.

The main question that is thus worth asking about any historical claim is not "Is it true?" but rather "What does it mean?"[46] This question of meaning, in turn, usually resolves into one of self-interest: "Who is appropriating what, when, where, how, to whose advantage?"

In a sense, despite all one's passion for accuracy in sifting through the annals of the past, it no longer matters what "really happened" in history. What's done is done. The victors of former struggles are now wrapped by the same earth that covers their victims. What does matter greatly is *what people believe* happened in history, *what they say* happened, for such beliefs and claims can have a passionate relation to rivalries of which the outcome is still in doubt. What does it mean for people to hold certain beliefs about the past, to make specific claims about it, to go out of their way to assert a direct link to it, or to be outraged by someone else's skewed version of it? These questions are always to be asked, for they may yield timely answers.

Let me then sum up what may have seemed at some points a circuitous argument.

By making a case for appropriation as a controlling element in the production of culture, I have wished first of all to develop an intellectual tool that can be used to make good sense of the phenomenon of Anglo-Saxonism. By "making good sense" of Anglo-Saxonism, what I mean is showing it to be a coherent phenomenon, one that is aligned with both the pressures and pulls of specific historical eras and the habits of cultural change in general.

Additionally, I have wished to make sense of the chronologically deep layering of human civilizations that is such a striking feature of the landscape of the British Isles. There, as in some other regions of the world, imposing records of civilization date back six thousand years, while traces of prior human habitation can be carbon dated to hundreds of thousands of years before that. The peoples who left behind this archeological record were not necessarily linked to one another by unbroken lines of tradition or descent. In archeology, as in geology, an unconformity may separate one stratum from the next. Still, every civilization has built on what it has found already in place as well as what it could invent or borrow from outside sources. While few traditions can be traced back in an unbroken sequence over more than a few centuries—certainly the tradition of Anglo-Saxon studies cannot be—never has there been an era when people have not made massive appropriations of the past.

The importance of any historical period lies in its complex relation to other periods, emphatically including our own. A continuing sense of the presentness of Anglo-Saxon England can do wonders toward making us aware of our own place amid the discontinuities and effacements that form the greater part of history. Through such self-consciousness we can discern the lay of the historical ground on which we stand, the means by which other people have shaped that ground, and the ways in which we continue to inhabit it today. At the least, we can be mindful of what Carlo Ginzburg has called the "historical mutilations" of which "we ourselves are the victims."[47]

This point is reinforced when we become aware of the silences that surround us, the legacies that have been lifted from our grasp. For every stone that tells a story, another holds its tongue. Whole civilizations have disappeared like smoke, sometimes to emerge anew to the eyes of human-kind and sometimes to remain effaced. Aerial photographs reveal crop marks that inscribe on the earth, with a draftsman's accuracy, the foundations of houses that have left not a single trace for strollers to stumble on. If you cock your ear, you hear voices on the wind. Whose voices? Why care? One person does not care. Others want to savor even the silences that are woven into the fabric of which they are made.

Sooner or later, a time comes in the life of many people when they feel they must lighten the burden of their education, discarding other people's stories in favor of their own. When such moments arrive, then one task that presents itself is to search out elements of past eras that have long been ignored or forgotten. Like stones that have tumbled in a heap, buried with shards and dung, the elements of past civilizations may be waiting patiently for someone with sufficient clarity of vision to discern their features and mark out their possible use. Each generation, with greater or less intensity, experiences the same need of anchoring itself by discovering a significant past and charging that past with ideals it can live by. This is the main function of the social language we call *Anglo-Saxonism*: that over the years, in conjunction with other discourses about other places and times, it has permitted people of many different backgrounds and persuasions to define their place in a continuing audacious human experiment.

If you should have difficulty sifting through the rubble of past ages, reading its shards and detecting its silences—never mind. Somewhere a stone has taken notes. But read the notes with care. As Simic has said, "My stones will not sing the song yours are singing."[48]

The beauty of the past is that it is never the same thing twice. Anglo-Saxon England confirms the truth of that maxim as clearly as does any other historical concept that has been formed by the imagination of humankind.

Notes

1. The epigraph is from Charles Simic's book of poems *Somewhere Among Us a Stone Is Taking Notes* (San Francisco: Kayak, 1969).

By *Anglo-Saxonism* I refer to attempts to create an Anglo-Saxon identity or to delineate the Anglo-Saxon past. The Anglo-Saxons themselves (or people who thought of themselves as English, at any rate) were the first people to practice Anglo-Saxonism, and the practice has continued at least intermittently up to the present day. Anglo-Saxonism has tended to gain intellectual solidity and moral authority as the ideological counterpart of Orientalism (that is, attempts by westerners to delineate the exotic East), as Allen J. Frantzen has pointed out in *Desire for Origins: New Language, Old English, and Teaching the Tradition* (New Brunswick, N.J.: Rutgers University Press, 1990), pp. 27–61, in a chapter that takes some of its inspiration from Edward Said's *Orientalism* (New York: Pantheon, 1978). Both Anglo-Saxonism and Orientalism often involve an antiquarian element, and both have regularly been exercises in values, status, sovereignty, and power.

2. In France, this move is indelibly associated with the post-war *Annales* school of historiography represented by such scholars as Fernand Braudel and Jacques Le Goff; for discussion of this work in its wider intellectual context see Stuart Clark, "The *Annales* Historians," in *The Return of Grand Theory in the Human Sciences,* ed. Quentin Skinner (Cambridge: Cambridge University Press, 1985), pp. 177–98. Celebrated recent gestures in this direction include Emmanuel Le Roy Ladurie, *Montaillou,* trans. Barbara Bray (New York: G. Braziller, 1978), and Carlo Ginzburg, *The Cheese and the Worms: The Cosmos of a Sixteenth-Century Miller,* trans. John and Anne Tedeschi (Baltimore: Johns Hopkins University Press, 1980). The general turn away from actor- and event-centered narrative history is underscored in such an anthology as Philippe Ariès and Georges Duby, gen. eds., *A History of Private Life,* 5 vols. (Cambridge: Harvard University Press, 1987–1991). A recent collection of essays edited by Allen J. Frantzen and Douglas Moffat, *The Work of Work: Servitude, Slavery, and Labor in Medieval England* (Glasgow: Cruithne, 1994), seeks to redress the "top-down" view of history whereby great men (and, more rarely, great women) are celebrated while social underclasses remain dispossessed and voiceless.

3. For a succinct orientation to the concept of *mentalité* seen in relation to English "mentality," with cautionary remarks on prospects and pitfalls in the history of mentalities, see Jacques Le Goff, "Mentalities: A History of Ambiguities," in *Constructing the Past: Essays in Historical Methodology,* ed. Jacques Le Goff and Pierre Nora (Cambridge: Harvard University Press, 1974), pp. 166–80. It is important to note that my own discussion of "mentalities" refers not just to the historical study of the thinking of past eras but also to the historical study of the place the past has taken in the thinking of successive eras.

4. J. Mordaunt Crook discusses the partnership of Burges and Lord Bute in chap. 6 of his *William Burges and the High Victorian Dream* (Chicago: University of Chicago Press, 1981). A brief but useful guidebook to Cardiff Castle has been published by Cardiff City Council (Cardiff: Westdale Press, n.d.). The third Marquess of Bute came into his fortune at age 21. Well traveled, and both devout and intellectual to a degree that was incomprehensible to most of his contemporaries, he was an ardent convert to Catholicism and medievalism and turned immediately to the project of rebuilding Cardiff Castle and nearby Castle Coch. There is a memoir by David Hunter Blair, *John Patrick, Third Marquess of Bute, K.T.* (London: J. Murray, 1921).

5. Crook, *William Burges,* p. 267.

6. A mild Welsh epithet, equivalent to "My word!"

7. One of Burges's masterworks, the clock tower is seven stories high. Its interiors are decorated with sculptures, inlays, and paintings depicting the signs of the zodiac, figures of the four seasons and the four elements, alchemical symbols and designs, characters drawn from Greek, Roman, and Old Norse mythology, and details modeled after medieval Italian, French, and Arab prototypes. One contemporary reviewer found the ensemble "truly fearful and wonderful"; other reviewers were at a loss how to respond (Crook, *William Burges,* p. 266).

8. The Marquess's fondness for opium was one of the characteristic vices of his time.

9. Although the phrase *concept of culture* is a pretentious one that may seem redolent of a grand theory that will serve as yet another impediment to knowledge, I shall use it for lack of a more exact term, with the understanding that what is hoped for is not so much a theory as a tool for understanding the mechanisms by which culture is produced. Theories are always with us; tools can be used for a specific task, then set aside for a while. For discussion of current controversies regarding the role of theory in humanistic studies, see Skinner, ed., *The Return of Grand Theory.* Two other debts are worth noting here. One is to Clifford Geertz, who has described deftly (although with few particulars) how "man has created himself" as a cultural artifact over time; see in particular his essay "The Impact of the Concept of Culture on the Concept of Mind," rpt. in his *The Interpretation of Cultures* (New York: Basic Books, 1973), pp. 33–54. Another is to Raymond Williams, whose many writings explore literature as one part of a whole system

of symbolic expression that evolves through the principles of reproduction. As for the term *culture,* I know of no more pointed guide to its complex range of meanings and associations than is offered by Williams in *Keywords: A Vocabulary of Culture and Society,* 2d ed. (New York: Oxford University Press, 1983), pp. 87–93; see further his short book *Culture* (London: Fontana, 1981). I use the term to refer to the whole set of symbolic representations and patterns of behavior in a society.

10. My perspective now departs from that of the stone, of course. The stone sees only the most important social and political changes, with no concept of how anything is connected to anything else. What is more, it has a biased view of the world, as it only takes note of those things that directly affect it. It has a vague sense of being either appropriated or neglected, but since it possesses only the most rudimentary historical consciousness, it fails to perceive what the large movements are that exert their influence on local events. This much said, it is also necessary to note that those people who lift stones into new configurations, like Lord Bute and his architects and masons, also often lack full understanding of those large movements in which their volition or employment plays a part.

11. Colin Platt, *The Abbeys and Priories of Medieval England* (New York: Fordham University Press, 1984), p. xiv.

12. *Webster's New World Dictionary of the American Language* (Cleveland: World Publishing Co., 1960), p. 72.

13. *Selected Prose of T. S. Eliot,* ed. Frank Kermode (New York: Harcourt Brace Jovanovich, 1975), p. 153. I have heard similar remarks attributed to Ezra Pound and Lionel Trilling.

14. See F. J. Levy, *Tudor Historical Thought* (San Marino, Calif.: Huntington Library, 1967), pp. 110–12.

15. Similarly, Tacitus (*Agricola* 21) speaks favorably of the Roman practice of building temples, public squares, and good houses so that barbaric tribesmen will more willingly embrace *Romanitas.*

16. Many examples of striking originality are cited, for example, in the essays brought together in Eric Hobsbawm and Terence Ranger, eds., *The Invention of Tradition* (Cambridge: Cambridge University Press, 1983). Hobsbawm notes that even invented traditions usually have a strong link to the past (5).

17. I draw here from Roland Barthes, whose *Mythologies* (Paris: Éditions du Seuil, 1957) established his reputation as the pop artist of the French intellectual scene.

18. A set of examples drawn from the history of the country house could show how the stones of specific monastic sites were incorporated into Tudor "power houses" like Burghley House, Northamptonshire, or Wilton House, Wiltshire, that were constructed in the period following the Dissolution. Examples of Tudor appropriations of monastic sites are presented by David Knowles, *Bare Ruined Choirs* (Cambridge: Cambridge University Press, 1959), pp. 266–73; Colin Platt,

Medieval England: A Social History and Archaeology from the Conquest to 1600 A.D. (New York: Charles Scribner's Sons, 1978), pp. 209–24; Platt, *Abbeys and Priories,* pp. 209–41; and David Crossley, *Post-Medieval Archaeology in Britain* (London: Leicester University Press, 1990), pp. 53–56.

19. See the spectacular Cambridge University aerial photographs on display in Richard Muir, *History from the Air* (London: M. Joseph, 1983), esp. pp. 55–81.

20. H. Munro Chadwick, *The Study of Anglo-Saxon,* 2d ed., rev. Nora K. Chadwick (Cambridge: Heffer, 1955), p. xi.

21. Michael Herzfeld, *Ours Once More: Folklore, Ideology, and the Making of Modern Greece* (New York: Pella Publishing, 1986).

22. Frantzen, in *Desire for Origins,* discusses many points of interest cited in the present "prospectus" while critiquing the disinterested pose of modern Anglo-Saxon scholarship. His book develops the argument he raises in an essay (coauthored with Charles L. Venegoni) titled "The Desire for Origins: An Archaeology of Anglo-Saxon Studies," *Style* 20 (1986): 142–56, to the effect that Anglo-Saxon England is an idea created by scholarship about Anglo-Saxon England in the image of scholars and their interests. Other, less controversial approaches to Anglo-Saxonism are taken in four recent books: Reginald Horsman, *Race and Manifest Destiny: The Origins of American Racial Anglo-Saxonism* (Cambridge: Harvard University Press, 1981); Hugh A. MacDougall, *Racial Myth in English History: Trojans, Teutons, and Anglo-Saxons* (Montreal: Harvest House; Hanover, N.H.: University Press of New England, 1982); Clare A. Simmons, *Reversing the Conquest: History and Myth in Nineteenth-Century British Literature* (New Brunswick, N.J.: Rutgers University Press, 1990); and *Anglo-Saxon Scholarship: The First Three Centuries,* ed. Carl T. Berkhout and Milton McC. Gatch (Boston: G. K. Hall, 1982). Horsman explores the intellectual basis of some pernicious aspects of nineteenth-century American racialism; MacDougall analyzes the postmedieval "history wars" that pitted the theory of the Trojan origins of the English people against the ascendant rival theory of their Anglo-Saxon origins; and Simmons studies the emergence of a strong sense of Anglo-Saxon resistance to Norman tyranny (hence Germanic as opposed to Gallic cultural allegiance) in England of the Victorian era. Concentration in the Berkhout/Gatch collection is on pre-nineteenth-century antiquarian scholarship rather than on ideological issues that extend into recent times.

23. Following Horsman, I use the term *racialism* (rather than *racism,* which often denotes mere personal bigotry) to denote distinctions based upon intellectual theories of racial superiority.

24. On the reputation of this king see David Hill, ed., *Ethelred the Unready: Papers from the Millenary Conference,* British Archaeological Reports, British Series, 59 (Oxford, 1978), and note further Theodore M. Andersson, "The Viking Policy of Ethelred the Unready," in *Anglo-Scandinavian England: Norse-English Relations in the Period before the Conquest,* ed. John D. Niles and Mark

Amodio (Lanham, Md.: University Press of America, 1989), pp. 1–11. By "myth of decadence," I mean to refer to the *ante hoc ergo propter hoc* principle whereby it is thought that since a land is conquered, it must previously have been corrupt.

25. Worth singling out among a spate of revisionist publications on the Vikings is James Graham-Campbell and Dafydd Kidd, eds., *The Vikings* (London: British Museum Publications, 1980), published on the occasion of a major exhibit of Viking artifacts at the British Museum.

26. See Colin Chase, ed., *The Dating of Beowulf* (Toronto: University of Toronto Press, 1981). I have reiterated a case for a relatively late dating of that poem in "Locating *Beowulf* in Literary History," *Exemplaria* 5 (1993): 79–109, with references to recent scholarship.

27. On the cultural centrality of this myth see Nicholas Howe, *Migration and Myth-Making in Anglo-Saxon England* (New Haven: Yale University Press, 1989). On its doubtful truth value see Richard Hodges, *The Anglo-Saxon Achievement* (Ithaca: Cornell University Press, 1989). The theory that the Anglo-Saxon kingdoms came into being chiefly through a process of Germanization of the inhabitants of Britain, rather than chiefly through conquest and migration, has its counterpart in the theory espoused by Martin Millett, *The Romanization of Britain: An Essay in Archaeological Interpretation* (Cambridge: Cambridge University Press, 1990), that still earlier, the Iron Age inhabitants of Britain had embraced *Romanitas* "to assert, project and maintain their social status" (212). Both Hodges and Millett speak for the stones, as it were.

28. Ronald Hutton, *The Pagan Religions of the Ancient British Isles: Their Nature and Legacy* (Oxford: Blackwell, 1991), pp. 284–341, offers a review of modern survivals and revivals of paganism, including witchcraft and goddess worship. For up-to-date information and insights bearing on neopaganism, see "Contemporary and New Age Religions in the British Isles," ed. Brian Bocking and Marion Bowman, a special issue of *Religion Today* 9, no. 3 (summer 1994).

29. John Cannon and Ralph Griffiths, *The Oxford Illustrated History of the British Monarchy* (Oxford: Oxford University Press, 1988), p. 31. Although endlessly repeated, the claim is a false one. This makes it more interesting. Cnut (Danish Knut, English Canute) is also commonly called "the Great," and even Cannon and Griffiths honor him with that surname (86). Apparently such a contradiction is supposed to be invisible. Cnut was an English king who did not enjoy the distinction of being of English birth, and he thus has a way of vanishing.

30. On the cult of King Alfred, see the introduction to *Alfred the Great: Asser's 'Life of King Alfred' and Other Contemporary Sources,* trans. Simon Keynes and Michael Lapidge (Harmondsworth: Penguin, 1983), pp. 44–48, and Simmons, *Reversing the Conquest,* pp. 25–41, 52–53, 185–91, passim.

31. The pet name *Englene durlyng* appears in the thirteenth-century "Proverbs of Alfred." Wordsworth praised Alfred in "Ecclesiatical Sonnet XXVI." The third quotation is from Antonia Fraser's introduction to Douglas Woodruff's *The*

Life and Times of Alfred the Great (London: Weidenfeld and Nicolson, 1974), p. 7. No comment should be needed on the wishful thinking that is involved in this last claim.

32. Alfred Bowker, *The King Alfred Millenary: A Record of the Proceedings of the National Commemoration* (London: Macmillan, 1902), p. 56. Were some of these rotten bones Alfred's, or had his remains already been lost, unmarked? It is impossible to tell. To judge from the reference to "idolatry," Cromwell's men thought that the "relics" pertained to putative saints, not kings, whatever they were in fact.

33. See McDougall, *Racial Myth in English History,* pp. 7–17, and note further my essay "The Wasteland of Loegria: Geoffrey of Monmouth's Reinvention of the Anglo-Saxon Past," to appear in *Reinventing the Middle Ages and Renaissance: Constructions of the Medieval and Early Modern Periods,* ed. William Gentrup (Turnhout, Belgium: Brepols, forthcoming).

34. Axel Olrik, "Epische Gesetze der Volksdichtung," *Zeitschrift für deutsches Altertum* 51 (1909): 1–12, trans. as "Epic Laws of Folk Narrative," in *The Study of Folklore,* ed. Alan Dundes (Englewood Cliffs, N.J.: Prentice-Hall, 1965), pp. 129–41.

35. On the vogue for tartan and related phenomena see Hugh Trevor-Roper, "The Invention of Tradition: The Highland Tradition of Scotland," in *The Invention of Tradition,* ed. Hobsbawm and Ranger, pp. 15–41.

36. See further Linda Dégh, "Grimm's *Household Tales* and Its Place in the Household: The Social Relevance of a Controversial Classic," *Western Folklore* 38 (1979): 83–103 (esp. pp. 94–97), and Christa Kamenetzky, "Folktale and Ideology in the Third Reich," *Journal of American Folklore* 90 (1977): 168–78.

37. H. Mattingly, in the introduction to his translation of Tacitus's *The Agricola and The Germania,* rev. ed. (Harmondsworth: Penguin, 1970), p. 12.

38. Williams, *Culture,* p. 182.

39. One of Blake's annotations to Sir Joshua Reynolds' *Works,* cited in *The Complete Poetry and Prose of William Blake,* ed. David V. Erdman, 2d ed. (Berkeley: University of California Press, 1982), p. 641.

40. R. G. Collingwood, *The Idea of History* (Oxford: Clarendon Press, 1946), pp. 229–30.

41. Jan Vansina, *Oral Tradition as History* (Madison: University of Wisconsin Press, 1985), p. 182.

42. By "genealogical wars" I refer chiefly to the claims of ancient lineage that attended the power struggle between Henry VI, Richard Duke of York, and Edward IV. See T. D. Kendrick, *British Antiquity* (London: Methuen, 1970), and Sydney Anglo, "The British History in Early Tudor Propaganda," *Bulletin of the John Rylands Library* 44 (1961–62): 21–44.

43. See Craig R. Davis, "Cultural Assimilation in the Anglo-Saxon Royal Genealogies," *Anglo-Saxon England* 21 (1992): 23–36, with further citations there.

44. On the translation of saints and the translation of documents as two analogous politically motivated acts, see David Rollason, *Saints and Relics in Anglo-Saxon England* (Oxford: Blackwell, 1989), pp. 133–63.

45. The new Globe, when complete, will then function as the equivalent of "Shakespeare's Tomb," analogous to Chaucer's sixteenth-century tomb in Westminster Abbey but far grander and thus more convincingly able to confirm the Elizabethan period as the great originary era of the present kingdom.

46. To minimize ire, let me stress that I do not mean to say that the first question, that of veracity, does not matter. It does. Some historical claims are based on good evidence, some are innocent distortions of the truth, and others are impudent lies. It is good to know which are which, as far as one can.

47. Ginzburg, *The Cheese and the Worms,* p. xxvi.

48. Simic, "Stone Inside a Stone," in *Somewhere Among Us,* p. 25.

Contributors

Robert E. Bjork is professor of English at Arizona State University, director of the Arizona Center for Medieval and Renaissance Studies, and general editor of MRTS (Medieval & Renaissance Texts & Studies). His book publications include *The Old English Verse Saints' Lives: A Study in Direct Discourse and the Iconography of Style* (1985), *Cynewulf: Basic Readings* (1996), and (with Daniel G. Calder, Patrick K. Ford, and Daniel F. Melia) *Sources and Analogues of Old English Poetry II: The Major Germanic and Celtic Texts in Translation* (1983). He has also published translations of seven modern Swedish novels for the University of Nebraska Press.

Allen J. Frantzen is professor of English at Loyola University Chicago. Among his books are *The Literature of Penance in Anglo-Saxon England* (1983), *King Alfred* (1986), and *Desire for Origins: New Language, Old English, and Teaching the Tradition* (1990). He has also edited *Speaking Two Languages: Traditional Disciplines and Contemporary Theory* (1991) and has coedited *The Work of Work: Servitude, Slavery, and Labor in Medieval England* (1994).

Suzanne C. Hagedorn is assistant professor of English at the College of William and Mary, Williamsburg, Virginia. She received a Ph.D. in medieval studies in 1995 from Cornell University. She is currently writing a book on representations of abandoned women in medieval vernaculars.

J. R. Hall is professor of English at the University of Mississippi. He is the author of a number of essays on the literature of Anglo-Saxon England

and related subjects and is working on a book on early *Beowulf* scholars and the *Beowulf* manuscript.

John D. Niles is professor of English at the University of California, Berkeley. He is the author of *Beowulf: The Poem and Its Tradition* (1983) and numerous essays on folklore and medieval literature. He has edited *Old English Literature in Context: Ten Essays* (1981) as well as special issues of *Scandinavian Studies* (1987) and *Mediaevalia* (1991) devoted to Anglo-Saxon topics, and, with Robert E. Bjork, he recently coedited *A Beowulf Handbook* (1997).

Mary P. Richards is professor of English and dean of the College of Arts and Science at the University of Delaware. She is the author of *Texts and Their Traditions in the Medieval Library of Rochester Cathedral Priory* (1988) and has edited *Anglo-Saxon Manuscripts: Basic Readings* (1994).

Velma Bourgeois Richmond is professor of English at Holy Names College, Oakland, California. Among her books are *The Popularity of Middle English Romance* (1975), *Geoffrey Chaucer* (1992), and *The Legend of Guy of Warwick* (1996), and she has produced *A Prologue to Chaucer* for Films for the Humanities (1986).

Janet Thormann teaches English composition and literature at the College of Marin in Kentfield, California. She received her Ph.D. from the University of California, Berkeley, in 1971. She has published articles on Old and Middle English poetry and on feminist and psychoanalytic theory and has published three volumes of poetry with White Rabbit Press of San Francisco.

Gregory A. VanHoosier-Carey is assistant professor in the School of Literature, Communication, and Culture at Georgia Institute of Technology, where he teaches courses in American culture, Southern culture, and cultural theory. He completed his doctorate in English in 1995 at the University of Texas, Austin.

Index